Reg

Economic integration

Contributions to Economics

www.springer.com/series/1262

Further volumes of this series can be
found at our homepage

Sardar M. N. Islam
Empirical Finance
2004. ISBN 978-3-7908-1551-1

Jan-Egbert Sturm/Timo Wollmershäuser
(Eds.)
**Ifo Survey Data in Business Cycle
and Monetary Policy Analysis**
2005. ISBN 978-3-7908-0174-3

Bernard Michael Gilroy/Thomas Gries/
Willem A Naudé (Eds.)
**Multinational Enterprises, Foreign Direct
Investment and Growth in Africa**
2005. ISBN 978-3-7908-0276-4

Günter S. Heiduk/Kar-yiu Wong (Eds.)
WTO and World Trade
2005. ISBN 978-3-7908-1579-5

Emilio Colombo/Luca Stanca
**Financial Market Imperfections
and Corporate Decisions**
2006. ISBN 978-3-7908-1581-8

Birgit Mattil
Pension Systems
2006. ISBN 978-3-7908-1675-4

Francesco C. Billari/Thomas Fent/
Alexia Prskawetz/Jürgen Scheffran (Eds.)
Agent-Based Computational Modeling
2006. ISBN 978-3-7908-1640-2

Kerstin Press
A Life Cycle for Clusters?
2006. ISBN 978-3-7908-1710-2

Russel Cooper/Gary Madden/
Ashley Lloyd/Michael Schipp (Eds.)
**The Economics of Online Markets
and ICI Networks**
2006. ISBN 978-3-7908-1706-5

Renato Giannetti/Michelangelo Vasta (Eds.)
**Evolution of Italian Enterprises
in the 20th Century**
2006. ISBN 978-3-7908-1711-9

Ralph Setzer
**The Politics of Exchange Rates
in Developing Countries**
2006. ISBN 978-3-7908-1715-7

Dora Borbély
**Trade Specialization in the Enlarged
European Union**
2006. ISBN 978-3-7908-1704-1

Iris A. Hauswirth
Effective and Efficient Organisations?
2006. ISBN 978-3-7908-1730-0

Marco Neuhaus
The Impact of FDI on Economic Growth
2006. ISBN 978-3-7908-1734-8

Nicola Jentzsch
**The Economics and Regulation
of Financial Privacy**
2006. ISBN 978-3-7908-9

Klaus Winkler
**Negotiations with Asymmetrical
Distribution of Power**
2006. ISBN 978-3-7908-1743-0

Sasha Tsenkova, Zorica Nedović-Budić
(Eds.)
The Urban Mosaic of Post-Socialist Europe
2006. ISBN 978-3-7908-1726-3

Brigitte Preissl/Jürgen Müller (Eds.)
Governance of Communication Networks
2006. ISBN 978-3-7908-1745-4

Lei Delsen/Derek Bosworth/Hermann Groß/
Rafael Muñoz de Bustillo y Llorente (Eds.)
Operating Hours and Working Times
2006. ISBN 978-3-7908-1759-1

Pablo Coto-Millán; Vicente Inglada (Eds.)
Essays on Transport Economics
2006. ISBN 978-3-7908-1764-5

Christian H. Fahrholz
**New Political Economy of Exchange Rate
Policies and the Enlargement of the
Eurozone**
2006. ISBN 978-3-7908-1761-4

Sandra Gruescu
Population Ageing and Economic Growth
2007. ISBN 978-3-7908-1905-2

Patrick S. Renz
Project Governance
2007. ISBN 978-3-7908-1926-7

Christian Schabbel
The Value Chain of Foreign Aid
2007. ISBN 978-3-7908-1931-1

Kerstin Groß
Equity Ownership and Performance
2007. ISBN 978-3-7908-1933-5

George M. Korres (Ed.)
**Regionalisation, Growth,
and Economic Integration**
2007. ISBN 978-3-7908-1924-3

George M. Korres (Ed.)

Regionalisation, Growth, and Economic Integration

With 39 Figures and 66 Tables

Physica-Verlag

A Springer Company

Series Editors

Werner A. Müller
Martina Bihn

Editor

Prof. Dr. George M. Korres
The University of the Aegean
Department of Geography
University Hill
811 00 Mytilene
Greece
gkorres@geo.aegean.gr

and

Visiting Fellow (Oct. 2006/ Feb. 2007) at the
University of Leeds
Institute of Communication Studies
Leeds LS2-9J
United Kingdom

Library of Congress Control Number: 2007928955

ISSN 1431-1933
ISBN 978-3-7908-1924-3 Physica-Verlag Heidelberg New York

Physica-Verlag is a part of Springer Science+Business Media
springer.com
© Physica-Verlag Heidelberg 2007

Typesetting: Integra, India
Cover design: WMX Design GmbH, Heidelberg

Printed on acid-free paper   SPIN: 11946267   5 4 3 2 1 0

*To the memory
of Michael I. Korres*

Preface

Europe suffers from an inadequate capacity to transform scientific and technological knowledge into business opportunities [...] A strong collective effort will be needed in the area of innovation [...]

To make any real impact on the unemployment problem and the future of forthcoming generations, macroeconomic policies must be backed up by an equally far-sighted range of microeconomic measures [...]

This range of measures must above all include an extra special effort in the area of training of all types of human resources, of stepping up investment in research and development and the development of an information society [...].

(Romano Prodi, Former President European Commission)

There is considerable empirical evidence that investment in Research and Technological Development and Innovation (RTD&I) has a positive correlation with the level of economic development. Efforts in the area of RTD&I have been associated in the economic literature with higher growth rates, increases in exports and trade, gains in productivity, growth in income and output, bigger business profits and lower inflation, international competitiveness, etc.

Innovation must apply to all aspects of the activity of a firm (markets, products, processes and services). In this sense, the concept of innovation embraces research and development, technology and training as well as marketing, design and quality, finance, logistics and not least the business management required to mesh these various functions together efficiently.

In short, as Professor Joseph Schumpeter said, innovation is at the root of the evolution of the economic system and its main engine for change and 'creative destruction'. Given the correlation between innovation and RTD&I efforts, and regional economic development, closing the interregional RTD&I gap in the European Union becomes a pre-condition for reducing the cohesion gap, which is the primary objective of regional policy. Less favoured regions are spending comparatively lower levels of public funds on innovation and on top of this, are having greater difficulties in absorbing these funds than more developed regions. These risks further widen the existing RTD&I gap and thus inter-regional disparities in the European Union.

European regional policy has to cope with fresh challenges, globalisation and rapid technological change in particular, in order to provide the economic opportunities and quality jobs needed in less favoured regions. As the technology gap remains substantial, the Commission aims to help Europe's regions gain a competitive advantage based on innovation rather than cost. To do so, innovative actions will have to promote strong and close partnerships between the public sector agencies dealing with RTD&I and innovation and the private sector.

These contacts should improve the exchange of know-how and facilitate integration of innovation into the productive fabric, resulting in the creation of regional innovative systems. All European regions have assets on which they can draw to develop a sustainable and competitive economy and to improve the living standrads of their residents. These assets and opportunities may lie in their cultural heritage or diversity, specific competencies, an exceptional natural environment, strategic location, the particular quality of the educational infrastructure, linguistic ability, traditional crafts, music or regional products. Less densely populated, rural or peripheral regions should therefore make better use of the potential offered by the specific way of life resulting from their natural environment or from the cultural differences vis-à-vis urban areas. Innovative actions should explore new avenues in this area.

The sources of wealth creation and economic growth in the new networked economy are Information Technology and Communications (ICT) and knowledge in the form of intellectual capital, rather than natural resources and the efficiency of physical labour as competitive factors. More than ever, human capital (and training) is the key to innovation and competitiveness. Moreover, network economies as they grow, increase the benefits of all those who are "connected", giving a "win/win situation". This is why, less favoured regions cannot afford not to be connected, and regional policy has to cope with the so-called "digital divide" between those regions that are connected and have got the ICT skills, infrastructures and the knowledge access, and those who have not.

Regional advantage will go to those places which can attract and quickly mobilise the best people ("knowledge workers"), resources and capabilities required to turn innovations into new business ideas and commercial products. This is precisely why regional policy should help the less advanced regions to anticipate and prepare for the new economy through a new type of regional policy.

Today, in the European Union, the R&TDI gap is nearly twice as great as the cohesion gap. Many of the causes of disparities among regions can be traced to disparities in productivity and competitiveness. Education, research, technological development and innovation are vital components of regional competitiveness. So let us look at some examples of the so-called inter-regional R&TDI gap.

The 25 least developed regions in Europe spend, as a percentage of GDP, less than a quarter of the E.U. average (0.5% compared to an EC average of 2% – 1995). On a regional level, business expenditure on RTD&I, as a percentage of GDP in the most developed 25 regions, is on average 1.9%, while in the 25 least developed regions this figure falls to around 1.1%.

This difference in financial input has also consequences in terms of innovation outputs. For example, there are over 20 times the number of patent application in Germany alone than in the four cohesion countries together (Ireland, Greece, Portugal and Spain). The "technology gap" is a particular cause for concern with regard to the human resources for RTD&I, since human capital is increasingly a source of the dynamic comparative advantage which governs regional potential for innovation. In an increasingly "knowledge-based" economy, the only real capital is human capital. In terms of High Technology employment, in the 25 most advanced regions high technology accounts for an average of 14.6% of total employment, compared to just over 4% on average in the 25 least developed regions. This is compared to a community average of around 10.5%.

Moreover, the inter-regional RTD&I gap is not only of a quantitative nature but also of a qualitative one. There are a number of characteristics of regional innovation systems in less advance regions which make them less efficient. Regional actors are also in a better position to act on local knowledge, they are aware of the economic situation in firms, the existing links and networks between firms, the quality of the local labour market as well as the capacity of relevant local institutions to provide services of a technical, training or commercial nature. There is an advantage of being on the ground and having an eye-witness account of the local situation.

Regional policy should evolve from supporting physical RTD&I infrastructure and equipment towards encouraging co-operation and a collective learning process among local actors in the field of innovation. A policy which facilitates the creation of rich, dynamic regional innovation systems and which assists in the exchange of skills and expertise which small and medium sized firms may not have available in-house.

Regional policy should evolve from supporting general RTD&I efforts towards innovation promotion. It should encompass all functions of a firm, including technological, organisational, financial and managerial aspects in order to help it remain competitive. It should also change the emphasis from a "technology-push" into a "demand-pull" approach, to identify and understand the demand for innovation in firms in the less favoured regions in particular.

Technological transfer is essential for regions which lag behind. It might even be more important than the development of indigenous RTD&I activities in the weaker regions. Regional policy should facilitate the identification, adaptation and adoption of technological developments elsewhere in a specific regional setting. It might be less costly, avoid duplicating previous errors and reinventing the wheel.

Regional policy should facilitate technology transfer and the flow of knowledge across regions, maximising the benefit of the European dimension by facilitating access from less favoured regions economic actors to international networks of "excellence" in this field. Innovation can be promoted through the help of the Structural funds 2000–2006, either through the mainstream operational programmes, Objective 1 and 2, or through the new generation of innovation actions.

The regional development programmes (operational programmes or single programming documents) are presented to the European Commission by the Member States in order to benefit from Structural Funds being co-financed within the framework of the priority regional Objectives. In some cases, the adoption of the programmes is preceded by the adoption of a Community support framework which lays down the general strategy for ERDF assistance in a certain number of regions within a Member State. The European Union's regional policy is based on financial solidarity inasmuch as part of Member States' contributions to the E.U.'s budget goes to the less prosperous regions and social groups. For the period 2000–2006, these transfers will account for one third of the Community budget, or €213 billion:

- €195 billion will be spent by the four Structural Funds (the European Regional Development Fund, the European Social Fund, the Financial Instrument for Fisheries Guidance and the Guidance Section of the European Agricultural Guidance and Guarantee Fund);
- €18 billion will be spent by the Cohesion Fund;
- The Structural Funds concentrate on clearly defined priorities;
- 70% of the funding goes to regions whose development is lagging behind. They are home to 22% of the population of the Union (Objective 1);
- 11.5% of the funding assists economic and social conversion in areas experiencing structural difficulties. 18% of the population of the Union lives in such areas (Objective 2);
- 12.3% of the funding promotes the modernisation of training systems and the creation of employment (Objective 3) outside the Objective 1 regions where such measures form part of the strategies for catching up.

- There are also four Community Initiatives seeking common solutions to specific problems. They spend 5.35% of the funding for the Structural Funds on:
- cross-border, transnational and interregional cooperation (Interreg III);
- sustainable development of cities and declining urban areas (Urban II);
- rural development through local initiatives (Leader +);
- combating inequalities and discrimination in access to the labour market (Equal).

There is a special allocation of funds for the adjustment of fisheries structures outside the Objective 1 regions (0.5%). One particular fund, the Cohesion Fund, provides direct finance for specific projects relating to environmental and transport infrastructure in Spain, Greece, Ireland and Portugal, as these are still inadequate. The Instrument for Structural Policies for Pre-Accession (ISPA) provides assistance along the same lines to the ten central and eastern European countries which have applied for Union membership. To improve the quality of regional development strategies the Commission intends to support the latest ideas which have not yet been adequately exploited. They are expected to provide the regions with the scope for experimentation which they sometimes lack and need to meet the challenges of the information society and to make their economies more competitive.

The European Union is increasingly becoming a knowledge-based economy and society. The development of knowledge has a direct effect on competitiveness and employment, as well as on the way society functions in general. Although the importance of knowledge was explicitly recognised at the European Summit in Lisbon in February 2000, research in Europe displays contrasting features. There are not only unquestionable strengths but also evident weaknesses, as reflected in a trade deficit in high tech-products of over 20 billions €. This, in turn, reflects a number of underlying factors – a lower level of expenditure on R&D in the EU (1.8% of GDP) than in the US (2.8%) and Japan (2.9%), a less dynamic environment for innovation and a relatively fragmented research system.

Regional and local authorities already support research, technological development and innovation. It is estimated that the finance they provide amounts annually to almost 1½ times the total appropriation of the EU Framework Programme (4.5 billions € compared with EUR 3 billion), over 90% of which is allocated on a regional basis. The establishment of a European Research Area, however, is not confined to the most central and competitive regions. The instruments available – the Framework Programme, the Structural Funds and action at national and regional level –

should be used together in a more coherent way, each according to its objectives, in order to enable all regions to participate fully in the area.

EU RTD policy has increased its support for those involved in research and technology in the cohesion countries, less favoured regions and candidate countries. The absence of statistics on funding prevents quantification of the extent to which funding has been directed towards the latter. The increased number of projects with participation from Objective 1 regions, however, and the relatively favourable position of research fellows from cohesion countries in the European Human Mobility schemes point towards a positive contribution towards reducing regional disparities. Moreover, various measures have helped improve the effectiveness of policies relating to innovation in a number of disadvantaged regions.

Overall, EU RTD policy has adopted an approach oriented more towards innovation than technological excellence as such, better addressing the deficiencies of less favoured regions as a result. The regional dimension of RTD policy has come to be featured explicitly in the Initiative 'Towards a European Research Area'. An improvement in the interaction between the deployment of the Structural Funds and RTD policy is important to accelerate the "catching up" of lagging regions.

We therefore propose to define regionalisation as the process which creates a capacity for independent action aimed at developing a specific area (sub-national but supra-local) through the mobilisation of its economic fabric and, where appropriate, of features of local and regional identity, and through the development of its potential. This process can occur on the basis of existing institutions, or can give rise to a new territorial organization(s) which will better fulfill these aims. It is always conditioned by the constraints imposed by the political and institutional framework, which in turn can be influenced by other factors. Although it may seem paradoxical, the creation of regions as new local authorities is only one manifestation of this process, in fact a rather exceptional one, and, when it does occur, it may be in response to considerations other than the process of regionalisation as defined above, even if the institutions then created do fulfill these needs (for example, the cases of Italy and Spain). The innovation that affects regionalisation becomes clearer when we compare it with the historical development of intermediate-level institutions in European States.

We may identify five types of regionalisation based on where regionalisation is located in the constitutional and administrative structure of the State.

- Administrative regionalisation;
- Regionalisation through the existing local authorities;

- Regional decentralisation;
- Political regionalisation, or regional autonomy (institutional regionalism);
- Regionalisation through the federate authorities;
- The book likes to tackle the following four issues:
  - *Why is innovation important for regional economic development;*
  - *Why is the regional dimension important for innovation promotion;*
  - *What has been our policy response so far and what lessons have we learnt from it;*
  - *And finally, what are our action lines for the future.*

The purpose of this book is to analyse the process of regionalisation and plot its likely future development in the 15 Member States of the E.U. Regionalisation certainly seems to be a common feature of the changing territorial organisation of European States today. Some have gone as far as to speak of a "Europe of the regions", in which the regions would function as intermediate-level public authorities in response to the localised requirements of certain Community policies, and provide the basis for a process of institutional convergence between the Member States of the Union. Then, regionalisation alone cannot produce any of the benefits we attribute to it all too often without looking into the conditions in which they occur.

The book is intended to provide a basic understanding of the current issues in and the problems of regional integration and examine many aspects and consequences of this integration that are obscure or yet to be explored. After addressing general issues in the field of economic integration, the discussion turns to empirical and theoretical aspects of monetary union, social policy reform and social union, public finance and technology policy. In particular, with its wide range of topics, methodologies and perspectives, the book offers stimulating and wide-ranging analyses that will be of interest to students, economic theorists, empirical social scientists, policy makers and the informed general reader.

The volume comprises four parts. Part I is devoted to macroeconomic issues and the problems of regional growth and economic integration. Part II investigates the microeconomic implications of regional growth and economic integration with regard to manufacturing, Foreign Direct Investment (FDI), and unemployment. Part III deals with institutional matters and the policies of regional growth and economic integration, including technology policy, shipping policy, the distribution of E.U. funds, regional development and productivity problems. Finally, Part IV discusses the challenges and policies for regional growth and economic integration, with emphasis on social policy, the welfare state, and political reforms.

The publication of this book has been a truly worthwhile project, involving 28 authors. I would like to thank all the contributors to this volume for their great enthusiasm and willingness to cooperate. I should also thank Dr. Ekaterini Nikolarea, University of the Aegean, for English-proofing towards this project. Finally, I would also like to thank the anonymous reviewer of the volume, and above all, my publisher for the great encouragement and support.

January 2007
George M. Korres
University of Leeds, U.K. and
The University of the Aegean, Greece

Contents

Part I

Macroeconomic Issues of Regional Growth
and Economic Integration

Economic Integration and Labour Markets: Ways Forward

Simonetta Longhi* and Peter Nijkamp

Department of Spatial Economics, Free University Amsterdam, The Netherlands

1 Introduction

Regions are economic systems that share many characteristics of national economies. However, regions are much more open – and, therefore, integrated with each other – than nations: spatial interactions among regions in one country are more intensive and remain generally easier and, therefore, more developed than spatial interactions across countries. For example, trade barriers across regions belonging to the same country are much lower than trade barriers across countries, and labour and capital are more mobile across regions than across countries.

The increasing globalisation and integration of national economies is likely to significantly increase the incidence of such spatial interactions across countries. In this framework, a better knowledge of the role of spatial interactions and spatial spillovers might, therefore, lead to a better understanding of the possible development of national economies. Up to now, however, the effect that spatial interaction might have in shaping adjustment paths in response to national or local economic shocks has not been completely analysed.

The impact of economic integration on production and economic specialisation has been extensively studied in the literature (see, e.g. Nijkamp et al., 2003). Yet much less attention has been paid to the analysis of the impact of economic integration on the labour market up to now. Changes in the location of production are likely to have a relevant effect on the labour demand, while bigger flows of workers' moving across countries are likely to have a relevant effect on the labour supply. Moreover, most of these (exogenous) shifts in labour demand and supply are likely to have

* Email: slonghi@feweb.vu.nl

markedly local effects. This suggests that increasing economic integration might have a relevant impact on regional economic disparities.

Where's on the other hand, because of differences in their location and size, some regions might behave like open and interacting labour markets, while other regions might behave like more isolated and therefore closed local labour markets. The way local labour markets adjust to local or national external changes might depend, among other regional characteristics, on the degree of isolation of each region. This suggests that the degree of openness and spatial interaction might have an (indirect) effect on regional disparities.

The aim of this paper is to give a brief summary of selected strands of the literature on local labour markets that might be related to issues of openness and integration. Unresolved questions on the effect of integration on local labour markets are identified and future research directions are suggested. The paper is organised as follows. Section 2 summarises the theoretical and empirical literature on the effects of economic integration on inter-regional movements of firms and, therefore, on regional specialisation. Such external shifts in local labour demand generate temporary adjustments in both unemployment and wages, followed by permanent adjustments in employment (see Blanchard and Katz, 1992; and Decressin and Fatás, 1995). In this framework, Sect. 3 focuses on the effect that regional unemployment disparities have on regional wage differentials in the context of the "wage curve" literature. The results by Blanchard and Katz (1992) and Decressin and Fatás (1995) also suggest that a local shock in labour demand might indirectly have an influence on the other regions, through migration. Because of the high interaction across local labour markets, a shift in local labour demand of one region might generate a shift in local labour supply of other regions. Then, Sect. 4 turns on the literature analysing the impact that (international) immigration has on local wages in the host country. A specific characteristic of European labour markets is the relevance of collective bargaining, at either national or sectoral level.

All the empirical literature mentioned up to now is usually based on the analysis of data about the past. To develop effective policy measures, reliable forecasts of future developments of socio-economic variables are needed. Thus, the focus of Sect. 5 is on the literature dealing with short-term forecasts. Finally, Sect. 6 proposes a research agenda for future analyses of the impact of openness and economic integration on local economies.

2 The Impact of Economic Integration on Firm Location

The increasing openness and economic integration among countries is likely to affect all regions belonging to the national economy. However, because of different economic and geographic characteristics, each region will probably respond to such institutional changes in a different way. There is a vast literature analysing the effects of economic integration on the location of economic activities. This literature belongs to international trade theory and can be grouped into three strands: the traditional trade theory, the new trade theory, and the new economic geography; for recent surveys of the theoretical literature see: Amiti (1998), Aiginger et al. (1999), Brülhart (1998), Hallet (2001), Nijkamp et al. (2003), Puga (2002) and Venables (1998). While offering different explanations of patterns of specialisation, all three theoretical approaches predict increasing specialisation as a result of trade liberalization, since regions/countries tend to exploit their comparative advantages in certain economic sectors (Baldwin and Brown, 2004).

Traditional trade theory explains patterns of specialisation on the basis of differences in productivity (technology) or endowments across countries and regions. The new trade theory and more recently new economic geography models underline increasing returns in production, agglomeration economies and cumulative processes as explanations for the concentration of activities in particular countries and regions.

More specifically, traditional trade theory explains specialisation patterns through differences in relative production costs that result from differences in productivity (Ricardo, 1817) or endowments (Heckscher, 1949; Ohlin, 1933) between countries. These are termed "comparative advantages". Traditional trade theory predicts that trade liberalisation will result in production relocation and increasing specialisation according to comparative advantages. The consequent changes in demand for factors of production will tend to equalise factor prices across countries and regions. A large portion of inter-industry specialisation can be explained by neoclassical trade models (Leamer and Levinsohn, 1995). However, comparative advantage is not sufficient as the sole explanation for specialisation (Venables, 1998), since different production structures are found in regions and countries with similar factor endowments and production technologies. Furthermore, trade between industrialised countries consists mainly of goods in the same product category, that is, it is intra-industry trade.

Mainly used for explaining intra-industry trade, new trade theory models were developed during the 1980s; see Helpman and Krugman, 1985, Krugman, 1979, 1980, 1981, Krugman and Venables, 1990. The new trade

theory models focus on the interactions between firms with increasing returns in product markets and explain location of industrial activity in terms
of the geographical advantage of countries and regions with good market
access. When trade barriers fall, activities with increasing returns will tend
to locate in areas with good market access ("the centre"), and move away
from remote ones ("the periphery"). Geographical advantage will be greatest at some intermediate trade cost (Krugman and Venables, 1990). This
implies that the relationship between trade costs and the location of activity has an inverse U-shape. When trade barriers and transport costs are
small, the geographical advantage of the regions with good market access
becomes less important. At this stage, factor production costs will motivate
firms to move back to peripheral regions.

The prediction of the new trade theory regarding the distribution of
economic activity between the core/centre and the periphery is relevant to
the accession of Central Eastern European countries to the E.U. (Hallet,
1998). The current economic integration situation could be seen as one
with "intermediate trade costs". Further integration could therefore result
in the relocation of manufacturing to Central Eastern European countries
due to factor cost considerations.

The new economic geography models assume that the geographical advantage of large markets is endogenous, and suggest that specialisation
patterns may be the result of the spatial agglomeration of economic activities (Krugman, 1991a, 1991b; Krugman and Venables, 1995; Venables,
1996). Krugman's analysis focusses on a two-sector two-region model.
The two regions are identical in terms of initial factor endowments, and the
factor specific to manufacturing (industrial workers) is mobile across regions. Relocation of firms and workers from one region to the other generates agglomeration via the cumulative effects of demand linkages. Assuming no barriers to the movement of firms or manufacturing workers
(Krugman, 1991b), a bleak scenario could be imagined: the manufacturing
sector in the "donor" region would collapse and manufacturing would concentrate in the "receiving" region. This scenario could develop gradually,
following the lowering of trade costs. Initially, when trade costs are high,
manufacturing is evenly split between the two regions (each region produces for its own local market). If trade costs are sufficiently low, demand
linkages bring about the agglomeration of activities. Regions with initial
scale advantage in particular sectors would attract more manufacturing activity, thus reinforcing their advantage in those sectors.

The new economic geography models imply that, in sectors where sup-
ply-side and demand-side linkages are important, European integration
would bring massive specialisation and concentration. However, given the
low inter-EU country mobility, in some cases this result might seem

unrealistic (Eichengreen, 1993; Obstfeld and Peri, 1998). Sufficient labour mobility within EU countries could result in agglomeration effects emerging around border regions similar to those effects identified by Hanson (1996, 1997b) for the case of US-Mexican economic integration.

There is a growing empirical literature on the impact of economic integration on geographical specialisation and on industrial concentration. In a series of papers, Hanson looked at the US-Mexican integration and assessed the locational forces identified by the new economic geography models. He found that integration with the US has led to a relocation of Mexican industry from Mexico City to states close to the US market (Hanson, 1996). In the case of Mexico, inter-regional wage differentials are increasingly explained by the distance from the border with the US, and less by the distance from the capital city, that is Mexico City (Hanson, 1997a, 1997b, 1998).

Using production data at current prices for 27 manufacturing industries, Amiti (1999) finds that there was a significant increase in specialisation between 1968 and 1990 in Belgium, Denmark, Germany, Greece, Italy, and the Netherlands. No significant change occurred in Portugal, while a significant decrease in specialisation occurred in France, Spain and the UK. Between 1980 and 1990, however, there was a significant increase in specialisation in all countries analysed. With more disaggregated data, the increase in specialisation is more pronounced. Other evidence of increasing specialisation in the EU countries in the 1980s and 1990s based on production data is provided by Aiginger et al. (1999), Greenway and Hine (1991), Hine (1990), Midelfart-Knarvik et al. (2000). Analyses based on trade – rather than employment – data indicate that the EU member states have a diversified rather than a specialised pattern of manufacturing exports (Brülhart, 2001; Sapir, 1996). The results obtained using trade data are not necessarily in contradiction with the ones obtained using employment data. These results might be explained by the different speed of these two processes – specialisation in terms of employment or in terms of export and trade – that follow a fall in trade barriers and costs (Brülhart, 2001).

With respect to Eastern European countries, the research is still at an early stage. The existing evidence suggests that these countries tend to specialise in labour- and resource-intensive sectors (Landesmann, 1995), and that the processes of internationalisation and structural change tend to favour metropolitan and Western regions, as well as regions with a strong industrial base (Petrakos, 1996, 2000). Increasing differences between core/central and peripheral regions, with respect to the EU, have also been documented (Raagmaa, 1996; Resmini, 2002).

Most of the empirical literature on EU integration focuses on the reallocation of economic activities across EU countries. However, the fast process of integration with the EU has probably also led to a relevant process of reallocation of economic activities among Eastern European countries. Furthermore, the benefits and costs resulting from increased integration might not be evenly distributed across space, thus leading to "win and lose" situation. A step forward from the previous literature consists in analysing the effects that economic integration might have on regions rather than on national economies. Furthermore, as will be clarified in the following sections, economic integration might have a relevant impact on local labour market variables such as the local unemployment rate and the local wages. Future research should aim at clarify the effect that economic integration across countries has on local labour markets.

3 Relocation of Firms and Local Wages: The Wage Curve Literature

With increasing openness and economic integration, it is becoming easier for firms to relocate across regions and countries. Shifts in local labour demand might therefore be a consequence of increasing openness. Shifts in local labour demand are likely to have a direct short-run effect on the regional unemployment rate (Blanchard and Katz, 1992). In turn, the local unemployment rate might be relevant in the explanation of local pay differentials (Molho, 1992). A well-studied phenomenon in regional economics, the "wage curve" suggests that wages adjust to changes in the local unemployment rate (Blanchflower and Oswald, 1995).

The literature on the wage curve dates back to the beginning of the 1990s. Using American and British data, Blanchflower and Oswald (1990) found a negative relationship between regional unemployment and individual wages, which becomes flat at relatively high levels of the unemployment rate. They labelled this relationship the "wage curve". In subsequent analyses Blanchflower and Oswald (1994a, 1994b) estimated the wage curve for most OECD countries and found that the estimated unemployment elasticity of pay is often close to –0.1. Their estimates are remarkably similar across countries and over time, suggesting that a ten percent increase in the local unemployment rate (e.g. from five percent to 5.5 percent) should cause a one percent decrease in local real wages, independent of the country and period of analysis.

The wage curve is essentially a Mincer (1974) equation regressing the log of individual wages on a number of individual characteristics such as gender, education, experience, etc. In the "wage curve" version, the unemployment rate appears among the explanatory variables. The negative coefficient of the log unemployment rate suggests that workers employed in labour markets characterised by higher unemployment rates receive lower wages than similar workers employed in similar labour markets but which have a lower unemployment rate.

In the literature, considerable attention has been paid to the relationship between the wage curve and the Phillips curve (Phillips, 1958). The wage curve describes the equilibrium phenomenon for which the level of real individual wages correlates negatively with the level of regional unemployment. The wage curve is estimated using cross-sectional or panel data on individuals. The Phillips curve describes the process by which the rate of wage change adjusts to the unemployment rate. The Phillips curve is estimated on aggregated time series data and suggests a negative correlation between the unemployment rate and wage changes. Although they might seem similar, the wage curve and the Phillips curve estimate different phenomena. Therefore, wage curve findings are not necessarily inconsistent with the Phillips curve (Card, 1995). In this respect, the wage curve hypothesis has been often tested versus the Phillips curve (see, for example Blanchflower and Oswald, 1994b; Blanchard and Katz, 1997; Bell et al., 2002; Pannenberg and Schwarze, 1998b). Since this study is only concerned with relationships between local labour markets, the focus will be exclusively on the wage curve.

In his review of Blanchflower and Oswald's book (1994a), Card (1995) adds further evidence for the US, the UK, Canada and Australia and concludes that the wage curve is a robust phenomenon. Further empirical analyses aiming at testing the wage curve relationship under different conditions have been carried out for the US (see, among others, Bratsberg and Turunen, 1996, Partridge and Rickman, 1997), Australia (Kennedy and Borland, 2000), New Zealand (Morrison et al., 2005; Papps, 2001) and Japan (Doi et al., 2003). For European countries, estimations of the wage curve have been computed for, among others, Austria (Winter-Ebmer, 1996), Belgium (Janssens and Konings, 1998), Italy (Chiarini and Piselli, 1997, Montuenga et al., 2003), the Netherlands (Groot et al., 1992), Norway (Johansen, 2002), Spain (Montuenga et al., 2003, Sanroma' and Raul, 2004), France, Portugal and the UK (Montuenga et al., 2003), as well as for Turkey (Ikkaracan and Selim, 2003). A number of estimations refer to West Germany (Baltagi and Blien, 1998, Bellmann and Blien, 2001, Buettner, 1999, Wagner, 1994) and East Germany (Baltagi et al., 2000, Elhorst et al., 2002, Pannenberg and Schwarze, 1998a). Despite the use of different data, control variables and estimation strategy, most of these studies find a negative relationship between unemployment and wages, which is often close to −0.10. This large amount of empirical findings has been summarised by means of a meta-analysis by Nijkamp and Poot (2005). They further confirm that the wage curve is a robust phenomenon, and compute a publication-bias corrected average wage curve estimate of about −0.07.

Various possible explanations for an inverse relationship between the unemployment rate and local wages have been put forward in the literature. One of these was put forward by Campbell and Orszag (1998), who modified a model of lump-sum labour turnover costs based on Salop (1979) and Phelps (1984). Here, firms economise on the costs associated with hiring new workers by paying higher wages to discourage workers from quitting at times of a tight labour market. Labour earnings and unemployment rates would have a negative correlation, ceteris paribus, and a wage curve would result. This suggests that the wage curve might reflect a monopsony situation (see also Morrison et al., 2005). When workers commute from different residential locations such costs generate heterogeneity among workers that leads to the limited number of local employers facing upward sloping labour supply curves (Bhaskar and To, 1999). Hence, if the wage curve is due to employers facing upward sloping labour supply curves, any spatial phenomenon that affects the wage elasticity of the labour supply curve will also affect the elasticity of the wage curve. Since the threat of unemployment is less when employment opportunities in surrounding regions are plentiful, firms located in regions close to other regions with large labour markets may not be able to respond to a local demand shock by lowering wages. Burgess and Profit (2001) found empirical evidence of spatial externalities in the British labour market: high unemployment levels in neighbouring areas tend to raise the number of local vacancies being filled and to lower the local outflow from unemployment.

Nevertheless, most of the empirical estimations of the wage curve tend to model local labour markets as closed and unconnected economies. However, given the openness of regional labour markets in a national economy, high levels of inter-relation among local labour markets may be expected. Evidence for New Zealand suggests a downward effect on wages of labour market isolation (Morrison et al., 2005). Tests for spatial autocorrelation on West German data find that the wage curve could be extended by including a spatial lag of wages on the right-hand side of the earning equation (Buettner, 1999). This suggests that local wages may also be affected by the level of wages in the neighbouring regions.

As previously mentioned, because of differences in their location and size, some regions might behave like open and interacting labour markets, while other regions might behave like more isolated and, therefore, closed local labour markets. Wage curves estimated separately for these two kinds of regions might show significant differences in the responsiveness of wages to changes in the unemployment rates. Future research may shed light into the effect of increasing openness and economic integration on local labour markets by explicitly analysing spatial heterogeneity and spatial stationarity of the unemployment elasticity of pay.

4 Relocation of Workers and Local Wages: Impacts of Immigration

The increasing openness and economic integration among European economies is also favouring cross-country movement of workers, which generates shifts in local labour supply. Such shifts are likely to generate adjustments in local labour market variables like unemployment, employment, and wages.

The short-run effects of migration are markedly local, since immigrants are likely to put downward pressure on wages only in the labour market area where they choose to locate. In addition, immigrants are likely to be unevenly distributed across regions (Borjas, 2001). If immigrants are attracted by growing regions, thus responding to regional differences in local labour market conditions, migration should reduce regional differences (Borjas, 2001, Topel, 1986). However, if immigrants tend to locate in areas where similar immigrants are already located (Gorter et al., 1999), an external shock due to immigration might trigger adjustments that might cause regional imbalances.

In the literature, considerable research has been undertaken to analyse different aspects of migration, such as the determinants of flows, the characteristics of immigrants, the adaptation or assimilation of migrants, as well as the consequences for labour markets. Surveys can be found in, among others, Borjas (1994, 1999), Friedberg and Hunt (1995) and Zimmermann and Bauer (2002).

The first empirical estimation of the effect of immigration on natives' wages dates back to Grossman (1982). Here, native and immigrant workers enter a translog production function as two separate production inputs. The effect of a supply shock, given a specific production technology, is then simulated, and the elasticities of substitution between native and immigrant workers – corresponding to the effect of immigration on natives' wages – are computed using US data for 1970. Further estimations of the effect of immigration on natives' wages using a similar approach have then been computed for different countries and periods (see, among others,

Borjas, 1987, and Greenwood et al., 1997 for the US; Bauer, 1998, for Germany; and Akbari and Devoretz, 1992 for Canada). This strand of the empirical literature is called the "factor proportion approach". Besides the high number of hypotheses needed for the estimation of the effect of immigration on wages, the factor proportion approach may also suffer from the omission of certain consequential influences on local labour markets, such as changes in the composition of demand and induced capital inflows.

In contrast to the factor proportion approach, the other strand of the empirical literature, called the "area approach", has a less strong theoretical basis. The area approach estimates the effect of immigration on local labour markets by exploiting the fact that immigrants are highly spatially concentrated. In such a situation, it may be expected that there will be a negative spatial correlation between the proportion of the labour force in local labour markets who are immigrants and the wages of natives for whom, they can substitute.

Similar to Blanchflower and Oswald's wage curve, the equation typically used in the area approach to estimate the impact of migration on wages is a Mincer (1974) equation, in which the share of immigrant workers in the population appears among the explanatory variables. The first area approach results (King et al., 1986) found no effect of Hispanic immigrants on Hispanic American workers. Further analyses using this approach can be found in, among others, Bean et al. (1988), Borjas et al. (1996), Card (2001), Friedberg (2001), Jaeger (1996), and Winter-Ebmer and Zweimuller (1996).

Consistent with the standard economic analysis, both strands of the literature – the factor and the area approach – generally find that immigration has a negative effect on natives' wages, but this effect is rather small, and almost negligible (Friedberg and Hunt, 1995). Natural experiments, such as the impact of the Mariel Boatlift on the Miami labour market (Card, 1990), the impact of the repatriates from Africa on the Portuguese labour market (Carrington and de Lima, 1996), and the impact of the repatriates from Algeria on the French labour market (Hunt, 1992) seem to find similar results. Interestingly, the empirical results also show a large variability both between and within studies (Borjas, 2003). Such variability might be due to different causes, ranging from problems in defining of the unit of analysis (the local labour market) to institutional and other factors that impede competitive forces.

In a recent meta-analysis of the effect of immigration on local wages, Longhi et al. (2004) suggests that, because of greater substitutability among workers, wages of earlier immigrants are more affected by immigration than wages of natives. As a result, since immigrants do not locate randomly across local labour markets, regional imbalances (such as grow-

ing intra-regional income inequality) might appear as a response to an exogenous increase of immigration. Future research might shed light into the
effect of integration on local labour markets by analysing more in detail
immigrants' location decision versus natives' location decisions.

As previously mentioned, in European countries collective bargaining
might limit the possibility of local wages to adjust to changes in labour
demand and supply, thus possibly contributing to the rise of imbalances
across local labour markets.

5 Adjustments, Spillovers and Regional Short-Term Forecasts

The increasing openness and integration among countries is likely to generate shifts in local labour supply and demand. The analysis of the economic causes and consequences of such shifts is necessary to identify
"problem areas" and counteract imbalances across regions. Obviously, this
analysis is based on data about the past. At the same time, to develop effective policy measures, reliable forecasts of future developments of socio-
economic variables are needed.

On the other hand, forecasts can be computed either by means of
"structural macroeconomic models" or by means of "time-series" models.
Macroeconomic models are designed on the basis of economic theories,
and are usually composed of a large number of simultaneous equations involving a large number of socio-economic variables. Their estimation usually requires a large amount of data and a certain amount of expertise (see,
for example, Hatch, 2003). Since structural macroeconomic models are designed on the basis of a certain theory, their popularity might closely follow the popularity of the economic theory on which they rely (Diebold,
1998). For more details on macroeconomic forecasting, see for example,
Diebold (1998), Hendry and Ericsson (2003). Being strictly related to economic theories, macroeconomic models require a high number of economic and econometric hypotheses. For the same reason, macroeconomic
models allow the analysis of alternative scenarios that might take place
under specific (simulated) policy measures (see, for example, Don, 2004;
Sims, 1980; and Turner, 2003).

On the other hand, non-structural time-series models neither rely on any
specific economic theory, not require any prior economic hypothesis. Such
models exploit the correlation in the past observations of a variable to predict its future development. Since they do not generally allow any meaningful economic interpretation of their results, non-structural models might

be considered as "black boxes". Though such black boxes might be useless for the analysis of the effect of policy measures (Don, 2004), they, none-theless, have become popular tools to forecast future developments of eco-nomic variables (Diebold, 1998). Furthermore, when the main focus is on forecasting rather than on interpreting, such a drawback might be consid-ered a minor side effect. Structural time-series models, which combine non-structural time-series models with restrictions arising from theory (Diebold, 1998), are also becoming very popular.

Since macroeconomic models are simplified (thus imperfect) represen-tations of real economies, and real economies are always subject to unan-ticipated shifts (Hendry and Clements, 2003), in many cases non-structural approaches to short-term forecasts have been found to perform rather well compared with macroeconomic models (Diebold, 1998). For example, Eitrheim et al. (1999) found that "badly-fitting extrapolative tools" are able to outperform the "Norges Bank" econometric model in short-term (up to four quarters) forecasts. However, given the lower variance, the "Norges Bank" model is preferred over long-horizon forecasts.

One of the most interesting advantages of non-structural forecasting models, compared with macroeconomic models, is that they usually do not require the availability of a large quantity of information about different aspects of the economy. Because they do not rely on economic assump-tions, non-structural models are more flexible than macroeconomic mod-els. The empirical analyses mentioned in the previous sections analyse how local labour markets adjust to specified external shifts in economic conditions, in a sort of partial equilibrium framework. In reality, however, more shifts happen simultaneously. A naïve combination of models with different sets of restrictions would generate a bad description of regional employment change, and therefore a bad forecasting model (see, for exam-ple, Sims, 1980). In such a situation, non-structural forecasting models should be preferred.

Nowadays, a large theoretical and empirical literature is concerned with the problem of forecasting economic variables, such as employment, by means of non-structural models. For example, employment forecasts have been computed by, among others, Boomsma (1999), Fauvel et al. (1999), Partridge and Rickman (1998), Rickman (2002), Stock and Watson (2002).

It has often been noted that the variability of labour market aggregates, such as employment and unemployment, is much higher across regions of the same countries than across national economies (see, for example, Overman and Puga, 2002, and OECD, 2000). Furthermore, empirical analyses show that regions are affected by local-specific shocks, and might react differently to national shocks (Blanchard and Katz, 1992; Decressin and Fatás, 1995). To counteract disparities among regional labour markets and to make efficient use of the available public funds, national governments need reliable forecasts at the regional level as a complement for forecasts computed at the national level.

To better represent similarities and differences across regions as well as the interactions among them, panel data sets should be used. In the context of regional forecasting experiments, the number of regions for which the forecasts have to be made is generally much higher than the number of time periods for which regional data are available. As a result, statistical techniques that are commonly used in time-series analysis – generally characterised by a large number of observations over time – are not easily generalised and applied to panel data. Nevertheless, the use of cross-section and panel data has important advantages.

Regions are open, small economies highly interacting with each other. The economic development of each region is probably highly affected by (and is likely to have a high impact on) the economic development of the other regions. One advantage of the use of space-time data is that it allows the increasing spatial spillovers to be explicitly modelled. First researches in this direction have already shown that more reliable forecasts can be computed using spatial econometric techniques; see Baltagi and Li, 2004 on the prediction of per-capita cigarette consumption. Future research should test and extend the models proposed by Baltagi and Li (2004) to forecasts of local labour market variables, such as employment and unemployment.

6 Research Agenda

The analysis of regional economies is a necessary complement to the analysis of the national economy. While some regions seem to be able to fully exploit their resources, some others seem to permanently lag behind the average national economic performance. As a result, the overall national economic performance is driven by just a limited number of regions, and regional disparities in economic conditions and developments seem to be rather persistent.

For this – and other – reasons the effectiveness of policy measures, as well as the effect of national external changes, such as economic integration, might differ across regions. This might, in turn, generate imbalances across local labour markets. Depending on its characteristics as well as on the characteristics of the neighbouring regions, each local labour market reacts to the national policy in a different way: open and highly interacting local labour markets might behave differently from more isolated ones.

Because of such spatial heterogeneity, national policies might be partly ineffective. As a result, the effect of national policy measures might be better understood when evaluated at local level, while national policy measures that are likely to generate unwanted regional imbalances might be more effective when "adjusted" at local level.

Depending on their level of spatial interaction among neighbouring local labour markets, regions may or may not respond to shifts in local labour demand with changes in wages. In this context, the spatial location of firms might have a relevant impact on the relationship among local labour market variables. As suggested in the previous sections, policy measures that try to favour location of firms in specific areas might have an indirect effect on the regional unemployment elasticity of pay as well as on the regional variability of wages. Future research might shed light into the effect of increasing openness and economic integration on local labour markets by explicitly analysing spatial heterogeneity and spatial stationarity of the relationships between labour market variables that are often assumed to be constant across regions.

Besides the spatial location of firms, the spatial location of workers too might have an effect on regional labour market disparities. For example, if immigrants are closer substitutes for earlier immigrants than for natives, immigration might have a bigger negative effect on wages of earlier immigrants, than on natives' wages. In such a situation, immigrants' wages might depend on regional characteristics, such as the percentage of immigrants in the labour force in the local labour market. Depending on immigrants' location decisions, regional wage disparities might then arise. If immigrants are attracted by growing markets, with above-average wages, then immigration might contribute to a reduction in inter-regional wage disparities, while at the same time generating growing intra-regional inequalities in immigrant clusters. In this case, incentives for immigrants to locate in specific regions might be considered as policy measures to partly counteract regional imbalances. In this context, further research on location decisions of immigrants and on their effect on regional disparities is needed.

Furthermore, in the context of regional forecasts, taking into account the degree of openness and spatial interaction, for example, by means of distances across regions, might contribute to the computation of better models.

In conclusion, openness and spatial interactions might have a non-negligible effect on the way local labour markets adjust to external changes. Spatial interactions not only might generate spillovers across regions, but also have an effect on the relationship between economic variables. To avoid the development of policy measures that are ineffective or produce unexpected results, it is therefore necessary to study the effect of spatial interactions.

In light of the previous remarks, there is still much potential for future research analysing the effect of spatial interaction. What is the role of openness and accessibility – and therefore of spatial interactions – versus other regional characteristics (for example the availability of a more educated labour force or fiscal incentives) on location decisions of firms? Which kinds of firms (for example grouped by size or economic sector of activity) are more likely to benefit more from openness and increased spatial interactions? And which of them are therefore more likely to be sensitive to changes in regional accessibility or to incentives to (re-)locate in less accessible regions? These are only questions/issues which can lead to possible researches on the effect of openness and accessibility on local labour demand.

What is the role of openness and accessibility versus other characteristics of local labour markets – such as higher wages or lower unemployment rate – on location choices of workers? Which kinds of workers (for example grouped by education, occupation or marital status) are more likely to benefit from more accessibility, and which ones are likely to be more sensitive to changes in regional accessibility or to incentives to locate in less accessible regions? These are only few possible researches on the effect of openness and accessibility on local labour supply.

Answers to these kinds of questions/issues are likely to have relevant policy implications. Useful suggestions for policy measures that aim at influencing disparities in regional developments and developing lagging regions might certainly be a product of a more careful analysis of spatial interactions of local economies.

7 References

Aiginger, K., Boeheim, M., Gugler, K., Pfaffermayr, M., Wolfmayr-Schnitzer, Y. (1999) Specialisation and (Geographic) Concentration of European Manufacturing, Enterprise DG Working Paper No 1, Background Paper for the The competitiveness of European industry: 1999 Report, Bruxelles.

Akbari, A. H., Devoretz, D. J. (1992) The Substitutability of Foreign-Born Labour in Canadian-Production: Circa 1980, The Canadian Journal of Economics, 25 (3), 604-614.

Amiti, M. (1998) New Trade Theories and Industrial Location in the Eu: A Survey of Evidence, Oxford Review of Economic Policy, 14 (2), 45-53.

Amiti, M. (1999) Specialisation Patterns in Europe, Weltwirtschaftliches Archiv, 134 (4), 573-593.

Baldwin, J. R., Brown, W. M. (2004) Regional Manufacturing Employment Volatility in Canada: The Effects of Specialisation and Trade, Papers in Regional Science, 83 (3), 519-541.

Baltagi, B. H. and Blien, U. (1998) The German Wage Curve: Evidence from the Iab Employment Sample, Economics Letters, 61 135-142.

Baltagi, B. H., Blien, U., Wolf, K. (2000) The East German Wage Curve 1993-1998, Economics Letters, 69 25-31.

Baltagi, B. H., Li, D. (2004) Prediction in Panel Data Model with Spatial Correlation, in Advances in Spatial Econometrics: Methodology, Tools and Application, ed. by L. Anselin, R. J. G. M. Florax and S. Rey. Heidelberg (Germany): Springer-Verlag, 283-295.

Bauer, T. (1998) Do Immigrants Reduce Natives' Wages? Evidence from Germany, Department of Economics Rutgers University Working, Paper No. 1998/02.

Bean, F. D., Lowell, B. L., Taylor, L. J. (1988) Undocumented Mexican Immigrants and the Earnings of Other Workers in the U.S., Demography, 25 (1), 35-52.

Bell, B., Nickell, S., Quintini, G. (2002) Wage Equations, Wage Curves and All That, Labour Economics, 9 341-360.

Bellmann, L., Blien, U. (2001) Wage Curve Analyses of Establishment Data from Western Germany, Industrial and Labor Relations Review, 54 851-863.

Bhaskar, V., To, T. (1999) Minimum Wages for Ronald Mcdonald Monopsonies: A Theory of Monopsonistic Competition, Economic Journal, 109 190-203.

Blanchard, O. J., Katz, L. F. (1992) Regional Evolutions, Brookings Papers on Economic Activity, 1 1-75.

Blanchard, O. J., Katz, L. F. (1997) What We Know and Do Not Know About Natural Rate of Unemployment, Journal of Economic Perspectives, 11 (1), 51-72.

Blanchflower, D. G., Oswald, A. J. (1990) The Wage Curve, Scandinavian Journal of Economics, 92 (2), 215-235.

Blanchflower, D. G., Oswald, A. J. (1994a) Estimating a Wage Curve for Britain 1973-90, The Economic Journal, 104 1025-1043.

Blanchflower, D. G., Oswald, A. J. (1994b) The Wage Curve. Cambridge: MIT Press.

Blanchflower, D. G., Oswald, A. J. (1995) An Introduction to the Wage Curve, The Journal of Economic Perspectives, 9 (3), 153-167.

Boomsma, P. (1999) Employment Forecasting in Fryslân in the Age of Economic Structural Changes, in Regional Development in an Age of Structural Economic Change, ed. by P. Rietveld and D. Shefer: Ashgate, 183-212.

Borjas, G. J. (1987) Immigrants, Minorities, and Labor Market Competition, Industrial and Labor Relations Review, 40 (3), 382-392.

Borjas, G. J. (1994) The Economics of Immigration, Journal of Economic Literature, 32 (4), 1667-1717.

Borjas, G. J. (1999) The Economic Analysis of Immigration, in Handbook of Labor Economics, ed. by O. Ashenfelter and D. Card: North Holland, 1697-1760.

Borjas, G. J. (2001) Does Immigration Grease the Wheels of Labor Market?, Brookings Papers on Economic Activity, 1:2001 69-133.

Borjas, G. J. (2003) The Labor Demand Curve Is Downward Sloping: Reexamining the Impact of Immigration on the Labor Market, Quarterly Journal of Economics, 118 (4), 1335-1374.

Borjas, G. J., Freeman, R. B., Katz, L. F. (1996) Searching for the Effect of Immigration on the Labor Market, The American Economic Review, 86 (2), 246-251.

Bratsberg, B., Turunen, J. (1996) Wage Curve Evidence from Panel Data, Economics Letters, 51 345-353.

Brülhart, M. (1998) Economic Geography, Industry Location and Trade: The Evidence, The World Economy, 21 (6), 775-801.

Brülhart, M. (2001) Growing Alike or Growing Apart? Industrial Specialisation of Eu Countries, in The Impact of Emu on Europe and the Developing Countries, ed. by C. Wyplosz. Oxford: Oxford University Press, 169-194.

Buettner, T. (1999) The Effect of Unemployment, Aggregate Wages, and Spatial Contiguity on Local Wages: An Investigation with German District Level Data, Papers in Regional Science, 78 (1), 47-67.

Burgess, S., Profit, S. (2001) Externalities in the Matching of Workers and Firms in Britain, Labour Economics, 8 313-333.

Campbell, C., Orszag, J. M. (1998) A Model of the Wage Curve, Economics Letters, 59 119-125.

Card, D. (1990) The Impact of the Mariel Boatlift on the Miami Labor Market, Industrial and Labor Relations Review, 43 (2), 245-257.

Card, D. (1995) The Wage Curve: A Review, Journal of Economic Literature, 33 (2), 785-799.

Card, D. (2001) Immigrant Inflows, Native Outflows, and the Local Market Impacts of Higher Immigration, Journal of Labor Economics, 19 (1), 22-64.

Carrington, W. J., de Lima, P. J. F. (1996) The Impact of 1970s Repatriates from Africa on the Portuguese Labor Market, Industrial and Labor Relations Review, 49 (2), 330-347.

Chiarini, B., Piselli, P. (1997) Wage Settings, Wage Curve and Phillips Curve: The Italian Evidence, Scottish Journal of Political Economy, 44 (5), 545-565.

Decressin, J., Fatás, A. (1995) Regional Labour Market Dynamics in Europe, European Economic Review, 39 1627-1655.

Diebold, F. X. (1998) The Past, Present, and Future of Macroeconomic Forecasting, Journal of Economic Perspectives, 12 (2), 175-192.

Doi, M., Hiyoshi, T., Poot, J. (2003) National and Regional Wage Curves in Japan, 1981-2001, Paper presented to the 50th North American Regional Science Conference, Philadelphia.

Don, F. J. H. (2004) How Econometric Models Help Policy Makers: Theory and Practice, De Economist, 152 (2), 177-195.

Eichengreen, B. (1993) Labour Markets and the European Monetary Unification, in Policy Issues in the Operation of Currency Unions, ed. by P. R. Masson and M. P. Taylor. Cambridge: Cambridge University Press.

Eitrheim, O., Husebo, T. A., Nymoen, R. (1999) Equilibrium-Correction Vs. Differencing in Macroeconometric Forecasting, Economic Modelling, 16 (4), 515-544.

Elhorst, J. P., Blien, U., Wolf, K. (2002) A Spatial Panel Approach to the East German Wage Curve, Paper presented at the 42nd Congress of the European Regional Science Association (ERSA) Dortmund, Germany.

Fauvel, Y., Paquet, A., Zimmerman, C. (1999) Short-Term Forecasting of National and Provincial Employment in Canada, Applied Research Branch - Strategic Policy - Human Resources Development Canada, Working Paper R-99-6E.

Friedberg, R. M. (2001) The Impact of Mass Migration on the Israeli Labor Market, The Quarterly Journal of Economics, 116 (4), 1373-1408.

Friedberg, R. M., Hunt, J. (1995) The Impact of Immigrants on Host Country Wages, Employment and Growth, The Journal of Economic Perspectives, 9 (2), 23-44.

Gorter, C., Nijkamp, P., Poot, J. (1999) (Eds.) Crossing Borders: Regional and Urban Perspectives on International Migration. Aldershot: Ashgate

Greenway, D. and Hine, R. C. (1991) Intra-Industry Specialisation, Trade Expansion and Adjustment in the European Economic Space, Journal of Common Market Studies, 29 (6), 603-622.

Greenwood, M. J., Hunt, G. L., Kohli, U. (1997) The Factor-Market Consequences of Unskilled Immigration to the United States, Labour Economics, 4 (1), 1-28.

Groot, W., Mekkelholt, E., Oosterbeek, H. (1992) Further Evidence on the Wage Curve, Economics Letters, 38 355-359.

Grossman, J. B. (1982) The Substitutability of Natives and Immigrants in Production, The Review of Economics and Statistics, 64 (4), 596-603.

Hallet, M. (1998) The Regional Impact of the Single Currency, Paper presented at the 38th Congress of the European Regional Science Association, Vienna.

Hallet, M. (2001) Real Convergence and Catching-up in the Eu, paper presented to the workshop Structural Funds and Convergence, The Hague.

Hanson, G. H. (1996) Economic Integration, Intra-Industry Trade, and Frontier Regions, European Economic Review, 40 941-949.

Hanson, G. H. (1997a) Increasing Returns, Trade, and the Regional Structure of Wages, Economic Journal, 107 113-133.

Hanson, G. H. (1997b) Localization Economies, Vertical Organization, and Trade, American Economic Review, 87 1266-1278.

Hanson, G. H. (1998) Market Potential, Increasing Returns, and Geographic Concentration, NBER Working Paper No. 6429.

Hatch, N. (2003) Modeling and Forecasting at the Bank of England, in Understanding Economic Forecasts, ed. by D. F. Hendry and N. R. Ericsson. Cambridge (Mass): The MIT Press, 124-148.

Heckscher, E. (1949) The Effect of Foreign Trade on Distribution of Income, Economisk Tidskrift, 497-512, Reprinted, in Readings in the Theory of International Trade, ed. by H. S. Ellis and L. A. Metzler. Philadelphia: Blakiston, 272-300.

Helpman, E., Krugman, P. (1985) Market Structure and Foreign Trade: Increasing Returns, Imperfect Competition and the International Economy. Brighton: Harvester Wheatsheaf.

Hendry, D. F., Clements, M. P. (2003) Economic Forecasting: Some Lessons from Recent Research, Economic Modelling, 20 (2), 301-329.

Hendry, D. F., Ericsson, N. R. (2003) (Eds.) Understanding Economic Forecasts. Cambridge (Mass): The MIT Press

Hine, R. C. (1990) Economic Integration and Inter-Industry Specialisation, University of Nottingham, CREDIT Research Paper 89/6.

Hunt, J. (1992) The Impact of the 1962 Repatriates from Algeria on the French Labor Market, Industrial and Labor Relations Review, 45 (3), 556-572.

Ikkaracan, I., Selim, R. (2003) The Role of Unemployment in Wage Determination: Further Evidence on the Wage Curve from Turkey, Applied Economics, 35 1589-1598.

Jaeger, D. A. (1996) Skill Differences and the Effect of Immigrants on the Wages of Natives, US Bureau of Labor Statistics, Mimeo.

Janssens, S., Konings, J. (1998) One More Wage Curve: The Case of Belgium, Economics Letters, 60 223-227.

Johansen, K. (2002) Regional Wage Curves Empirical Evidence from Norway, Dept. of Economics, Norwegian University of Science and Technology Working Paper No. 3/2002.

Kennedy, S. and Borland, J. (2000) A Wage Curve for Australia?, Oxford Economic Papers, 52 774-803.

King, A. G., Lowell, B. L., Bean, F. D. (1986) The Effects of Hispanic Immigrants on the Earnings of Native Hispanic Americans, Social Science Quarterly, 67 (4), 673-689.

Krugman, P. (1979) Increasing Returns, Monopolistic Competition and International Trade, Journal of International Economics, 9 469-479.

Krugman, P. (1980) Scale Economies, Product Differentiation, and the Pattern of Trade, American Economic Review, 70 950-959.

Krugman, P. (1981) Intraindustry Specialization and the Gains from Trade, Journal of Political Economy, 89 959-973.

Krugman, P. (1991a) Geography and Trade. Cambridge: MIT Press.

Krugman, P. (1991b) Increasing Returns and Economic Geography, Journal of Political Economy, 99 (3), 483-499.

Krugman, P. and Venables, A. (1990) Integration and the Competitiveness of Peripheral Industry, in Unity with Diversity in the European Community, ed. by C. Bliss and J. Braga de Macedo. Cambridge: Cambridge University Press.

Krugman, P. and Venables, A. (1995) Globalisation and the Inequality of Nations, The Quarterly Journal of Economics, 110 (4), 857-880.

Landesmann, M. (1995) The Patterns of East-West European Integration: Catching up or Falling Behind?, in Transforming Economies and European Integration, ed. by R. Dobrinsky and M. Landesmann. Aldershot: Edward Elgar, 116-140.

Leamer, E. E. and Levinsohn, J. (1995) International Trade Theory: The Evidence, in Handbook of International Economics, ed. by G. M. Grossman and K. Rogoff: Amsterdam, Elsevier-North Holland.

Longhi, S., Nijkamp, P. and Poot, J. (2004) A Meta-Analytic Assessment of the Effect of Immigration on Wages, Tinbergen Institute Discussion Paper TI 2004-134/3; Population Studies Centre Discussion Paper No. 47.

Midelfart-Knarvik, K. H., Overman, H. G. and Venables, A. J. (2000) The Location of European Industry, Economic Papers No. 142 - Report prepared for the Directorate General for Economic and Financial Affairs, European Commission.

Mincer, J. (1974) Schooling, Experience and Earnings. New York: Columbia University Press.

Molho, I. (1992) Local Pay Determination, Journal of Economic Surveys, 6 155-194.

Montuenga, V., Garcia, I., Fernandex, M. (2003) Wage Flexibility: Evidence from Five Eu Countries Based on the Wage Curve, Economics Letters, 78 169-174.

Morrison, P. S., Papps, K. L. and Poot, J. (2005) Wages, Employment, Labour Turnover, and the Accessibility of Local Labour Markets, Labour Economics, In press.

Nijkamp, P., Poot, J. (2005) The Last Word on the Wage Curve?, Journal of Economic Surveys, Forthcoming.

Nijkamp, P., Resmini, L. and Traistaru, I. (2003) European Integration, Regional Specialization and Location of Industrial Activity: A Survey of Theoretical and Empirical Literature, in The Emerging Economic Geography in Eu Accession Countries, ed. by I. Traistaru, P. Nijkamp and L. Resmini. Aldershot: Ashgate Publishing Ltd., 28-45.

Obstfeld, M., Peri, G. (1998) Asymmetric Shocks: Regional Non-Adjustment and Fiscal Policy, Economic Policy, 28 206-259.

OECD (2000) Disparities in Regional Labour Markets, in Employment Outlook: OECD, Organization for Economic Co-operation and Development.

Ohlin, B. (1933) Interregional and International Trade. Cambridge, MA: Harvard University Press.

Overman, H. G., Puga, D. (2002) Regional Unemployment Clusters, Economic Policy 115-144.

Pannenberg, M., Schwarze, J. (1998a) Labor Market Slack and the Wage Curve, Economics Letters, 58 351-354.

Pannenberg, M., Schwarze, J. (1998b) Phillips Curve or Wage Curve: Is There Really a Puzzle? Evidence for West Germany, Otto-Friedrich Universitat, Bamberg, Volkswirtschaftsliche Diskussionsbeitrage No. 83.

Papps, K. L. (2001) Investigating a Wage Curve for New Zealand, New Zealand Economic Papers, 35 218-239.

Partridge, M. D., Rickman, D. S. (1997) Has the Wage Curve Nullified the Harris-Todaro Model? Further Us Evidence, Economics Letters, 54 277-282.

Partridge, M. D., Rickman, D. S. (1998) Generalizing the Bayesian Vector Autoregression Approach for Regional Interindustry Employment Forecasting, Journal of Business and Economic Statistics, 16 (1), 62-72.

Petrakos, G. (1996) The Regional Dimension of Transition in Eastern and Central European Countries: An Assessment, Eastern European Economics, 34 (5), 5-38.

Petrakos, G. (2000) The Spatial Impact of East-West Integration, in Integration and Transition in Europe: The Economic Geography of Interaction, ed. by G. Petrakos, G. Maier and G. Gorzelak. London: Routledge.

Phelps, E. (1984) Structural Slumps: The Modern Equilibrium Theory of Unemployment, Interest and Assets. Cambridge (MA): Harvard University Press.

Phillips, A. W. (1958) The Relation between Unemployment and the Rate of Change of Money Wage Rates in the United Kingdom, 1861-1957, Economica, 25 (100), 283-299.

Puga, D. (2002) European Regional Policies in Light of Recent Location Theories, Journal of Economic Geography, 2 373-406.

Raagmaa, G. (1996) Shifts in Regional Development in Estonia During the Transition, European Planning Studies, 4 (6), 683-703.

Resmini, L. (2002) Specialization and Growth Prospects in Border Regions of Accession Countries, Center for European Integration Studies, University of Bonn, ZEI Working Paper B02-17.

Ricardo, D. (1817) On the Principles of Political Economy and Taxation. London.

Rickman, D. S. (2002) A Bayesian Forecasting Approach to Constructing Regional Input-Output Based Employment Multipliers, Papers in Regional Science, 81 (4), 483-498.

Salop, S. (1979) A Model of the Natural Rate of Unemployment, American Economic Review, 69 117-125.

Sanroma', E., Raul, R. (2004) Further Evidence on Disaggregated Wage Curves: The Case of Spain, Universitat de Barcelona.

Sapir, A. (1996) The Effects of Europe's Internal Market Programme on Production and Trade: A First Assessment, Weltwirtschaftliches Archiv, 132 (3), 457-475.

Sims, C. A. (1980) Macroeconomics and Reality, Econometrica, 48 (1), 1-48.

Stock, J. H. and Watson, M. W. (2002) Macroeconomic Forecasting Using Diffusion Indexes, Journal of Business and Economic Statistics, 20 (2), 147-162.

Topel, R. H. (1986) Local Labor Markets, The Journal of Political Economy, 94 (3 Part 2), S111-S143.

Turner, P. (2003) Economic Modeling for Fun and Profit, in Understanding Economic Forecasts, ed. by D. F. Hendry and N. R. Ericsson. Cambridge (Mass): The MIT Press, 42-53.

Venables, A. (1996) Equilibrium Locations of Vertically Linked Industries, *International Economic Review*, 37 341-359.

Venables, A. J. (1998) The Assessment: Trade and Location, Oxford Review of Economic Policy, 14 (2), 1-6.

Wagner, J. (1994) German Wage Curves, 1979-1990, Economics Letters, 44 307-311.

Winter-Ebmer, R. (1996) Wage Curve, Unemployment Duration and Compensating Differentials, Labour Economics, 3 425-434.

Winter-Ebmer, R., Zweimuller, J. (1996) Immigration and the Earnings of Young Native Workers, Oxford Economic Papers, 48 (3), 473-491.

Zimmermann, K. F., Bauer, T. K. (2002) The Economics of Migration. 4 Volumes. Cheltenham, UK and Northampton, Mass: Edward Elgar.

An Assessment of the Integration of Eastern European Economies in the European Union

George M. Korres[1,*], Emmanuel Mamatzakis[2,**] and Christos Staikouras[3]

[1] Assistant Professor, Department of Geography, University of the Aegean, University Hill, Mytilene 81100, Greece. Also Visiting Fellow (Oct. 2006/Feb. 2007) at University of Leeds, Institute of Communication Studies, Leeds LS2-9J, United Kingdom
[2] Assistant Professor, Department of Economics, University of Macedonia, Thessaloniki Member of Advisors Committee, Ministry of Finance, Greece
[3] Athens University of Economics and Business, Athens, Greece

1 Introduction

The issue of economic convergence has attracted considerable attention from many researchers during the last decade. This issue is of particular interest for Europe after the launch of the euro currency in 1999 and following the importance attached to economic and social cohesion. Structural funds and cohesion policies became important instruments in reducing regional disparities in the European Union (EU).

The Eastern enlargement of the EU represents one of the most challenging components of the EU construction process. The accession of eight countries (Czech Republic, Estonia, Hungary, Latvia, Lithuania, Poland, Slovak Republic and Slovenia) to the EU was an important milestone in the integration process of Central Eastern European countries and the Baltic states with Western Europe. The fundamental role played by regional policies, notably in the aftermath of the Economic and Monetary Union (EMU), has led European authorities to promote the administrative capacity of potential candidates to undertake sound regional development plans in an integrated economic, social and legal environment. To become a full EU member, candidate countries are expected to fulfil certain economic criteria, predominantly in nominal terms, with the issue of real convergence somehow shading into the background. In neo-classical models the technology is such that, all things equal, poor countries, in terms of Gross Domestic Product (GDP) per capita, grow faster than rich ones (absolute

* Email: gkorres@hol.gr
** Email: tzakis@uom.gr

β-convergence). If poor and rich countries only differ by their initial level of per capita GDP – that is, they face identical levels of technology and preferences – then the inequality eventually disappears in the long run. If countries differ in other aspects too, then convergence takes the form of the stabilization of the distribution of relative per capita income across regions (conditional β-convergence and σ-convergence).

A great number of empirical studies have appeared testing the convergence issue, mostly focussed on real convergence referring to per capita income as a measure of living standards, using the neo-classical framework (Smith and Venables, 1991; Sala-i-Martin, 1996; Siriopoulos and Asteriou, 1998). The popular approaches which are used explore the concepts of σ-(sigma) and β-(beta) convergence where the former measures the dispersion of per capita income or productivity among different economies (or countries) over time and the latter predicts the inverse relationship between the growth of per capita income or productivity and their initial levels. The σ-(or variance) convergence implies that wealth differences diminish among a set of countries or economies over time. The evidence of σ-convergence is useful, since one can observe periods of convergence or divergence through time.

The evidence of β-(or regression) convergence is different, showing directly the rate of convergence across economies, implying that poor economies or countries grow faster than richer ones. The two measures are complementary, but not exclusive; β-convergence is exclusive necessary, but not a sufficient condition for σ-sigma convergence to take place. Sala-i-Martin (1996) further argues that β-convergence is of special interest, since its value shows whether there exists convergence pattern among different economies, measures the pace of the convergence process, and identifies whether it is partial (limited to specific time-period) or total (for the whole time-period) convergence.

On the other hand, in endogenous growth models, rich countries grow faster than poor ones and inequality is expected to increase infinitely. Moreover, Quah (1996) argues that the concept of β-convergence, by observing a negative correlation for growth rates and levels of per capita income (or productivity), reveals no information on the way that poor economies are catching up with the richer ones. Given this criticism, one needs to take into account the limitations of the β-convergence analysis, when economic policy implications drawing.

The purpose of this paper is thus twofold; firstly, we review recent progress towards the nominal convergence of the new EU Member States from Eastern Europe along the lines of the Maastricht Treaty. The nominal convergence entails several criteria that act as prerequisites to join the Exchange Rate Mechanism (ERM-II) and subsequently the eurozone. Secondly step, we empirically investigate the concept of real convergence of the new EU Member States based on the principles of the neo-classical analysis, as stated above. This paper focuses mostly on the eight new economies; Cyprus and Malta, which are not transition economies, possess a financial sector whose structure is closer to that of the eurozone. This is why we exclude these two countries from our analysis.

The rest of the paper is organised as follows. Section 2 presents a comprehensive insight regarding the impact of the nominal economic integration of the new EU Member States (EU-8 thereafter). Section 3 reports the process of real convergence in the EU-8 based on an analysis of the β-convergence measure. Finally, Sect. 4 draws some conclusions on policy intervention and convergence prospects.

2 Nominal Convergence

In 2004, the EU-8 countries (together with Cyprus and Malta) joined the EU and, as a consequence, became subject to the budgetary requirements of the Stability and Growth Pact, as well as to the country-specific recommendations reported in the Broad and Economic Policy Guidelines (BEPGs) of the EU Commission. In June 2004, three of the countries (namely Estonia, Lithuania and Slovenia) took the first step towards adopting the euro currency with their accession to the ERM II. All the EU-8 share the view that their integration within EU will lead them into the euro zone within the next few years. For this development to take place, it is necessary to conform to all the conditions of the EMU prior to entering the euro-zone as stated in the Maastricht treaty.

The EU-8 went through comprehensive adjustments and moved a long way in converging to the rest of the EU member states, but important disparities remain as captured by on average lower income per capita levels than their euro zone counterparts (see Table 1). The Baltic States, with relatively low per capita GDP levels and a longer remaining process for convergence with other EU members, outpaced the other countries in the region. The region therefore remains on a path towards higher living standards and eventually convergence with the richer industrial nations. In many instances, economic growth has been accompanied by a rapid rise in domestic bank lending. This has stimulated the financial system and boosted investment and consumption.

Table 1. Gross Domestic Product [GDP, %]

	Average annual real growth rate [%]		GDP/head [PPS in % of EU average]	
	1998–2002	2003–2006	2002	2006
Czech Rep.	1.5	3.0	59.8	62.0
Estonia	4.7	5.5	41.7	47.6
Hungary	4.3	4.0	55.9	60.2
Latvia	5.7	6.2	35.2	41.2
Lithuania	4.5	6.4	39.1	46.1
Poland	5.4	4.7	39.4	43.5
Slovak Rep.	3.0	4.3	47.3	51.6
Slovenia	3.9	3.9	73.7	79.0

Source: EU Commission. Forecasts are based on Commission's projections Autumn 2004.

The first criterion of nominal convergence refers to price stability. The assessment of price stability and inflation convergence is based on the Harmonised Index of Consumer Prices (HICP). Of the EU-8 countries three are below the average rate of inflation (2.1%), namely the Czech Republic, Estonia, and Lithuania; this implies the significant progress that some of these countries have made, as depicted in Table 2; from the previous stratospheric inflation rates observed in some of the former transition economies of the Eastern European region, all countries achieved in recent years single digit inflation levels. A clear policy orientation towards price stability has been a key economic policy.

Next, we assess the criterion for the government budgetary position. This criterion is of critical importance for the smooth operation of EMU, as it is linked to the decisions made in accordance with the excessive deficit procedure in Article 104 of the Treaty which claims that a member state is considered to have attained sustainable convergence if it has

Table 2. Inflation [HICP, %]

	2002	2006
Czech Rep.	1.8	2.5
Estonia	3.6	3.2
Hungary	5.3	3.0
Latvia	1.9	3.0
Lithuania	0.3	2.6
Poland	1.9	2.9
Slovak Rep.	3.3	3.0
Slovenia	7.5	3.7

Source: EU Commission. Forecasts are based on Commission's projections of Autumn 2004.

achieved a budgetary position without an excessive deficit. In turn, the existence of an excessive deficit is determined in relation to the two criteria for budgetary discipline, namely the government deficit and the government debt. As reported in the latest European Commission Convergence Report for 2003 (published in 2004), the Czech Republic, Hungary, Poland and Slovak Rep. recorded a general government deficit in excess of the maximum three percent of GDP reference value set by the Treaty; the remaining Member States had either a lower deficit or a surplus. Based on this evidence for the existence of an excessive deficit, the Commission initiated the excessive deficit procedure for these four countries. The other examined Member States, namely Estonia, Latvia, Lithuania, and Slovenia, are not the subject of such a Council decision and therefore fulfil the budgetary convergence criterion (Table 3).

According to the Stability and Growth Pact, Poland and Slovak Rep. should correct their excessive deficits by 2007 and the Czech Republic and Hungary by 2008. These four countries, which have excessive deficits, are being allowed a longer period to adjust to the three percent deficit norm. Only one Member State, namely Estonia, has generally maintained a balanced or surplus position. A gradual trend towards fiscal consolidation is visible in the other Member States fulfilling the budgetary convergence criterion (that is for Latvia, Lithuania and Slovenia). While the government debt ratio remains below the 60 percent of GDP reference value in all the new member states over the last five years, it has increased significantly in the Czech Republic, Poland and Slovak Rep. and remains only slightly below the reference value in Hungary (Table 3). In 2004, the debt ratio was projected to increase further in all the Member States with significant stocks of debt, except for Hungary.

Table 3. General government balance [% of GDP]

	Revenue		Expenditure		Total balance		Primary balance	
	2002	2006	2002	2006	2002	2006	2002	2006
Czech	42.4	42.7	49.1	46.8	−6.7	−4.0	−5.0	−2.4
Estonia	39.7	40.7	38.4	40.7	1.3	0.0	1.6	0.3
Hungary	44.5	43.6	53.7	46.1	−9.2	−2.5	−5.5	0.4
Latvia	41.9	42.2	44.9	44.2	−3.0	−2.0	−2.6	−1.3
Lithuania	33.8	35.6	35.6	37.4	−1.7	−1.8	−0.2	−0.5
Poland	42.1	42.1	45.9	45.5	−3.8	−3.4	−1.0	−0.8
Slovak .	41.8	38.3	49.0	41.2	−7.2	−2.9	−3.5	−0.6
Slovenia	41.5	41.7	43.9	43.0	−2.4	−1.3	−0.2	0.0

Source: EU Commission. Forecasts are based on Commission's projections of Atumn 2004.

The Treaty also refers to the exchange rate criterion. The currencies of the new member states are required to follow the normal fluctuation margins of the ERM II for at least two years without severe tensions, and in particular without devaluing against the currency of any other Member State. Table 4 depicts the prospects of participation in ERM II of the new Member States. Moreover, on June 28th, 2004, the Estonian kroon, Lithuanian litas and Slovenian tolar joined ERM II with a standard fluctuation band of ±15 percent around their central rate.

Over the period of reference, Estonia and Lithuania have maintained successfully their currency board within ERM II while the Slovenian tolar, after having continuously depreciated against the euro currency in the previous years, has remained very stable. The Czech koruna, Hungarian forint, Latvian lats, Polish zloty, and Slovak koruna have not yet joined ERM II. These currencies are characterised by different exchange rate regimes. The Latvian lats has displayed in recent year a fairly stable

Table 4: Exchange rate criterion

	Current exchange rate regime	Euro introduction target date	ERM II partici-pation target date	Envisaged changes to exchange rate regime
Czech Rep.	Managed float	In 2009–2010	Entry date conditional upon date of compliance with convergence criteria	None
Estonia	Currency board based on the euro	In 2007	Participation in June 2004	None
Hungary	Peg to the euro with wide band (± 15%)	In 2008–2009	Entry date conditional upon date of compliance with convergence criteria	None
Latvia	Peg to SDR	In 2008–2009	2005	None
Lithuania	CBA based on the euro	None	Participation in June 2004	None
Poland	Float	2009	None	None
Slovak Rep.	Managed float with the euro as reference currency	2009	None	None
Slovenia	Managed float	None	Participation in June 2004	None

development vis-à-vis its anchor currencies (respectively the SDR, a currency basket and the euro). The peg of the Hungarian forint to the euro was less stable in a context of increasing inflation and substantial fiscal deficit. Among the floating currencies, the Czech koruna was relatively stable against the euro currency in the last two years, while the Slovak koruna strengthened and the Polish zloty initially depreciated but appreciated recently. The minimum stay of two years in ERM II was not respected by any of the new Member States and hence none did not fulfil the exchange rate criterion (see the European Central Bank Convergence Report, 2004).

Moreover, in the single-currency EU area, convergence must ensure that the single interest rate set at the level of the EMU is appropriate for all its participants. This condition is set so as in case that euro zone is hit by a shock, a high degree of convergence limits the emergence of asymmetric economic developments at the country level, taking into account that the individual member state can use the exchange rate as a policy tool. In recent years, sovereign ratings have been upgraded for most of the new Member States, which has further contributed to the decreasing levels of their long term interest rates and their spreads vis-à-vis the euro area rates (see European Commission's Convergence Report, 2004).

At the beginning of 2001, the countries with the highest long-term interest rates among the new Member States were Lithuania and Poland (with rates in the range of 9.5–10.5 percent). In August 2004, Hungary and still Poland had the highest long-term interest rates among the new Member States, well above the euro area average (with rates above seven percent), while the countries with the lowest long term interest rates were Lithuania and Slovenia (with rates around 4.6–4.7 percent). Excluding Hungary and Poland, where developments in long-term interest rates have diverged from the euro area developments, the degree of the long-term interest rate convergence among the new Member States is strong. In this sub-group (EU-8 excluding Hungary and Poland) the spread between the highest and the lowest long-term interest rates declined from 2.0 percentage points on average in 2001 to around 0.9 percentage points on average in the period January–August 2004, clustered within a range of 0.4 percentage points (Lithuania) above the euro area average. In Hungary and Poland, the process of interest rate convergence has been interrupted in the second half of 2003 on concerns about the authorities' resolve to tackle the mounting government deficits.

There are other additional factors that assert an impact on the integration process. The advent of the euro has had, and continues to have, a major impact on the European financial sector, towards further integration. Specifically, all countries have made strides towards financial integration. Most countries have completed, or advanced to a substantial degree, the restructuring and privatisation of their banks and, usually with some lag, of their non-bank financial sectors – with the notable exceptions of Slovenia, where delays in restructuring and privatisation complicate the development of the financial markets. In spite of these developments, the financial sector in the transition countries has so far remained relatively small in size and not fully developed in terms of market segments or instruments and, notwithstanding considerable progress there still remains more to become room for enhancing efficiency. This is particularly true for capital markets, which play only a marginal role in many of the new EU countries' financial sectors, but it is also true for most indicators of banking activities.

Altogether, the sector's intermediation role and its supportive function for economic growth and macroeconomic stability need further strengthening. Despite the remarkable progress made in recent years and the ongoing adjustments to euro zone standards, it is likely that the financial sectors of the new EU countries will undergo further significant changes in the future. One way to gauge the potential for further changes is to compare the current situation with the average of financial sector indicators in the euro zone, motivated by the fact that the integration process can be expected eventually to make the new EU countries broadly comparable to current euro zone member states.

In this comparison, the following picture would emerge: financial sectors of accession countries are relatively small, even when taking the countries' lower income levels into account; as percentage of GDP, bank deposits, bank loans and bank holdings of securities as well as capitalisation of bond and stock markets are far below the euro zone average. Financial sectors are dominated even more strongly by the banking sector than those of euro zone countries; banking sectors are, by and large, well-capitalised and characterised by strong foreign involvement. Limited financial sector intermediation has in particular been detrimental to small and medium-sized enterprises, which are usually not able to tap direct foreign financing and to use it as a substitute for domestic credit. In most countries, the private sector credit-to-GDP ratio is still only about one third or less of the euro-zone.

Financial sectors in the new EU countries have undergone fundamental changes since the beginning of transition about a decade ago. In the formerly planned regimes, financial markets were non-existent, and these sectors consisted almost entirely of the, so-called, non banks that collected deposits, remunerating them at regular rates, and provided loans based on decisions in planning bureaus. Upon transition, the mono banks were broken up to form a two-tier structure of a central bank and commercial banks, with the latter being restructured, recapitalised and privatised. In addition, newly founded private banks entered the market, often supported by fairly liberal licensing and rather loose regulatory regimes.

In many cases, this process went through – at times severe – banking crises, involving a collapse of financial assets and intermediation and often requiring massive amounts of public funds. Tightening supervision, consolidation and liquidation of insolvent institutions as well as a massive entry of foreign banks, however, have ultimately led to a stable commercial banking sector. At the same time, money, bond and stock markets have been set up. At the current stage, the financial sectors can be characterised by overall financial stability and a trend of gradual financial development in most of the sectors' segments (see Caviglia et al., 2002).

This process of integrating the EU-8 into a market-oriented economy was also associated with a large initial decline of GDP and an important reorientation of trade, in particular exports to the EU counties. As a result, current accounts in the examined countries recorded only moderate deficits, or even turned positive, at the very beginning of the 1990s. The overall surge of economic activity towards in the mid-1990s, including a progressive resumption of investment activity, explains the progressive widening of the current account deficits in the transition economies. At that time, the new Member States also liberalised transactions on the current and capital accounts. Financing of the current account shifted from loans and transfers from official lenders, such as the IMF, to private capital, mostly Foreign Direct Investment (FDI) and, in some cases, debt-creating flows. With the progressively widening current account imbalances leading to increasing doubts about current account sustainability, capital flows started to reverse and provoked in some countries adjustments to their exchange rate regimes (Czech Republic, Hungary, Poland, and Slovak Rep.).

The impact of the 1998 Russian crisis and the economic slowdown contributed to an overall decrease of current account deficits in the late 1990s in most of the countries, with the exception of Hungary and Poland. More recently, the slowdown of economic growth in the EU with a stronger growth momentum in most of the new Member States led to a gradual widening of the current account deficits in five out of the eight Member States (Czech Republic, Estonia, Latvia, Lithuania, and Hungary). At the same time Slovenia's current account went into surplus; Poland saw their deficit narrowing and Slovak Rep. experienced a sharp deficit reduction in 2003.

Overall, the review on the nominal convergence of EU-8 shows that, although countries have performed differently in being adjusted to and meeting the Maastricht criteria, they have clearly achieved some significant convergence. One would consider that such differentiation could have a bearing impact on how EU-8 will adjust prior to their accession in the ERM II and eventually in the euro zone. Notice, however, that there might be in operation a trade-off between meeting the ERM II criteria and real convergence. In this respect, the recent current account widening in the Baltic States could have been associated with strong investment activity underlying the catching-up process. This, in turn, may also have implications for the real convergence.

3 The Real Convergence

Having reviewed the nominal convergence of the EU-8 we turn our attention to the real convergence hypothesis. The economic policy of the EU has been focused on the promotion of a higher degree of nominal and real convergence between its member states, and, although nominal convergence has been achieved, the same is not observed for the real convergence. In particular, as far as we are aware, the tendency of real convergence between the EU-8 in the last decade has not been investigated. The enlarged EU poses new challenges in terms of achieving real convergence among Member States in a timely manner. To proceed with our analysis, we adopt the concept of convergence in per capita output, as it is perceived that economies reach a common long-run steady-state growth. This concept of absolute (or unconditional) β-convergence assumes a unique steady-state economy which, in turn, requires that technology, saving rates, population growth and depreciation rates take similar values across the different economies. The main element behind the force for convergence is the diminishing returns to reproducible capital, so that, poor economies with low capital-labour ratios will have a higher marginal productivity of capital and, hence, will grow faster than richer ones, given the same level of savings and investments. This analysis is contingent to free factor mobility and free trade, as those conditions are essential and contribute to the acceleration of the convergence through the equalisation of prices of goods and factors of production and are particularly valid within the enlarged EU. In a cross country context, the mobility of production factors, such as are capital and labour, across economies within a union, like the EU, enhances the working of the market mechanism and, therefore, accelerates the absolute β-convergence on per capita income. This is so, since factor movements are at work and reinforce the equilibrating tendency towards the real convergence. For instance, if wages are too high in the more developed countries, labour will migrate from the less developed ones. Then, labour will become scarce in the latter and abundant in the former. Indeed, the wages and the marginal product of capital are inversely correlated and, therefore, capital will move to labour-intensive sector in low wage economies; this will diminish the trend for labour to migrate outwards.

In the long-run, any tendency for disparities declines over time, given that factor costs are lower and profit opportunities are higher in poor compared to rich economies. In this context, transitory shocks have a short-run effect but not a lasting effect. The role of government policy is limited to the promotion of market forces and the provision of macroeconomic stability. Given perfect competition, the unaffected working of the market mechanism will be equilibrating and any disparities in regional determinants of growth will tend to disappear over time. Exogenous technical progress is treated as a public good freely available to the poor countries, facilitating the imitation process and allowing these economies to grow faster. Under these conditions, policies have no role in shaping long-term economic growth. Empirical studies give support to the absolute convergence hypothesis only as a special case in which the sample involves economies with a high degree of homogeneity. This is known as the convergence club hypothesis.

At empirical level, the neo-classical prediction of convergence has been tested by the hypothesis of β-convergence predicting a negative relationship between the growth of per capita income over a given period and the initial level of per capita income across different economies. The absolute β-convergence is interpreted as a convergence to the same steady-state growth of per capita income (or productivity) for all economies (Barro and Sala-i-Martin, 1991). Absolute (or unconditional) convergence derives from the neo-classical growth theory based on diminishing returns to capital properties (Solow, 1956). According to the neo-classical theory, convergence is the rule, and divergence is a transitory short-term phenomenon. Free trade and perfect factor mobility will guarantee the convergence result through the equalisation of factor prices.

Next, we investigate the empirical validity of the neo-classical long-run absolute β-convergence prediction on the level of real per capita income across the new EU-8 for the whole period 1994–2003, as well as for the sub-period 1999–2003 (time period closer to the accession in the EU). Moreover, we estimate the convergence growth specification by using the following equation:

$$\Delta(y_{i,t}) = \alpha - \beta \ln(y_{i,0}) + \varepsilon_{i,t} \tag{1}$$

where the dependent variable is the real growth rates in per capita income for each economy into the sample. On the right hand side, the explanatory variable is the logarithm of the level of real per capita income in the starting year, β is the annual convergence rate of the GDP per head to the common stationary state, while α is a constant and ε is an error term. Table 5 reports the results of the traditional β-convergence test following (1). The regression has been performed assuming that EU-8 countries share the same GDP-per-head stationary state, and that the relationship between the growth rate of that variable and its initial value is not conditioned by other parameters. The data for national GDP series and population sizes is derived from Eurostat. As it can be seen from Table 5, β-coefficient has a very significant and negative value, indicating that the per capita income of the EU-8 countries is converging at the annual 3.9% rate along the whole sample period. This speed of convergence is higher than the stylised value that Barro and Sala-i-Martin (1991 and 1992) obtained for a large variety of less homogeneous (and less integrated) groups of countries. The important difference in these results, apart from the degree of homogeneity of the countries analysed, might be explained by the fact that our sample includes some recent years during which improvements in convergence could have been intense.

Indeed, the cross-country regression for the period 1999–2003 (Table 6), shows a significant β-coefficient (at 4.3%) and is higher in magnitude than for the whole sample. The test statistics are satisfactory, while the R^2 indicates that there is good fit. Thus based on these findings, there is evidence of absolute β-convergence across the EU-8 countries, while the pace of convergence increases over time. One could argue that the process of the accession of the new member States to the EU has also been beneficial in terms of real convergence, since late in the nineties until mid 2000 in the differences in EU-8 became less pronounced.

Table 5. Real convergence [β-convergence measure, 1994–2003]

Cross country regression				
Sample period	A	B	R^2	SE
1994–2003	3.38	0.039	0.83	2.63
	(12.89)	(3.61)		

Test statistics	
LM test for serial correlation	7.98
Functional form	2.87
Heteroscedasticity	4.63

Table 6. Real convergence [β-convergence measure, 1999–2003]

Cross country regression				
Sample period	A	B	R^2	SE
1999–2003	4.71	0.043	0.78	2.37
	(2.90)	(2.18)		
	Test statistics			
LM test for serial correlation	Hetero-scedasticity	6.38	2.13	3.76
Functional form				

Although, according to the preceding results, the EU-8 countries seem to converge on a unique and common GDP per head stationary state, a word of caution would suggest that national values of the underlying variables tend to be at different levels in the long run. This possibility derives from the neo-classical model of economic growth claiming that countries have very different structural parameters, such as preferences, technology and population growth rates. Though the EU-8 countries share many similar characteristics, with their transition to a market based economy as the most pre-dominant, some degree of heterogeneity among them should not been overseen.

4 Concluding Remarks

This paper tests empirically the validity of the neo-classical growth model across the new EU Member States from Eastern Europe from 1994 to 2003. Moreover, it investigates the validity of the neo-classical predictions on absolute β-convergence in terms of per capita income.

The results from our analysis support the unconditional convergence hypothesis among the eight new EU member states (we exclude Cyprus and Malta from the analysis). Moreover, the absolute convergence tests indicate that the EU-8 countries converge to a unique and common stationary state of income per capita at an annual rate ranging from 3.9%–4.3%. However, given some criticism (see, for example, Quah, 1996), one needs to bare into account the limitations of the β-convergence analysis when drawing economic policy implications for the enlarged EU. In addition, the nominal convergence of EU-8 countries shows that countries have performed different in terms of progress towards meeting the Maastricht criteria. Such differentiation in nominal criteria could have a bearing, impact on how EU-8 countries will adjust prior to their accession in ERM II and, eventually in euro zone. This, in turn, has implications for the real convergence. Overall, however, it appears that the impact of the E.U. enlargement has been beneficial for the convergence process of the new EU countries.

5 References

Barro, R., Sala-i-Martín, X. (1991) Convergence Across States and Economies. Brooking Papers on Economic Activity, 1, 107-182

Barro, R., Sala-i-Martin X. (1992) Convergence. Journal of Political Economy, 100, 223-251

Caviglia, G., Krause, G., Thimann, C. (2002) Key features of the financial sectors in EU accession countries. Chapter in European Central Bank's Report entitled: Financial Sectors in EU Accession Countries, July

European Commission (2004) European Economy: Convergence Report 2004. EC

European Central Bank (2004) Convergence Report 2004. ECB

Quah, D. (1996) Twin Peaks: Growth and Convergence in Models of Distribution Dynamics, Economic Journal, 106, 1045-1055

Sala-i-Martin, X. (1996) Regional Cohesion: Evidence and Theories of Regional Growth and Convergence, European Economic Review, 40, 1325-52

Siriopoulos, C., Asteriou, D. (1998) Testing for Convergence Across the Greek Economies. Regional Studies, 32, 537-546

Smith, A., Venables, A. (1991) Economic Integration and Market Access. European Economic Review, papers and prodeedings, 35, 388-395

Solow, R.M. (1956) A Contribution to the Theory of Economic Growth. Quarterly Journal of Economics, 70, 65-94

Looking at the Monetary Integration: Modeling Interest Rate Transmission Dynamics in Greece. Is There any Structural Break After EMU?

Dionysios Chionis* and Costas Leon

Democritus University of Thrace,
Department of International Economic Relationships and Development,
Greece

1 Introduction

The European Monetary Union (EMU) is understood as an area with common monetary and exchange rate policy aiming at common economic objectives, such as liberalization of capital and labor movements, monetary and financial integration and elimination of the fluctuations of exchange rates of the participating member states. For the time being, and still under the gradual integration process, the convergence of the interest rates in the EMU makes many authors to believe that asymmetries in the monetary policy shocks will tend to disappear.

Within to this framework, an interesting question is how shocks of the policy-controlled interest rate are propagated in the deposit and lending rates. This propagation/transmission is a part of the transmission mechanism of monetary policy. Monetary transmission mechanism is a core issue in modern macroeconomics, although a very controversial one. Its main question is how a change in a nominal variable, e.g. the interest rate, is translated into changes in output, prices and employment. We may identify two fundamental stages in this mechanism. In the first stage, the reaction function, i.e. the function that determines the short run policy-controlled interest rate, is derived under optimization conditions given the optimal growth and inflation mix. Given the determination of this policy rate, we firstly ask how the changes in this rate are propagated in the rest interest rates. The process is usually called in the economic literature pass-through

* Email: dchionis@ierd.duth.gr

of interest rates or interest rate transmission. Secondly, we ask how the changes in these interest rates are translated into changes in output, prices and employment. This second stage is described by means of the channels of monetary policy.

Various studies referring to European countries have been concerned with the aforementioned transmission of interest rates, among others, *inter alia,* Mojon (2000), Sander and Kleimeier (2000, 2001, 2004), Angeloni and Ehrman (2003), Toolsema et al (2001), Burgstaller (2003), Bredin et al (2001), Petursson (2001), De Bondt (2003). From these studies one can realise the following: stickiness in the transmission process, non-completeness at least in some cases, significant variations across countries and indications of convergence after the introduction of the single currency on 1/1/1999 and the creation of the EMU.

In this paper, we continue the above line of research and focus on the transmission dynamics of interest rates in Greece. We ask how the shocks of the policy-controlled interest rate are transmitted to deposit and lending rates in Greece during the last eight years. Greece has been a participating member since 2001, and its monetary policy is conducted in line with the ECB targets. Therefore, an interesting question is whether there has been a structural break after the EMU (by this, we mean the period after the accession of Greece to EMU in January, 2001) in comparison with the pre-EMU period. To our knowledge, the propagation mechanism from the policy rate to the lending and deposit rates and the issue of a possible structural break after the EMU in Greece have not been dealt with. For example, the study by Mylonidis and Nikolaidou (2001) refers to the testing of expectation hypothesis of the term structure of interest rates with Greek money market data up to October 2001, but it does not refer to the propagation of the policy rates to the lending or deposit rates. In this paper, we make use of the most recent available data, up to September 2004, and we address the following questions:

- What is the impact multiplier in lending and deposit rates before and after EMU?
- Is the process completed and how long does it take for completion?
- Is there any structural break in the transmission dynamics after the accession of Greece to EMU?

In brief, our findings are a completely new situation coming into view after the EMU: the impact multipliers are now active and the speed of convergence to the new equilibria is very fast. However, the transmission is not complete. If our null hypothesis is that there is no structural break after the EMU, this clearly cannot be maintained on the basis of our statistical findings.

The paper is organized as follows: In Sect. 2, we present a summary of findings in the literature. In Sect. 3, we describe the data and the statistical framework to be employed. Sect. 4 discusses the transmission in the lending and deposit interest rates. The paper concludes in Sect. 5.

2 Studies on the Transmission Dynamics of Interest Rates

A common element found by all researchers is the stickiness of the interest rates. Stickiness simply means that a change in the policy interest rate, controlled by the Central Bank, is not propagated immediately to the retail rates (lending and deposit). Thus, these retail rates respond later and, in some cases, to a lesser degree than the initial impulse on the policy interest rate. In these cases, the process is characterised as incomplete.

Three issues have been the subject of theoretical and empirical research on the interest rate transmission, (Toolsema et al., 2001). First, the theoretical explanation on the interest rate stickiness. Agency costs due to asymmetric information (adverse selection and moral hazard), (Stiglitz and Weiss, 1981), adjustment costs (Cottarelli and Kourelis, 1994), switching costs (Klemperer, 1987) and risk sharing (Fried and Howitt, 1980) are the four theoretical contributions to the interest rate stickiness. Second, the degree of stickiness across countries. Cottarelli and Kourelis (1994) show a significant difference in the degree in both impact and long-run multipliers across EMU countries. A similar view is obtained from the studies of Borio and Fritz (1995), Kleimeier and Sander (2000), Donnay and Degryse (2001) and Toolsema et al. (2001). Further, issues of asymmetric propagation seem to arise, depending on whether there is a positive or negative impulse on the policy rate (see among others De Bondt, 2002; Borio and Fritz, 1995; Mojon, 2000) or whether the rates are below or above their equilibrium level (Hofmann, 2000; Kleimeier and Sander, 2000). Third, the relationship between interest rate stickiness and the financial system. Despite of the adoption of the common currency in the EMU area, significant differences still exist across EMU countries in their financial system (Mojon, 2000). These differences may be attributed to heavy investments in brand names which are country specific, networks of branches and different marketing policies, (Gual, 1999), and different setting and legal expertise (Cecchetti, 1999).

Although different statistical methodologies have been applied, involving different data sets, countries, time periods and underlying assumptions, most authors seem to agree on the following results, see among others Burgstaller, 2003. First, a high degree on stickiness of retail lending rates, for example, in the EMU area, only 30% of the change on a given market rate is passed to the lending rates within a month. Second, strong empirical evidence for significant differences among EMU area. Third, the average full adjustment of the retail rates to market rates varies between three and ten months (De Bondt, 2002). Fourth, the final pass-through of market retail rates is typically complete or, in some cases (Cottarelli and Kourelis, 1994) even more than complete, reaching 110% and the speed at which the market rates are completely transmitted to retail rates can vary between three months and two years.

3 Data Set, Statistical Methodology and Some Preliminary Tests

3.1 Data Set

The data set comprises of three interest rates series, that is policy, lending and deposit rates. The lending rate concerns short-run loans to enterprises and the deposit rates concern deposits from households. Both rates are of one year maturity. We use monthly data covering July 1996 to September 2004; that is, 99 observations in total. This period has been chosen for two reasons. First, it is this period when money market started to function and became important in Greece; and, second, interest rates prior to this period were principally administered by the Central Bank and show no variation for long periods. Thus, statistical estimates from series without variation would not be meaningful. Here, an important issue is which of the various interest rates that the Central Bank identifies as instruments will be used as a proxy for the policy rate. We have selected the money market rate to be used as the policy rate since this rate is the one which is more strongly correlated with monetary policy as a whole (Donnay and Degryse, 2001). Preliminary experimentation (not shown in this research) of two money market rates, with maturity of one and three months respectively, with the lending and deposit rates, shows that it is the rate of one month which possesses slightly better properties in terms of statistical adequacy. Therefore, we have chosen the interest rate of one month as our policy rate. More on the sources of data is given in the Appendix.

3.2 Statistical Methodology

The paper employs bivariate cointegration methods and the associated Error Correction Model (ECM) for the estimation of parameters. If the bank rate (lending or deposit) forms a linear long run relationship with the policy rate, a possible structure is the following equilibrium model:

$$BR_t = \theta_0 + \theta_1 M_t + \varepsilon_t \qquad (1)$$

Short-run dynamic adjustments (assuming one lag) are possible with the following disequilibrium model:

$$BR_t = \gamma_0 + \gamma_1 M_t + \gamma_2 M_{t-1} + \gamma_3 BR_{t-1} + \xi_t \qquad (2)$$

However, due to non-stationarity frequently encountered in the applied research, an estimable model in the analysis of interest rate dynamics is in the error correction form. This is known in the literature as the Granger Representation Theorem (Granger, 1987). This estimable form is the Error Correction Model (ECM), which is a reparameterisation of the disequilibrium model taking into account the long-run model. In particular, in a dynamic setting governed by possible non-stationarity and provided that cointegration exists, the ECM avoids the issue of spurious regression, ensures orthogonality among regressor, and allows parameters estimation in a statistically valid fashion. The ECM has the form:

$$\Delta BR_t = \delta + \gamma_1 \Delta M_t + (\gamma_1 + \gamma_2) M_{t-1} - (1 - \gamma_3) BR_{t-1} + u_t \qquad (3)$$

where, BR_t is the bank rate (lending or deposit) and M_t is the policy rate. Δ is the difference operator and $\delta, \gamma_1, \gamma_2, \gamma_3$ are short run parameters to be estimated. The parameter γ_1 is the impact multiplier. The long run parameters θ_0 and θ_1 are computed as $\dfrac{\delta}{1-\gamma_3}$ and $\dfrac{\gamma_1+\gamma_2}{1-\gamma_3}$, respectively. In all these models, we assume that the stochastic perturbations ε_t, ξ_t and u_t are i.i.d. processes. Given these assumptions, the estimates from the ECM are consistent and asymptotically efficient.

If the transmission process is complete then $\theta_1 = 1$ and all the change in the policy rate will be transmitted to the bank rate but, typically, it will take some months for the process to be completed. If $\theta_1 < 1$ then the process is incomplete, i.e. not all the change in the policy rate is transmitted to the bank rate. Finally, if $\theta_1 > 1$ then the bank rate change is even higher than the policy rate change. We experimented with several model structures, within the class of the ECMs, with various ARMA components and dummy variables to account for the shift of the regime in January 2001. Our final estimates are given in Tables 3–7.

3.3 Some Preliminary Tests

As it is customary in empirical analyses, we examine the dynamic properties of the employed interest rate series. We are interested if they are stationary or not, and if not, what their data generating processes are. Two means of analysis are employed: visual display of the series and their autocorrelation and partial autocorrelation functions, as well as formal unit root testing.

Figures 1 and 2 show the graphs of the rates and their autocorrelation and partial autocorrelation functions. It is obvious from these graphs that the series appear to be non-stationary and downward trending. To establish the non-stationarity property of the series on statistical ground, we proceed to formal unit root testing, i.e. ADF (Dickey and Fuller, 1979) and PP (Phillips and Perron, 1988) tests with several combinations of constant, constant with a trend, and various lags. Since these tests are sensitive to the deterministic components (constant and trend) and the selected lag length, we used a variety of optimal length information criteria such as AIC (Akaike) and SIC (Schwartz). Our experimentation verifies the visual impression: all the series are indeed non-stationary governed by one unit root process and, in some cases, with a drift. The implication is that all series are integrated of order one, a necessary condition for cointegration in a bivariate context. Since all experimentation leads to the same conclusion, i.e. the existence of one unit root, we present in Table 1, only the test statistics from the ADF test, based on the AIC. A next step in the analysis is to see if these series are cointegrated; that is, if the bank rate (lending or deposit) form a stable long-run linear relationship with the policy controlled rate. It is only in this case that ECM provides statistically sound and economically interpretable parameters estimations. On the basis of cointegration test and the Granger critical values (Engle and Granger, 1987; Engle and Yoo, 1987, Table 3), and from the cointegrating Durbin Watson (CRDW) statistic, both shown in Table 2, it turns out that our two regressions form a stable long-run linear relationship, marginally, though, at 10% significance level. Therefore, we proceed to the ECM estimation. Tables 3 and 5 present the estimates of the ECM for both interest rates equations.

4 The Transmission Dynamics: Findings

The preceding statistical analysis leads to the following findings: We may identify two periods of interest rate dynamics: the period prior to EMU, 1996:07–2000:12 and the period 2001:01–2004:09, i.e. the period after the accession to EMU. In both periods, there is a common property: the downward trend in all interest rates, although with very different speeds. Given the downward trends, a comparison of the interest rates between these two periods by means of simple averages would not be sensible. Instead, we prefer to fit a linear trend as an approximation of the downward movements of the interest rates. These regressions show that the downward trend is fast in the period prior to EMU, while in the second, it is clearly of much lower speed, almost of zero speed. For example, the lending rate downward trend was –0.22 percentage units per month before the EMU and just –0.02 after the EMU. For the deposit rates the figures are –0.10 and –0.04, respectively. The very low speeds in the second period, for both retail rates, imply a sort of convergence, a finding in accordance with the European integration literature. Table 8 shows the estimates of the trends.

Further, both lending and deposit rates seem to form a long-run relationship with the money market policy rate, marginally though, at 10% significance level. This is established on both the cointegrating Durbin Watson and the cointegration ADF test. The interest rate of one month is correlated somewhat more strongly with both retail rates than the rate of three months does.

The statistical fitness of the ECMs for the whole period 1996:07–2004:09 is not particularly strong, especially for the lending rate. The R^2 for lending rate equation is weak, just 0.16, while for the deposit rate R^2 is 0.44. However, given that, in general, the fitness of the ECMs is not particularly high, 0.44 is considered satisfactory. To find a more precise indication of the fitness of the model for the two periods under consideration, we performed two separate regressions (not shown), instead of including dummies. We found that for both retail rates, the first period was characterized by very low R^2s, less than 0.10 in both cases, while, on the contrary, in the second period R^2s were very satisfactory (0.70 for the lending rate and 0.77 for the deposit rate). A possible reason for this is that during the first period the transmission from the policy rate to the lending rate was quite noisy, reflecting low effectiveness of the policy rate as a means to influence the retail rates. The inclusion of dummy variables in the ECM equations (zero for the period before EMU and one after the EMU) improves the statistical adequacy of the model and reveals a structural break in the estimated parameters. This, of course, reflects the regime shift due to the accession of Greece to the EMU and the adoption of the ECB monetary policy guides since 2001:01. The change in impact multiplier, γ_1, is obvious. For the lending rate, the impact multiplier before EMU is 0.09, very low indeed, while after the EMU γ_1 rises to 0.508. The same picture is emerged for the deposit rates. Before EMU, γ_1 is 0.063, while after EMU it rises to 0.64. In fact, these are very significant changes for both retail rates.

Tables 3–7 present estimates and diagnostics of the estimated models. The estimates of the short-run parameters are presented in Tables 3 and 5. The high volatility of the interest rates in the prior to EMU period and the associated low fitness are shown in Fig. 3. Diagnostics for the ECMs are presented in Table 7. No autocorrelation or ARCH effects are statistically significant at 5% s.l. However, the normality assumption of the residuals, on the basis of the Jarque-Berra statistics, is clearly rejected, probably due to non-linearity frequently met in transition processes; see Fig. 4. The stability of the coefficients is evaluated by the Cusum of Squares Test, shown on Fig. 5. No parameters instability is apparent for both ECMs on the basis of the test.

For the long-run multipliers θ_1 we provide two different ways of estimation. The first is by means of the equilibrium model, while the second is by means of the error correction model. For example, for the lending rate before the EMU, the long run multiplier obtained from the ECM is 1.86, while the same multiplier obtained from the static regression is 0.926. After the EMU, the figures are 0.52 and 0.78, respectively. For the deposit rate before the EMU, the multipliers are 0.50 from the static regression and 1.24 from the ECM. For the period after the EMU, these multipliers are 0.63 and 0.68, they are in fact identical.

We may ascribe these differences of the estimates from the two models in the noisy and non-effective transmission mechanism (reflected by low R^2s) before the EMU. In the period after the EMU, the estimates from the two models are close, as it is expected from the econometric theory, given the consistency of the ECM estimates and the superconsistency of the cointegrating vector properties. Therefore, concluding that the process is complete in the first period, due to higher long-run multipliers θ_1, is rather misleading, due to low explanatory power of the models involved for this period. We think that direct comparison of the multipliers for both periods should be done cautiously; see Tables 2 and 6 for the estimates from the static regression, and Tables 3 and 5 for the estimates from the ECM.

The dynamic adjustments towards equilibrium are very different in the two periods. We perform a simulation on the assumption that a negative 100 basis points shock takes place. The simulation is conducted with the aid of the short-run disequilibrium model whose parameters $\delta, \gamma_1, \gamma_2, \gamma_3$ have been obtained indirectly from the ECM, (Tables 3 and 5). For example, for the lending rate, in the first period, we assume that the equilibrium policy rate is 11.4 (the average in the period) and due to the negative shock, the new equilibrium value of the lending rate, on the basis of the long run parameters θ_0 and θ_1 obtained indirectly from the ECM, will be 10.8. The dynamic adjustment from the initial value of 11.4 to the new value 10.8 will last about 70 periods, an extremely long period for the working of the monetary policy. This reflects the ineffectiveness of the monetary policy for the influence of the policy rate to the lending rate. For the lending rate again, the situation is completely different in the after EMU period. The speed of convergence is very fast. It should be emphasized, however, that the speed of convergence depends critically on the precision we wish to have. If, for example, we want a precision with two decimal points for our new equilibrium value, then the convergence is of course of lower speed. We think, however, that a precision with one decimal point is satisfactory in practice. Given this assumption, the transmission is complete within three months. The same picture is emerged from the dynamic adjustment of the deposit rate. After the EMU, the convergence is instantaneous. Figure 6 shows the dynamic adjustments for the two interest rates before and after the EMU.

5 Conclusion

This paper studies the transmission process of interest rates in Greece, before and after the EMU, with monthly data from 1996:07–2004:09. As a policy rate we have chosen the one month interest rate. We study how the changes of the policy rate are propagated into the lending and deposit rates with maturity of one year. Our findings are consistent with the relevant literature, although not fully. Using a cointegration and error correction framework, we find the following: First, downward trends are clear and fast before the EMU, while after the EMU downward trends are very slow, a consequence of the common monetary policy in the Eurozone area and an indication of convergence of the interest rates. Second, in the period before the EMU, and in common with all the relevant literature, the process was characterized by high stickiness, as measured by the impact multipliers, which in our data set is very low. The situation changes dramatically in the after the EMU period. Then the impact multipliers became indeed active. Third, as for the completion of the process, that is, the long-run multipliers, the picture was not clear in the first period. In the second period, the estimates from the two models (ECM and the equilibrium model) are comparable for both interest rates. Here, still the process is not complete, since the long-run multiplier θ_1 is less than one, being 0.52 for the lending rate and 0.63 for the deposit rate. That is, 100 basis points change in the policy rate will change the equilibrium lending rate by 52 basis points and by 63 basis points the deposit rate.

This finding of the non-completion of the transmission process differs from the findings of most of the papers in the literature. Finally, we think that structural break due to the accession in the EMU is clear from our empirical evidence, despite any model drawbacks of statistical nature for the first period. The implications of the structural break are important. Interest rate transmission now works and monetary policy has become an active tool since, the ECB is responsible for monetary policy.

This is clearly the positive effect. On the negative side, the issue of the non-completion still remains since the benefits of the monetary policy do not fully arrive at the final target groups, the debtors and depositors. It is probable, however, that if the intra-EMU credit mobility could be accelerated, the transmission process could also be complete at some later time. Concluding the paper, some other issues may be addressed for future research. For example, the propagation of policy rates, beyond the two rates we studied here, to other series of retail interest rates or bond yields. Moreover, instead of the one or three month interest rate as an instrument of the monetary policy, other similar rates could be tried. Another extension would be the possible interaction between the various rates and the feedback to the policy rates, by means of VAR models. Or, probably, asymmetries during the business cycle or asymmetries with regard to the direction of the shock (i.e. positive or negative shock). These are to be answered in another paper.

6 References

Angeloni I., Ehrman, M., (2003), Monetary Transmission in the Euro Area: Early Evidence, Economic Policy, October, 469-501.

BIS, (1994), National Differences in Interest Rate Transmission, C.B. 393, Basel, March.

Borio, C. E. V., Fritz, W., (1995), The Response of Short-Term Bank Lending Rates to Policy Rates: A Cross-Country Perspective, in Financial Structure and the Monetary Policy Transmission Mechanism. BIS, Basle.

Bredin, D., Fitzpatrick T., O'Reilly G., (2001), Real Interest rate Pass-Through: The Irish Experience, Technical Paper 06/RT/01, Central Bank of Ireland.

Burgstaller, J., (2003), Interest Rate Transmission to Commercial Credit Rates in Austria, Working Paper No 0306, Johann Kepler University of Linz, Austria.

Cecchetti, S.G., (1999), Legal Structure, Financial Structure, and the Monetary Transmission Mechanism, Economic Policy Review, 5, 9–28, Federal Reserve Bank of New York.

Cottarelli, C., Kourelis, A., (1994), Financial Structure, Bank Lending Rates, and the Transmission Mechanism of Monetary Policy, IMF Staff Papers, 41(4), 587–623.

De Bondt, G., (2002), Retail Bank Interest Rate Pass-Through: New Evidence at the Euro Area Level, Working Paper No 136, ECB.

Dickey, D.A., Fuller, W.A., (1979), Distributions of the Estimators for Autoregressive Time series with a Unit Root, Journal of the American Statistical Association 74, 427-431.

Donnay, M., Degryse. H., (2001), Bank Lending Rate Pass-through and Differences in the Transmission of a Single EMU Monetary policy, Discussion Paper DPS 01.17, Center of Economic Studies, Katholieke Universiteit, Leuven.

Engle, R. F., Granger C.W.J., (1987), Co-integration, and Error Correction: Representation, Estimation, and Testing, Econometrica 55, March, 251-276.

Engle, R.F., F Yoo, B.S., (1987), Forecasting and Testing in Co-integrated Systems, Journal of Econometrics 35: 143-159.

Fried, J. Howitt, P., (1980), Credit Rationing and Implicit Contract Theory, Journal of Money, Credit, and Banking, 12(3), 471–487.

Gual J. (1999), Deregulation, Integration and Market Structure in European Banking, Journal of the Japanese and International Economies No. 13, pp. 372-96

Hofmann, B., (2000), Non-linear Adjustment of Loan Rates to Money Market Rates: Some Evidence for the Euro Area, Paper Presented at Internal ECB Seminar, 18 October.

Kleimeier, S., Sander, H., (2000): Regionalisation versus Globalisation in European Financial Market Integration: Evidence from Co-Integration Analyses, Journal of Banking and Finance, 24(6), 1005–1043.

Klemperer, P., (1987), Markets with Consumer Switching Costs, Quarterly Journal of Economics, 102(2), 375–394.

Lowe, P. (1994), The Cash Rate, Lending Rates, and the Real Economy, in National Differences in Interest Rate Transmission, BIS CB 391, 1-30.

Mojon, B., (2000), Financial Structure and the Interest Rate Channel of ECB Monetary Policy, ECB Working Paper No 40.

Mozzami, B., (1999), Lending Rate Stickiness and Monetary Policy Transmission: the Case of Canada and the United States, Applied Financial Economics, 9, 533-538.

Mylonidis, N., Nikolaidou, E., (2003), The Interest Rate Term Structure in the Greek Money Market. European Review of Economics and Finance, 2(1), pp. 21-37.

Petturson, T.G., (2001), The Transmission Mechanism of Monetary Policy: Analyzing the Financial Market Pass-Trough, Working Paper No 14, Central Bank of Iceland.

Phillips, P.C.B., Perron, P., (1988), Testing for a Unit Root in Time Series Regression, Biometrika, 75, 335-346.

Sander, H., Kleimeier, S., (2004), Convergence in Eurozone Retail Banking; What Interest Rate Pass-through Tells Us About Monetary Policy Transmission, Competition and Integration, Journal of International Money and Finance, Vol. 23, 461-492.

Sander, H., Kleimeier, S., (2001) Asymmetric Adjustment of Commercial Bank Interest Rates in the Euro Area: Implications for Monetary Policy, mimeo, University of Applied Sciences Cologne, Cologne.

Sander, H., Kleimeier, S., (2000), Regionalisation versus Globalisation in European Financial Market Integration: Evidence from Co-Integration Analyses, Journal of Banking and Finance, 24(6), 1005–1043.

Stiglitz,, J.E., Weiss, A., (1981), Credit Rationing in Markets with Imperfect Information, American Economic Review, 71(3), 917–926.

Toolsema, L., Sturm, J.E., De Haan, J., (2001), Convergence of Monetary Transmission in EMU: New Evidence. Working Paper 465, Center for Economic Studies & Ifo Institute for Economic Research.

7 Tables

Table 1. Unit root tests

Variable	ADF t statistic	Unit Root yes/no
M1	−2.867146	Yes
LD	−1.557129	Yes
DP	−1.667944	Yes

The test statistics are not significant at the usual significance levels (5% and 10%). All the series are non stationary with one unit root. The AIC has been employed for the determination of the optimal lag length.

$$\hat{BR}_t = \hat{\theta}_0 + \hat{\theta}_1 M_t, \qquad \hat{\varepsilon}t = BR_t - \hat{BR}_t \qquad (4)$$

Table 2. Cointegration ADF tests on the Residuals in the Static Regressions

Residuals from	t statistic	CRDW statistic	Unit Root Yes/No
LD regression	−3.938190	0.478090	No
DP regression	−3.704290	0.315726	No

The static regression for the lending rate on the one month money market rate, based on the ADF test, show evidence of cointegration at the significance level (s.l.) 10%. The CRDW statistic shows cointegration at 5% s.l. The deposit rate, on the basis of the ADF test, is marginally cointegrated at s.l. 10% with the one month money market rate. The conclusion is the same if we take into account the CDRW for the deposit rate. The critical value for the t statistics with $m = 4$, sample size =100 and s.l. 10% is 3.71.

Table 3. Lending Rate: Estimates from the ECM

Before EMU		After EMU	
S-R Parameters	L-R Parameters	S-R Parameters	L-R Parameters
$\delta = -0.40$	$\theta_0 = -8.89$	$\delta = 0.989$	$\theta_0 = 5.75$
$\gamma_1 = 0.09$	$\theta_1 = 1.86$	$\gamma_1 = 0.508$	$\theta_1 = 0.527$
$\gamma_2 = -0.006$		$\gamma_2 = -0.417$	
$\gamma_3 = 0.955$		$\gamma_3 = 0.828$	

Table 4. Lending rate: Estimates from the Cointegrating Equation

L-R Parameters Before EMU	L-R Parameters After EMU
$\theta_0 = 6.128$	$\theta_0 = 5.010$
$\theta_1 = 0.926$	$\theta_1 = 0.780$

Table 5. Deposit rate: Estimates from the ECM

before EMU		after EMU	
S-R Parameters	L-R Parameters	S-R Parameters	L-R Parameters
$\delta = -0.41$	$\theta_0 = -8.34$	$\delta = -0.187$	$\theta_0 = -0.50$
$\gamma_1 = 0.064$	$\theta_1 = 1.24$	$\gamma_1 = 0.641$	$\theta_1 = 0.63$
$\gamma_2 = -0.002$		$\gamma_2 = -0.407$	
$\gamma_3 = 0.95$		$\gamma_3 = 0.632$	

Table 6. Deposit Rate: Estimates from the Cointegrating Equation

L-R Parameters before EMU	L-R Parameters after EMU
$\theta_0 = 2.62$	$\theta_0 = -0.64$
$\theta_1 = 0.50$	$\theta_1 = 0.68$

Table 7. Diagnostics of the ECMs

Lending rate equation	Deposit rate equation
R^2 0.16	R^2 0.44
DW 2.1	DW 1.99
LM Serial Correlation (2 lags) F 0.134	LM Serial Correlation (2 lags) F 2.23
ARCH (2 lags) F 2.78	ARCH (2 lags) F 0.919
Jarque – Berra 869.74	Jarque – Berra 37.43

Note for Tables 3-7: Parameters Estimates from the ECM and from the Cointegrating Equations. The short run parameters are estimated from the ECM.

$$\Delta BR_t = \delta + \gamma_1 \Delta M_t + (\gamma_1 + \gamma_2)M_{t-1} - (1 - \gamma_3)BR_{t-1} + four\ dummies + u_t \quad (5)$$

The long run parameters θ_0 and θ_1 from the ECM are computed as $\dfrac{\delta}{1 - \gamma_3}$

and $\dfrac{\gamma_1 + \gamma_2}{1 - \gamma_3}$, respectively. The cointegrating vector is estimated from the

cointegrating equation: $BR_t = \theta_0 + \theta_1 M_t + two\ dummies + \varepsilon_t$

$$\text{Regression Equation: } BR_t = \phi + \lambda t + h_t \quad (6)$$

Table 8: Linear Trend Approximations: Estimates for λ

Lending Rate	Deposit Rate
Period 1996:07–2000:12: $\lambda = -0.22$	Period 1996:07–2000:12: $\lambda = -0.10$
Period 2001:01–2004:09: $\lambda = -0.02$	Period 2001:01–2004:09: $\lambda = -0.04$

8 Figures

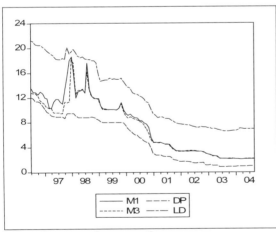

M1: policy rate of one month. .
M3: policy rate of three months (not used in the regression functions).
LD: Lending rate.
DP: Deposit rate.

Fig. 1. Time Plot of Money Market and Retail Rates, 1996:07–2004:09

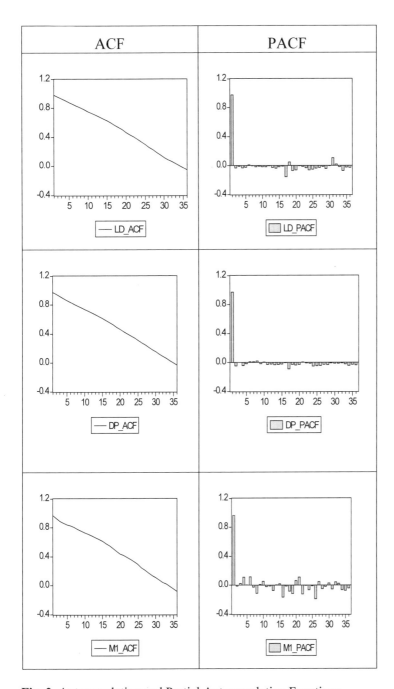

Fig. 2. Autocorrelation and Partial Autocorrelation Functions

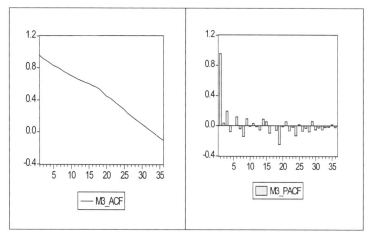

ACF AutoCorrelation Function, *PACF* Partial AutoCorrelation Function,
LD lending rate, *DP* deposit rate.

Fig. 2. continued

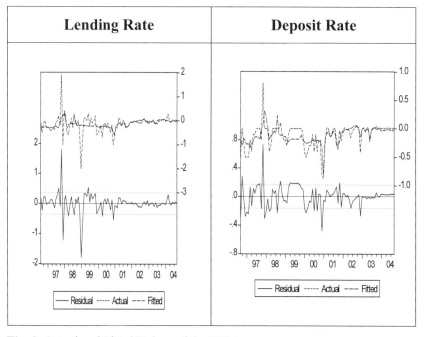

Fig. 3. Actual and Fitted Values of the ECM

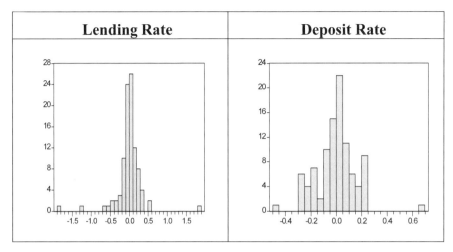

Fig. 4. Residuals Histograms

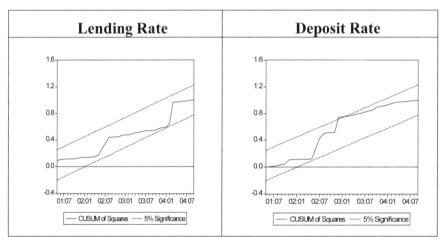

Fig. 5. Cusum of Squares Test

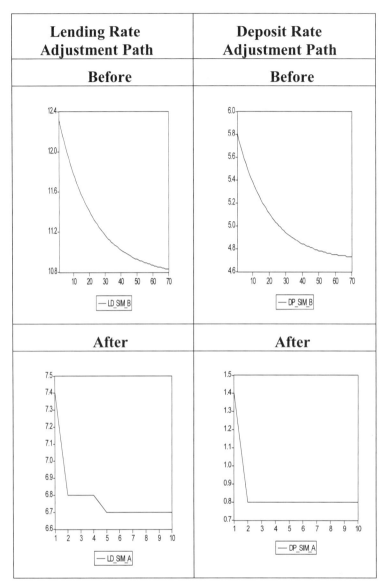

LD_SIM_B lending rate adjustment before EMU,
DP_SIM_B deposit rate adjustment before EMU,
LD_SIM_A lending rate adjustment after EMU,
DP_SIM_A deposit rate adjustment after EMU.

Fig. 6. Dynamic Adjustments to Equilibrium after a 100 bp Negative Shock

9 Appendix

9.1 Data Sources

The interest rate data set has been obtained from the Bulletin of Conjuctural Indicators, various issues, of the Bank of Greece. It is worth noting that several definitions and methods of computations have been applied to this data set over time, and, therefore, the same rate over different periods is not absolutely comparable.

How Harmful Is International Tax Competition?

Pantelis Kammas[1,*] and Apostolis Philippopoulos[2]

[1] Athens University of Economics & Business, Greece
[2] Athens University of Economics & Business, and CESifo. Department of Economics, 76 Patission Street, Athens 10434, Greece

Acknowledgements: We thank Hyun Park and Vangelis Vassilatos for helpful discussions. All errors are ours. The first co-author wishes to acknowledge financial support from the Greek Ministry of Education and the European Union under the "Iraklitos" Research Fellowship Programme.

1 Introduction

International tax competition for mobile tax bases is a key policy issue (known as the race-to-the-bottom problem). Non-cooperative (Nash) tax policies lead to inefficiently low tax rates, low tax revenues and under-provision of public goods.[1] Hence, there is an argument for international cooperation. And this argument becomes stronger as the degree of economic integration increases and tax competition gets fiercer.

International tax competition might be welfare inferior to international tax cooperation,[2] but how inferior is it quantitatively? To answer this

---

[1] See e.g. Gordon (1983), Zodrow and Mieszkowski (1986), Wilson (1986), Razin and Sadka (1991) and Persson and Tabellini (1992). The standard race-to-the-bottom result is usually derived in a setup where the only cross-country spill-over effect, or externality, is generated by international capital mobility. This externality is positive: an increase in the tax rate abroad, switches capital to the domestic country, and this increases tax revenues, public good provision and welfare at home. Then, a positive externality implies that Nash policies are inefficiently low (see below for details). This is the setup we also use here.

[2] International cooperation can become counter-productive if there are domestic policy failures (like time inconsistent national policies). This is a second-best story. Here, we do not study such issues. Thus, cooperation always increases aggregate welfare.

* Email: kammas@aueb.gr

question, we use a simple two-period two-country world economy adapted from Persson and Tabellini (1992). In each country, there are a private agent and a benevolent national government. Private agents consume and invest at home and abroad, where investment abroad implies a mobility cost. National governments tax domestic and foreign investors at the same tax rate (this is, the so-called source principle of taxation) to finance the provision of a domestic public good. National policies are chosen either non-cooperatively (Nash) or cooperatively, where the latter serves as a benchmark.

Our results are as follows. As expected, the Nash tax rate is lower than the cooperative one, and the general equilibrium utility level is higher under cooperation. Nevertheless, the difference between equilibrium utility in the non-cooperative case and equilibrium utility in the cooperative case is very small quantitatively. In our setup, this is a robust result. For instance, it holds even when capital is very mobile, and so there are large differences between Nash and cooperative tax rates.

To understand why welfare differences are negligible, one has to study the resulting macroeconomic outcomes. Welfare depends on the paths of both private consumption and public goods. Higher tax rates (as we move from Nash to cooperation) are good for public good provision but particularly bad for future private consumption. This happens because higher tax rates hurt private investment and, in turn, future private consumption. As a result, Nash tax rates are not that bad quantitatively (although, by construction, always inferior to cooperative ones qualitatively).

Thus, in a dynamic model, inefficiently low tax rates are good for private capital accumulation and economic growth, and this mitigates the welfare problem of under-provision of public goods. This is different from a static model, where higher tax rates can increase the provision of public goods without hurting the economy in the future. Therefore, the standard argument – that tax competition is harmful in the presence of cross-country spillovers – becomes weaker as one moves from static to dynamic setups.

Mendoza and Tesar (2003) have also provided a quantitative assessment of tax competition and the welfare benefits of tax coordination. By using a richer model, they reach the same result: coordination yields very tiny welfare gains over the Nash outcome. Our work differs mainly because we get a closed-form analytic solution that enables us to reveal the implications of Nash policies for macroeconomic outcomes and aggregate welfare and, hence, explain why the welfare benefits of tax coordination are negligible. The rest of the paper is as follows. Section 2 solves for a world competitive equilibrium. Section 3 solves for optimal national policies. Section 4 concludes.

2 The Model and World Competitive Equilibrium

Let us consider a two-period and two-country world economy adapted from Persson and Tabellini (1992).[3] Each country is populated by a representative private agent and a benevolent national government. Both countries produce the same commodity and have access to a linear technology. The private agent in each country consumes and can invest at home and abroad, where investment abroad implies a mobility or transaction cost. The national government in each country can tax domestic and foreign investors at the same rate (source principle of taxation) to finance a domestic public good.

The sequence of events is as follows. National governments choose their tax rates, and the associated provision of public goods. In turn, private agents maximise their life-time utility by choosing the paths of consumption and investment. We will solve the problem backwards. Thus, we will first solve the private agents' optimisation problems by taking prices and policies as given. This will give a World Competitive Equilibrium (WCE). In turn, we will solve for Nash national policies. Specifically, each national government will choose its own tax rate optimally subject to WCE by taking as given the tax policies of the other national government. We will also solve for cooperative national policies; this will serve as a benchmark. We present the problem in country i. Country j is analogous.

2.1 Behaviour of Private Agents

The representative household in country i maximises:

$$U^i = U(c_1^i, c_2^i, g^i) \tag{1}$$

Where, c_1 and c_2 are private consumption in the first and second period respectively, and g is provision of public goods. The utility function is increasing and quasi-concave. For algebraic simplicity, we use an additively separable function of the form:

$$U^i = \log c_1^i + c_2^i + v^i g^i \tag{2}$$

Where, the parameter $v > 0$ is the weight given to public services relative to private consumption.

The first-period budget constraint of private agent in country i is:

---

[3] Park and Philippopoulos (2003) use the same model to address the problem of optimal membership in an economic union.

$$c_1^i + k^{ii} + k^{ij} = e^i \tag{3}$$

thus, the private agent begins with an exogenous endowment, e^i, and uses this endowment for consumption, c_1^i, and investment at home, k^{ii}, and abroad, k^{ij}.

The second-period budget constraint of private agent in country i is:

$$c_2^i = (1 - t^i) A^i k^{ii} + (1 - t^j) A^j k^{ij} - \frac{m^{ij} (k^{ij})^2}{2} \tag{4}$$

where $0 < t^i < 1$ and $0 < t^j < 1$ are income tax rates in countries i and j respectively, the parameters $A^i > 0$ and $A^j > 0$ are the exogenous capital returns in i and j respectively, and $m^{ij} \geq 0$ is a measure of transaction costs when an investor in i invests in j[4]. Thus, the last term on the right-hand side of (2b) captures costs of investing abroad.

Private agents take policy variables as given. Substituting (2a) and (2b) into (1b), the first-order conditions with respect to k^{ii} and k^{ij} give respectively (these are Euler equations):

$$\frac{1}{c_1^i} = (1 - t^i) A^i \tag{5}$$

$$\frac{1}{c_1^i} = (1 - t^j) A^j - m^{ij} k^{ij} \qquad \text{for } i \neq j \tag{6}$$

so that $(1 - t^i) A^i = (1 - t^j) A^j - m^{ij} k^{ij}$. Thus, without uncertainty, net returns are equalized across countries via capital mobility.

2.2 National Government Budget Constraint

According to the source principle of taxation, national governments tax domestic and foreign investors at the same rate. Thus, assuming a balanced budget, the budget constraint of the national government in country i is:

$$g^i = t^i A^i k^i \tag{7}$$

where $k^i = k^{ii} + k^{ji}$ denotes the total capital stock in country i (k^{ji} is the capital invested in country i by investors located in country j).

---

[4] We use a quadratic function for simplicity.

2.3 World Competitive Equilibrium (Given Policies)

We now characterise a World Competitive Equilibrium (WCE) for any feasible policy. As (7) shows, only one of the two policy instruments (g and t) can be set independently in each country. We choose to express the WCE in terms of national tax rates (t). Then, it is straightforward to show that (2)–(7) imply:

$$c_1^i = \frac{1}{(1-t^i)A^i} \tag{8}$$

$$c_2^i = (1-t^i)A^i k^{ii} + (1-t^j)A^j k^{ij} - m^{ij}\frac{(k^{ij})^2}{2} \tag{9}$$

$$g^i = t^i A^i (k^{ii} + k^{ji}) \tag{10}$$

where

$$k^{ij} = \frac{(1-t^j)A^j - (1-t^i)A^i}{m^{ij}} \tag{11}$$

$$k^{ii} = e^i - \frac{1}{(1-t^i)A^i} - k^{ij} \tag{12}$$

where (5a), (5b), (5c), (5d) and (5e) give respectively the first-period consumption, the second-period consumption, government expenditure on the public good, capital invested abroad and capital invested at home, all from the point of view of country i in a WCE.

In an analogous way, we have for country j in a WCE:

$$c_1^j = \frac{1}{(1-t^j)A^j} \tag{13}$$

$$c_2^j = (1-t^j)A^j k^{jj} + (1-t^i)A^i k^{ji} - m^{ji}\frac{(k^{ji})^2}{2} \tag{14}$$

$$g^j = t^j A^j (k^{jj} + k^{ij}) \tag{15}$$

where

$$k^{ji} = \frac{(1-t^i)A^i - (1-t^j)A^j}{m^{ji}} \tag{16}$$

$$k^{ji} = e^j - \frac{1}{(1-t^j)A^j} - k^{ji} \tag{17}$$

We sum up this section. We have solved for a World Competitive Equilibrium (WCE). This is for any feasible policy as summarized by the national tax rates (t^i and t^j). In this equilibrium: (i) private agents maximize their utility; (ii) all constraints are satisfied; (iii) all markets clear. This WCE is given by (5a)–(5j). Notice that, thanks to the model specification, we have managed to get closed-form solutions for equilibrium allocations as functions of t^i and t^j. This will be convenient algebraically when we endogenize the choice of t^i and t^j.

3 Choice of National Policies and General Equilibrium

We move on to the first stage of the game and endogenize national policies, t^i and t^j. National policies will be chosen by benevolent national governments that either play Nash or cooperatively. We will focus on symmetric (Nash and cooperative) equilibria in which optimal strategies are symmetric ex post.[5]

3.1 Symmetric Nash Equilibrium (SNE) in National Policies

The national government in country i chooses t^i to maximize (1b) subject to (5a)–(5j). In doing so, it takes t^j as given. The national government in country j solves an analogous problem when choosing t^j.

It is straightforward to show that, in a SNE, the non-cooperative tax rate (denoted as t^{nc}) is determined by the following equation:

$$A\left(e - \frac{1}{A(1-t)}\right) = v\left[A\left(e - \frac{1}{A(1-t)}\right) - \frac{t}{(1-t)^2} - \frac{2A^2t}{m}\right] \tag{18}$$

which is a non-linear equation in t^{nc} only. Then, Appendix A shows:

Result 1. *A Symmetric Nash Equilibrium (SNE) in national policies is summarized by the tax rate that solves (6). This non-cooperative tax rate, $0 < t^{nc} < 1$, is unique. Also comparative static exercises imply*

---

[5] See e.g. Cooper and John (1988) for the properties of symmetric equilibria (Nash and cooperative).

$t^{nc} = t(\overset{+}{m}, \overset{+}{v}, \overset{+}{e})$; *thus, the tax rate increases with mobility costs, the weight given to public goods and the initial endowment.*

3.2 Symmetric Cooperative Equilibrium (SCE) in National Policies

Consider now the benchmark case in which national tax policies are chosen by maximizing the sum of individual countries' welfare. That is, a fictional worldwide social planner chooses t^i and t^j jointly to maximize the sum of (1b) over countries i and j subject to (5a)–(5j).

It is straightforward to show that, in a SCE, the cooperative tax rate (denoted as t^c) is determined by the following equation:

$$A\left(e - \frac{1}{A(1-t)}\right) = v\left[A\left(e - \frac{1}{A(1-t)}\right) - \frac{t}{(1-t)^2}\right] \tag{19}$$

which is a non-linear equation in t^c only. Then, Appendix B shows:

Result 2. *A Symmetric Cooperative Equilibrium (SCE) in national policies is summarized by the tax rate that solves (7). This cooperative tax rate,* $0 < t^c < 1$, *is unique. Also comparative static exercises imply* $t^c = t(\overset{+}{v}, \overset{+}{e})$; *thus, the tax rate increases with the weight given to public goods and the initial endowment, but it is independent of mobility costs.*

3.3 Comparison of SNE with SCE: Analytical Results

Comparison of (6) and (7) implies (see Appendix-Result 3):

Result 3. *(i) The Symmetric Nash Equilibrium and the Symmetric Cooperative Equilibrium coincide only when* $m \to \infty$. *(ii) For any finite value of* m, t^c *exceeds* t^{nc}, *i.e.* $0 < t^{nc} < t^c < 1$, *and the difference becomes larger as* m *decreases.*

Thus, the Nash tax rate is sub-optimally low. This is the standard result in the literature on international taxation. The two tax rates coincide only when the mobility cost is very large, $m \to \infty$, which basically means that there is no capital mobility and the economies become closed. The mechanism behind Result 3 is as follows. In the background, there is a positive spillover across countries. Namely, an increase in the foreign tax rate leads to a capital inflow in the domestic country and this is good for domestic welfare.[6] Then, the standard game-theoretic result follows: in the presence of positive spillovers, Nash strategies are inefficiently low relative to co-operative ones; (see for instance, Cooper and John (1988)). Notice that as capital mobility increases, that is, the parameter m becomes smaller and smaller-tax competition gets fiercer and this increases the degree of ineffi-ciency in the form of divergence between the two tax rates. Furthemore, notice that, since the planner internalises the inefficiencies arising from tax competition (and since tax competition depends on the mobility cost, m), the cooperative tax rate is independent of m; see Result 2 above.

3.4 Comparison of SNE with SCE: Numerical Results

We now present numerical results.[7] Tables 1, 2 and 3 below will illustrate the equilibrium tax rates, the associated macroeconomic outcomes, and the resulting utilities in general equilibrium, in both the non-cooperative and cooperative cases. To get results for the non-cooperative case, we solve (6) for the Nash tax rate, use this solution into (5a)–(5e), and, in turn, plug (5a)–(5e) into the objective function (1b). We work similarly with the co-operative case in which the tax rate is given by (7).

Table 1 shows results for changing values of the parameter m, where recall that m measures the mobility cost from investing abroad. Table 2 does the same for changing values of the parameter v, where v is the weight given to public goods relative to private consumption in the house-hold's utility function. Table 3 reports the effects of a changing e, which is the exogenous initial endowment. We present results for both the Nash equilibrium and the cooperative solution.

---

[6] Using the WCE given by (5a)–(5j) into the utility function (1b), we get

$$\frac{\partial U^i}{\partial t^j} = v^i t^i A^i \left(\frac{A^j}{m^{ij}} + \frac{A^i}{m^{ji}} \right) - A^j k^{ij} .$$ The first term on the right-hand side captures

the effect of t^j on public good provision in country i, while the second term captures the effect of t^j on second-period consumption in country i. The first effect is positive, while the second effect can be negative or positive depending on whether the country is capital exporter ($k^{ij} > 0$) or capital importer ($k^{ij} < 0$). The first effect is known as the "tax competition effect", while the second one is known as the "tax-the-foreigner effect". In a symmetric equilib-rium, we have $k^{ij} = k^{ji} = 0$ (see (5d) and (5i)), so that only the first effect is present. Therefore, in our model, the cross-country externality is unambiguously positive. Then, the general game theoretic result follows.

[7] We use Mathematica, version 4.00. We will report well-defined solutions only. For instance, we will not report solutions for the tax rate that are higher than one.

Table 1. Effects of m on Nash tax policies, outcomes and utility

m	t^{nc}	$c_1[t^{nc}]$	$c_2[t^{nc}]$	$g[t^{nc}]$	$U[t^{nc}]$
$m \to 0$	$t^{nc} \to 0$	1	99	0	99
0.1	0.39	1.64	60	38.36	102.691
0.2	0.57	2.32	42	55.67	104.086
0.3	0.63	2.70	36	61.29	104.421
0.5	0.67	3.03	32	64.97	104.575
1.0	0.69	3.23	30	66.77	104.623
2.0	0.70	3.33	29	67.67	104.637
$m \to \infty$	0.714	3.49	27.6	68.90	104.646

Notes: (i) $A^i = A^j \equiv A = 1$, $v^i = v^j \equiv v = 1.1$, $e^i = e^j \equiv e = 100$.
(ii) The cooperative solution is independent of m (see Result 2).
Then, for the same parameter values as in (i), the cooperative
solution is $t^c = 0.714$, $c_1(t^c) = 3.49$, $c_2(t^c) = 27.6$, $g(t^c) = 68.9$ and
$U(t^c) = 104.646$.

Table 2a. Effects of v on Nash tax policies, outcomes and utility

v	t^{nc}	$c_1[t^{nc}]$	$c_2[t^{nc}]$	$g[t^{nc}]$	$U[t^{nc}]$
1.0	0	1	99	0	99
1.05	0.37	1.58	62	36.41	100.695
1.1	0.57	2.32	42	55.57	104.086
1.2	0.71	3.44	28	68.55	111.500
1.5	0.81	5.26	18	76.73	134.776
2.0	0.85	6.66	14	79.33	174.564
3.0	0.87	7.69	12	80.30	254.963

Notes: $A^i = A^j \equiv A = 1$, $m^{ij} = m^{ji} \equiv m = 0.2$, $e^i = e^j \equiv e = 100$.

Table 2b. Effects of v on cooperative tax policies, outcomes and utility

v	t^c	$c_1[t^c]$	$c_2[t^c]$	$g[t^c]$	$U[t^c]$
1.0	0	1	99	0	99
1.05	0.62	2.63	37	60.36	101.354
1.1	0.71	3.44	28	68.55	104.645
1.2	0.77	4.34	22	73.65	111.852
1.5	0.84	6.25	15	78.75	134.958
2.0	0.86	7.14	13	79.85	174.680
3.0	0.88	8.33	11	80.66	255.120

Notes: $A^i = A^j \equiv A = 1$, $m^{ij} = m^{ji} \equiv m = 0.2$, $e^i = e^j \equiv e = 100$.

Table 3a. Effects of e on Nash tax policies, outcomes and utility

e	t^{nc}	$c_1[t^{nc}]$	$c_2[t^{nc}]$	$g[t^{nc}]$	$U[t^{nc}]$
10	0.07	1.07	8.03	0.62	9.059
50	0.35	1.53	31.5	16.96	50.588
100	0.57	2.32	42	55.67	104.086
200	0.73	3.70	53	143.29	211.935
500	0.84	6.25	79	414.75	537.058
1000	0.89	9.09	109	881.91	1081.031

Notes: $A^i = A^j \equiv A = 1$, $v^i = v^j \equiv v = 1.1$, $m^{ii} = m^{ji} \equiv m = 0.2$.

Table 3b. Effects of e on cooperative tax policies, outcomes and utility

e	t^c	$c_1[t^c]$	$c_2[t^c]$	$g[t^c]$	$U[t^c]$
10	0.34	1.51	5.6	2.88	9.188
50	0.62	2.63	18	29.36	51.272
100	0.71	3.45	28	68.55	104.645
200	0.79	4.76	41	154.24	212.223
500	0.86	7.14	69	423.86	537.209
1000	0.9	10	99	891	1081.40

Notes: $A^i = A^j \equiv A = 1$, $v^i = v^j \equiv v = 1.1$, $m^{ii} = m^{ji} \equiv m = 0.2$.

In all three tables, the Nash tax rate is lower than the cooperative one, and the general equilibrium utility is higher under cooperation. Concerning tax rates, some useful details are as follows. In Table 1, the smaller is m, the stronger is international competition, and the lower gets the Nash tax rate relative to the cooperative one. On the other hand, the cooperative tax rate and the associated utility are independent of m (see the Notes of Table 1). Also, in the extreme case in which $m \to \infty$, the two solutions coincide.

In Table 2, a higher v leads monotonically to higher tax rates in both the non-cooperative and the cooperative case. Intuitively, when economic agents value public goods a lot, there is a strong incentive to go for higher tax rates anyway, and this pushes the sub-optimally low Nash tax rate towards the cooperative one. In Table 3, a higher e leads monotonically to higher tax rates in both the non-cooperative and cooperative case. Intuitively, richer societies can afford higher tax rates. Again, this reduces the difference between Nash and cooperative tax policies.

What is more interesting is the comparison of utilities. In all three tables, the difference between utility in the non-cooperative case and utility in the cooperative case is very small quantitatively. Notice that this happens even if the tax rates differ a lot between the two cases. For instance, consider Table 1. When the mobility cost is pretty low (say $m = 0.1$), the Nash tax rate is $t^{nc} = 0.39$, while the socially optimal tax rate is $t^c = 0.714$. However, despite this difference in policies, the utility is almost the same, $U^{nc} = 102.691$ versus $U^c = 104.646$, so that the welfare gain of coordination is only two percentage points. As m increases, the difference in utilities becomes even smaller. Tables 2 and 3 deliver a similar message. In other words, the welfare differences between non-cooperative and cooperative policies are very small quantitatively. The explanation is given by the results for macroeconomic outcomes also reported in the tables. Recall that utility depends on both private consumption and public good provision (see (1b)). Then, the numerical simulations imply that higher tax rates are good for public good provision (i.e. they mitigate the problem of under-provision of public goods), but particularly bad for second-period private consumption. This happens because higher tax rates hurt current private investment and in turn future private consumption (see (5b) and (5g)). As a result, in a dynamic setup, the Nash tax rates are not that bad quantitatively.

4 Conclusions

We used a simple two-period model of a world economy to show that the welfare gain of international tax coordination is very small quantitatively. Thus, the standard argument – that tax competition is harmful in the presence of cross-country spillovers – becomes weaker as one moves from static to dynamic setups. We believe our result is consistent with general public finance results which can change many things once we move to dynamic setups where which long-run tax bases are fully endogenous (see e.g. Philippopoulos and Economides (2003)). Although here we used a rather standard model, it would be interesting to study whether our result holds in richer models with, for instance, heterogeneous economies and/or other types of cross-country externalities. Concerning cross-country externalities, it would be interesting to add international public goods (i.e. public goods with cross-country spillovers) like the ones suggested in e.g. Tabellini (2003). We leave these extensions for future research.

5 Appendix

Result 1:

Consider (6). Define the left hand side as $LHS \equiv A\left(e - \dfrac{1}{A(1-t)}\right)$, and the

right hand side as $RHS \equiv v\left[A\left(e - \dfrac{1}{A(1-t)}\right) - \dfrac{t}{(1-t)^2} - \dfrac{2A^2 t}{m}\right]$. Then,

$$LHS_t = -\frac{1}{(1-t)^2} < 0 \quad \text{and} \quad RHS_t = -v\left[\frac{1}{(1-t)^2} + \frac{t+1}{(1-t)^3} + \frac{2A^2}{m}\right] < 0.$$

Also, from the second-order condition of the maximization problem, $|RHS_t| > |LHS_t|$ for $0 < t < 1$. Hence, assuming existence of a $0 < t < 1$, there is a unique solution t^{nc} as shown in Fig. 1.

In turn, total differentiation in (6) implies $\dfrac{\partial t^{nc}}{\partial m} = \dfrac{2A^2 t v}{m^2 (LHS_t - RHS_t)}$,

which is positive because $(LHS_t - RHS_t) > 0$. Also,

$\dfrac{\partial t^{nc}}{\partial e} = \dfrac{A(v-1)}{(LHS_t - RHS_t)}$, which is positive for $v > 1$. Finally,

$$\frac{\partial t^{nc}}{\partial v} = \frac{\left[A\left(e - \dfrac{1}{A(1-t)}\right) - \dfrac{t}{(1-t)^2} - \dfrac{2A^2 t}{m}\right]}{LHS_t - RHS_t} = \frac{RHS}{v(RHS_t - LHS_t)},$$ which is

also positive.

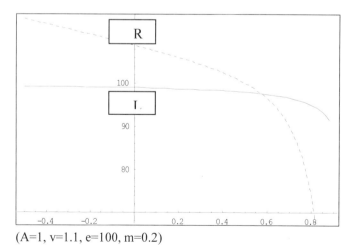

(A=1, v=1.1, e=100, m=0.2)

Fig. 1. Unique solution (1)

Result 2:

Consider (7). Define the left hand side as $LHS \equiv A\left(e - \dfrac{1}{A(1-t)}\right)$, and the

right hand side as $RHS \equiv v\left[A\left(e - \dfrac{1}{A(1-t)}\right) - \dfrac{t}{(1-t)^2}\right]$. Then,

$LHS_t = -\dfrac{1}{(1-t)^2} < 0$ and $RHS_t = -v\left[\dfrac{1}{(1-t)^2} + \dfrac{t+1}{(1-t)^3}\right] < 0$. Also, from

the second-order condition of the maximization problem, we have $|RHS_t| > |LHS_t|$ for $0 < t < 1$. Hence, assuming existence of a $0 < t < 1$, there is a unique solution t^c as shown in Fig. 2.

In turn total differentiation in (7) implies $\dfrac{\partial t^c}{\partial m} = 0, \dfrac{\partial t^c}{\partial e} = \dfrac{A(v-1)}{(LHS_t - RHS_t)}$, which is positive for $v > 1$, and

$\dfrac{\partial t^c}{\partial v} = \dfrac{A\left(e - \dfrac{1}{A(1-t)}\right) - \dfrac{t}{(1-t)^2}}{LHS_t - RHS_t}$, which is also positive.

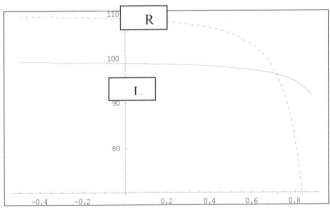

$(A=1, v=1.1, e=100, m=0.2)$

Fig. 2. Unique solution (2)

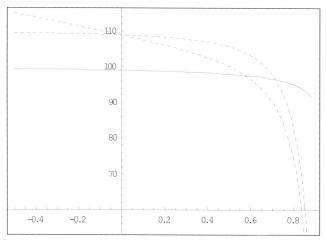

(A=1, v=1.1, e=100, m=0.2)

Fig. 3. Unique solution (3)

Result 3:
Since, other things equal, the RHS in the cooperative case is larger than the RHS in the Nash case, while the LHS is the same in both cases, it follows that t^c is higher than t^{nc} as illustrated in Fig. 3. In the special case in which $m \to \infty$, the RHS of the cooperative case coincides with the RHS of the Nash case so that the two tax rates also coincide. Then, by taking into account the comparative static properties of the two tax rates with respect to m, the difference between t^c and t^{nc} increases as m decreases.

6 References

Bucovetsky, S. (1991) Asymmetric tax competition, Journal of Urban Economics, September 1991, 30(2), pp. 167-81.

Cooper, R., John, A. (1988) Coordinating coordination failures in Keynesian models, Quarterly Journal of Economics, August 1988, 103(3), pp. 441-463.

Gordon, R. (1938) An optimal taxation approach to fiscal federalism, Quarterly Journal of Economics, 1983, 98, pp. 567-586.

Mendoza, E., Tezar, L. (2003) A quantitative analysis of tax competition versus tax coordination under perfect capital mobility, May 2003, NBER Working Paper, no. 9746.

Park, H., Philippopoulos, A. (2003) Choosing club membership under tax competition and free riding, July 2003, CESifo Working Paper, no. 985.

Persson, T., Tabellini, G. (1992) The politics of 1992: Fiscal policy and European integration, Review of Economic Studies, October 1992, 59(4), pp. 689-701.

Philippopoulos, A., Economides, G. (2003) Are Nash tax rates too low or too high? The role of endogenous growth in models with public goods, Review of Economic Dynamics, 2003, 6, pp. 37-53.

Razin, A., Sadka, E. (1991) International tax competition and gains from trade harmonization, Economics Letters, 1991, 37, pp. 69-76.

Tabellini, G. (2003) Principles of policymaking in the EU: An economic perspective, CESifo Economic Studies, 2003, 49(1), pp. 75-102.

Wildasin, D. (1988) Nash equilibria in models of fiscal competition, Journal of Public Economics, March 1988, 35(2), pp. 229-240.

Wilson, J. (1986) A theory of interregional tax competition, Journal of Urban Economics, May 1986, 19(3), pp. 296–315.

Zodrow, G., Mieszkowski, P. (1986) Pigou, Tiebout, property taxation, and the underprovision of local public goods, Journal of Urban Economics, May 1986, 19(3), pp. 356–70.

Part II

Microeconomic Issues of Regional Growth and Economic Integration

Foreign Direct Investment (FDI) and Exchange Rate Uncertainty in Imperfectly Competitive Industries

Ray Barrell*, Sylvia D. Gottschalk and Stephen G. Hall

National Institute of Economic and Social Research (NIESR), 2 Dean Trench Street, Smith Square, London SW1H 3PE, United Kingdom

1 Introduction

Recent empirical research on Foreign Direct Investment (FDI) and exchange rate uncertainty has highlighted the ambiguous effects of exchange rate volatility on FDI. Cushman (1985) and Cushman (1988) found evidence of a positive relationship between US FDI and exchange rate uncertainty, whereas Bénassy-Quéré, Fontagné and Lahrèche-Révil (2001) show that exchange rate volatility in emerging economies has a negative impact on OECD outward FDI to these countries. Cushman (1985) shows that exchange rate risk may increase direct investment bilateral flows between the US and Canada, France, Germany, Japan and the UK, whilst Cushman (1988) finds an analogous relationship between exchange rate risk and inward US FDI. In both papers, Cushman develops a mean-variance framework in which a firm's utility is a positive function of expected profit and a negative function of the variance of profit. The latter derives solely from exchange rate risk. FDI is mainly determined by the host country's relative factor cost competitiveness, which is influenced by exchange rate volatility.

The importance of exchange rate risk depends on whether the firm produces domestically or abroad, and on the share of imported inputs in production. Although Cushman attempts to apply conventional portfolio theory to the analysis of US foreign direct investment, none of the models

* Email: r.barrell@niesr.ac.uk

presented in Cushman (1985) and Cushman (1988) considers that a risk-averse firm would try to minimize the variance of its total profit by exploiting the correlation between exchange rate movements. Bénassy-Quéré, Fontagné and Lahrèche-Revil (2001) extend Cushman's work and investigate the role of exchange rate correlation on Foreign direct investment from OECD countries into developing economies. In their paper, the typical investing firm is a multinational company producing abroad and exporting from there to the home country. Its location choice will be determined by the potential host relative competitiveness, which is proxied by the relative real exchange rate of the potential host against the investor's real exchange rate. An increase in competitiveness is measured by the depreciation of the host country's currency. Their empirical analysis indicates that, irrespective of the sign of exchange rate correlation between alternative locations, inward FDI to one country decreases if the competitiveness of an alternative host rises.

In this paper, we investigate the role of exchange rate risk diversification as a determinant of the location of US FDI in Europe. We apply standard portfolio theory to the q theory of investment to show that risk-averse firms can reduce the negative impact of exchange rate volatility on their profits by diversifying their investments across two alternative locations in a single market. Unlike Cushman (1985), Cushman (1988) and Bénassy-Quéré, Fontagné and Lahrèche-Révil (2001), we focus exclusively on the impact of exchange rate risk on Foreign Direct Investment (FDI) conditional to the level of exchange rate and assume that firm-level specificities–e.g., competitive factor costs are captured by the profits reported by affiliates. In the papers surveyed above, firms are assumed perfectly competitive. On the contrary, we do consider that firms are imperfectly competitive, since there is ample theoretical and empirical evidence that market power moderates the negative impact of exchange rate volatility on domestic investment, we are not aware of any analysis of the interaction between market power and exchange rate volatility in the case of inward or outward foreign direct investment. We thus extend the works of, among others, Campa and Goldberg (1995), Campa and Goldberg (1995), Nucci and Pozzolo (2001).

Following this introduction, Section 2 presents the theoretical framework that will be estimated in Section 3, and discusses measures of industrial concentration. Section 3 shows the results of the panel data estimation. Section 4 concludes.

2 The Model

A firm chooses investment in locations A and B to maximize the present value of the utility of its profits:

$$V_t = \int_0^\infty e^{-rt} [U(E[(\pi(.)], Var[\pi(.)]) - C(I_A, I_B) - I_A - I_B] dt \tag{1}$$

where $E[\pi(.)]$ and $Var[\pi(.)]$ are the expected value of profits and the variance of profits respectively. We assume the firm is risk-averse, so $U(E[\pi(.)], Var[\pi(.)])$ is increasing in the expected value of profits and decreasing in the variance of profits. r is the discount factor and is constant over time and identical in both countries. $C(I_A, I_B)$ is the adjustment cost of capital. The profit function of the firm is given by $\pi(K_A, K_B, e_A, e_B)$.

The firm maximizes (1) subject to the following accumulation equations:

$$I_i = \frac{dK_i}{dt} \tag{2}$$

The solution to this maximization is obtained by forming the Hamiltonian:

$$H(U(\pi(.)), C(I_A, I_B), I_A, I_B) = e^{-rt} U(\pi(.)) - C(I_A, I_B) - I_A - I_B - \lambda_A(t)(I_A) - \lambda_B(t)(I_A) \tag{3}$$

The necessary conditions for the solution of the Hamiltonian are:

$$\frac{\partial H}{\partial \lambda_i} = \frac{dK_i}{dt} \tag{4}$$

$$\frac{\partial H}{\partial I_i} = 0 \tag{5}$$

$$-\frac{\partial H}{\partial K_i} = \frac{\lambda_i}{dt} \tag{6}$$

Let $\mu_i = \lambda_i e^{rt}$. From (5)

$$\mu_i = 1 + \frac{\partial C}{\partial I_i} \tag{7}$$

from (6)

$$\int \frac{\lambda_i}{dt} dt = \int e^{-rt} \frac{\partial U}{\partial K_i} dt \tag{8}$$

for i=A, B. Integrating (8) results in

$$\lambda_i(t)e^{rt} = \int \frac{\partial U}{\partial K_i} dt \tag{9}$$

Since $\mu_i = \lambda_i e^{rt}$ and substituting (9) in (7) we have

$$\int \frac{\partial U}{\partial K_i} dt = 1 + \frac{\partial C}{\partial I_i} \tag{10}$$

i=A, B. We assume the cost of investment follows the specification given in haya

$$C(I_A, I_B) = \frac{\gamma}{2}[(I_A - \mu)^2 + (I_B - \mu)^2] \tag{11}$$

Differentiating (11) with respect to K_i i=A,B and substituting in (10) yields

$$\int \frac{\partial U}{\partial K_i} dt = 1 + \gamma(I_i - \mu) \tag{12}$$

Solving for I_i we obtain an expression for investment, which depends on the firms' utility $U(\pi(.))$

$$I_i = (\int \frac{\partial U}{\partial K_i} dt - 1)\gamma^{-1} - \mu \tag{13}$$

At this stage we must specify a profit function for the investing firm. We consider that capital is a quasi-fixed cost, so that the cost-minimizing function $C_1^*(w_A, w_B, q_1^A, q_2^B, K_A, K_B)$ is a function of the capital stock in country A and country B. The nominal profit function of firm 1 in industry k, with plants in countries A and B, can thus be described as

$$\pi_{1,k}^* = \max_{q_{1,k}^A \cdot q_{1,k}^B} p^{A,k}(Q^{A,k})q_{1,k}^A s_A + p^{B,k}(Q^{B,k})q_{1,k}^B s_B \\ -(w_A + K_A)s_A q_{1,k}^A - (w_B + K_B)s_B q_{1,k}^B \tag{14}$$

where $q_{1,k}^i$ is output of a firm in industry k, producing in country $i = A, B$. $Q^{i,k}$ is the aggregate demand in country i in industry k, and is equal to the sum of production of firm 1 and firm 2 in country i. $Q^i = q_1^i + q_2^i$. e_i is the exchange rate in units of country i's currency per units of the investing firm's currency. So, the firm's profits are given in the currency of its home country. K_i is the stock of capital and is fixed in the short-run. w_i, i=A, B is the price of factors in country i. We assume that industry k is oligopolistic. Firm 1 maximizes its profit making certain assumptions about the reaction of its competitors in the industry. These assumptions are summarized in the derivative of the demand function with respect to the aggregate demand, $\frac{\partial P(Q_i)}{\partial Q_i}$.

The first order conditions for firm 1 are:

$$\frac{\partial \pi}{\partial q_1^A} = p^{A,k}(Q^{A,k})(1 + \frac{q_1^A}{Q_A}\frac{1}{\varepsilon_A})s_A - (w_A + K_A)s_A \qquad (15)$$

$$\frac{\partial \pi}{\partial q_1^B} = p^{B,k}(Q^{B,k})(1 + \frac{q_1^B}{Q_B}\frac{1}{\varepsilon_B})s_B - (w_B + K_B)s_B \qquad (16)$$

ε_i is the elasticity of the aggregate demand in country i. In (15) and (16), $\frac{\partial P(Q_i)}{\partial Q_i}$ was multiplied by $Q_i/Q_i P(Q_i)$, which yields the inverse of the elasticity of the aggregate demand.

Solving (15) and (16) for $P(Q_i)$, and defining the market share of firm 1 in country i as $m_i = \frac{q_i}{Q_i}$, gives

$$P(Q_i) = \frac{w_i + K_i}{1 + \frac{m_i}{\varepsilon_i}} \qquad (17)$$

Substituting (17) in the profit function gives the optimum profit given the capital stock

$$\pi^* = (w_A + K_A)(1 + \frac{m_A}{\varepsilon_A})^{-1} m_A q_{1,k}^{A*} + (w_B + K_B)(1 + \frac{m_B}{\varepsilon_B})^{-1} s_B q_{1,k}^{B*}$$
$$-(w_A + K_A)s_A q_{1,k}^{A*} - (w_B + K_B)s_B q_{1,k}^{B*} \qquad (18)$$

where the starred variables are the optimum outputs of firm 1 in country A and in country B.

Finally, we adopt a mean-variance specification for the firm's function $U(\pi)$, which reflects the assumption of risk aversion,

$$U(\pi(.)) = E[\pi(.)] - \phi Var[\pi(.)] \tag{19}$$

where $E[.]$ and $Var[.]$ are the expectation and the variance operators. Clearly, $U(.)$ varies positively with mean profits and negatively with the variance of profits. The derivative of $U(.)$ with respect to K_i in (13) is thus the derivative of the expected value of the profit minus the derivative of the variance of profits. This specification also has the advantage of highlighting the role of the correlation between the exchange rates of country A and country B. In effect, suppose a firm has a total amount of assets to be invested (K) that can be split between a number of foreign investments r_i (i=1,...,n). Suppose also that uncertainty is due to exchange rate risk (σ_i^2). If the firm chooses to invest w_i as a proportion of its assets in each country ($w_i < 1, \forall i, \sum w_i = 1$) then the total expected return on the firms assets will be

$$E[r] = \sum -i^n w_i E[r_i] \tag{20}$$

and the expected variance of the returns will be given by

$$\sigma^2 = \sum_1^n w_i^2 \sigma_i^2 + \sum_i^n \sum_j^n w_i w_j \sigma_{ij} \tag{21}$$

from which we obtain,

$$\sigma^2 = \sum_1^n w_i^2 \sigma_i^2 + \sum_i^n \sum_j^n w_i w_j \rho_{ij} \sigma_i^2 \sigma_j^2 \tag{22}$$

where ρ_{ij} is the correlation coefficient. A firm which is purely interested in maximizing expected profits should therefore invest only in the country or countries with the highest returns but a firm which is concerned with both maximizing profits and minimizing risk would exploit any correlation between returns which is less than one to reduce the variance of the total return. A correlation coefficient of 1 of course means that there are no benefits to diversification between the two regions and only the region with the higher return should receive any investment.

Given (19) and (18), $U(E[\pi(.)], Var[\pi(.)])$ can now be written as

$$U(.) = E[s_A \pi_1^{A*} + s_B \pi_1^{B*}] - \phi Var[s_A \pi_1^{A*} + s_B \pi_1^{B*}] \tag{23}$$

where $\pi^* = s_A \pi_1^{A*} + s_B \pi_1^{B*}$. Differentiating (23) with respect to K_i and substituting the result in (13) gives

$$I_i = (\int_0^\infty E[\frac{\partial \pi^*}{\partial K_i}] - \phi Var[\frac{\partial \pi^*}{\partial K_i}]dt - 1)\gamma^{-1} - \mu \tag{24}$$

where

$$E[\frac{\partial \pi^*}{\partial K_i}] = [(1 + \frac{m_i}{\varepsilon_i})^{-1} - 1]E[s_i]q_{1,k}^i \tag{25}$$

$$Var[\frac{\partial \pi^*}{\partial K_i}] = [(1 + \frac{m_i}{\varepsilon_i})^{-1} - 1]^2 \sigma_i^2 q_{1,k}^{i*2} + 2Cov(s_i,sj)[(1 + \frac{m_i}{\varepsilon_i})^{-1} - 1]$$

$$[(1 + \frac{m_j}{\varepsilon_j})^{-1} - 1]q_{1,k}^i q_{1,k}^j \tag{26}$$

$\sigma_i^2 \equiv Var(s_i)$. It should be noted that the sign of the expression involving $Cov(s_i, s_j)$, depends on the sign of the exchange rate covariance. Here, we implicitly assume that the weight of investment in each location is $w_i = \frac{I_i}{\sum I_i}$. (26) can be related to (21) by noting that $\rho_{i,j} = \frac{Cov(s_i,s_j)}{Var(s_i)*Var(s_j)}$.

2.1 Comparative Statics

The impacts on investment of exchange rate volatility and correlation between exchange rates can be shown by differentiating (24) with respect to the variance of s_i and the covariance of s_i and s_j.

$$\frac{\partial I_i}{\partial Var[\pi^*(s_i)]} = -\phi\gamma^{-1} \int_0^\infty [(1 + \frac{m_i}{\varepsilon_i})^{-1} - 1]^2]q_{1,k,i}^2 dt \tag{27}$$

where $q_{1,k,i}$ is the production of firm 1 of industry k in country i. (27) is clearly negative and unsurprising. Since we assume a risk-averse firm, volatility should have a negative impact on investment. More interesting is the fact that the negative impact of volatility is reduced when the firm's market power increases. To simplify notation, we replace the mark-up expression in (27) by its equivalent in terms of the Lerner index of market power. From (15), we can write

$$\frac{p_i - c_1}{p_i} = -\frac{m_1}{\varepsilon_i} \tag{28}$$

The left-hand side of (28) is the Lerner index of market power, denoted L. Substituting L in (27) and differentiating with respect to L, we found

$$\frac{\partial I_i^2}{\partial Var[\pi^*(s_i)] \partial L} = -2\phi\gamma^{-1} \int_0^\infty (1-L)^{-2}[(1-L)^{-1} - 1]q_{1,k,i}^2 dt \tag{29}$$

which is also clearly negative. Finally, we show that the impact of exchange rate correlation on investment depends on the sign of the derivative of (24) with respect to $Cov(s_i, s_j)$.

$$\frac{\partial I_i}{\partial Cov[s_i s_j]} = -2\phi\gamma^{-1} \int_0^\infty [(1-L_i)^{-1} - 1][(1-L_j)^{-1} - 1]q_{1,k,i}q_{1,k,j} dt \tag{30}$$

Considering that $Cov(s_i, s_j) = \rho_{i,j}\sigma_i^2\sigma_j^2$, two cases can be characterised.

Case 1: $-1 \le \rho_{i,j} < 1$. Risk diversification can be achieved by relocating investment from one country to the other, since exchange rates are either partially correlated or cancel each other.

Case 2: $\rho_{i,j} = 1$. Exchange rates are perfectly correlated. There is little possibility for risk diversification. Investment location will be determined by other factors, e.g. rate of return, market size, labour market conditions.

Finally, we can show that the derivative of (30) with respect to the Lerner index is negative, suggesting that an increase in market power diminish the impact of exchange rate correlation on investment.

2.2 Measures of Concentration

The most appropriate measure of a firm's market power is the Lerner index, which is given by the ratio of price less marginal costs over price. As marginal costs are not directly observable, a proxy for market power is generally used. Here, we use an industry-wide measure of market power. We construct a market Lerner index, defined as the weighted sum of individual firm Lerner indices, defined in (28) above. The weights are their market shares. Assuming that firms engage in Cournot competition, the market Lerner index can be written as function of the Herfindalh index (H) of industrial concentration and the demand elasticity, (η),

$$L = \frac{-H}{\eta} \tag{31}$$

Table 1. Herfindahl Index in the U.K. and European Union

Industry	U.K.	European Union
Food and Kindred Products	0.30	0.16
Chemicals and Allied Products	0.24	0.24
Primary and Fabricated Metals	0.13	0.13
Machinery	0.14	0.15
Electrical and Electronic Equipment	0.19	0.24
Transportation Equipment	0.42	0.54
Other Manufacturing	0.14	0.14

The Herfindahl index has been shown to be a good measure of monopoly power, and will be used in this paper as a proxy for market power.[1]

Herfindahl Indices can be constructed from various measures of firm size, gross output per firm, value added per firm, number of employees per firm. We use the share of value added at factor prices per firm as a measure of firm size. Eurostat data on value added at factor prices are more complete than other measures of firm sizes. We construct a Herfindahl index for 7 two-digit industries in the European Union for 1995, the only data point available in Table 1. We construct a Herfindahl index for 7 two-digit industries in the European Union for 1995. For this reason, we will assume in the empirical analysis of investment that the Herfindahl index is constant over time. Eurostat data for the U.K. were available from 1995–2000. We used the average over those five years as the constant Herfindahl Index for the U.K.

2.3 Measures of Uncertainty

In order to derive estimates of the conditional variance and covariance terms we employ a bivariate BEKK(1,1) (Engle and Kroner 1995) model between the real dollar-sterling rate and the real dollar-euro rate. A number of studies have already extended the basic GARCH framework to a multivariate context so that we may consider complete conditional covariance matrices, Kraft and Engle (1982), Bollerslev et al. (1988), Hall et al. (1990), Hall and Miles (1992), and Engle and Kroner (1995). Let us consider a set of n variables Y that may be assumed to be generated by the following VAR process.

$$A(L)Y_t = e_t \tag{32}$$

This varies from a conventional VAR model as we assume that

$$E[e_t] = 0 \tag{33}$$

---

[1]See Kwoka (1998).

$$E[e_t e_t] = \Omega_t \tag{34}$$

so that the covariance matrix is time varying, we then make the standard ARCH assumption that this covariance matrix follows an autoregressive structure. Estimation of such a model is, in principle, quite straightforward as the log likelihood is proportional to the following expression.

$$l = \sum_{t=1}^{T} \ln | \Omega_t | + e'_t \Omega_t^{-1} e_t \tag{35}$$

and so standard maximum likelihood (or quasi maximum likelihood) procedures may be applied. If we define the VECH operator in the usual way as a stacked vector of the lower triangle of a symmetric matrix then we can represent the standard generalization of the univariate GARCH model as

$$VECH(\Omega_t) = C + A(L)VECH(e_t e_t') + B(L)VECH(\Omega_{t-1}) \tag{36}$$

where C is an *(N(N+1)/2)* vector and *A* and *B* are *(N(N+1)/2)x(N(N+1)/2)* matrices. This general formulation presents a couple of drawbacks. First, (36) rapidly produces huge numbers of parameters as N rises. For instance, for one lag in A and B and a five variable system we generate 465 parameters to be estimated. So, beyond the simplest system, (36) will almost certainly be intractable. Second, without fairly complex restrictions on the system the conditional covariance matrix cannot be guaranteed to be positive semi definite. Much of the literature has thus focused on finding a parameterization which is both flexible enough to be useful and yet is also reasonably tractable.

One of the most popular formulations was first proposed by Baba, Engle, Kraft and Kroner, sometimes referred to as the BEKK (see Engle and Kroner(1993)) representation, this takes the following form

$$\Omega_t = C'C + \sum_{i=1}^{q} A_i e_{t-1} e_{t-1} A_i + \sum_{j=1}^{p} B_{t-j} \Omega_{t-j} B_{t-j} \tag{37}$$

this formulation guarantees positive semi definiteness of the covariance matrix almost surely and reduces the number of parameters considerably.

We define a pair of simple first order autoregressions for the log of the real exchange rate, $e_{i,t}$ i=1,2, and estimate a bivariate BEKK model of the conditional covariance and the conditional correlation between the real dollar-sterling rate and the real dollar-euro rate. The A and B matrices are restricted to be diagonal, maximum likelihood estimation. Consumer price

Table 2. The bivariate real exchange rate model.
For $i \neq j = 1, 2$

Variable	Coefficient	Std. Error	t-stat
D11	0.626276	0.253210	2.5
D12	0.942173	0.020272	46.4
D21	0.253396	0.156416	1.6
D22	0.956215	0.012994	73.5
A11	0.142521	0.101197	1.4
BG11	0.001000	0.175105	0.0
C11	0.018854	0.001291	14.6
C12	0.011676	0.001640	7.1
C22	0.000003	0.001411	0.0
A22	0.640873	0.166676	3.8
BG22	0.576504	0.097145	5.9

indices were used to obtain the real exchange rates. Results are presented in Table 2. D11 and D12 are the constant and lagged dependent variable-coefficients in the sterling dollar equation and D21 and D22 are the corresponding coefficients in the euro dollar equation. $A_{i,j}$, $B_{i,j}$ and $C_{i,j}$ are elements of the matrices defined in (37).

Figure 1 shows the estimated conditional correlation. There is a clear positive correlation between the dollar-sterling and the dollar-Euro exchange rates over the whole sample period. This clearly indicates that variations in both exchange rates tend to be in the same direction. These variations are considerable. Starting from an average of 60 percent in the 1970s, the correlation drops to almost zero in 1981 before peaking at more than 80 percent in 1986. From 1987 to 1996 the exchange rate correlation presented an upward trend before a plummeting to approximately zero in 1998. The positive correlation between the dollar-sterling exchange rate and the dollar-Euro exchange rate does not indicate a complementarity between U.S. foreign direct investment in the U.K. and U.S. Foreign Direct Investment (US FDI) in the Euro Area. Such a conclusion depends on the sign of the coefficient of the correlation in the econometric estimation of (24) above, which will be carried out in Sect. 3 below.

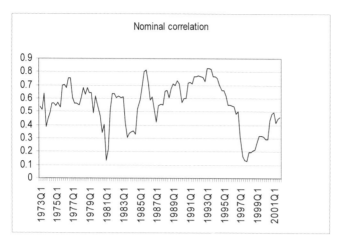

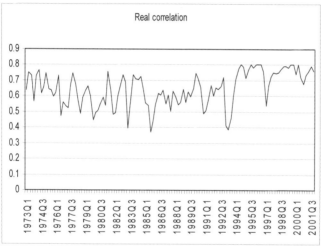

Fig. 1. Correlation between real sterling dollar and real euro dollar exchange rates. 1973Q1–2001Q4

3 Econometric Analysis

3.1 Data

Annual data from the U.S. Bureau of Economic Analysis (BEA) survey of US direct investment abroad were used in the empirical analysis. We used foreign direct investments by non-bank U.S. firms in Europe. The countries covered are the UK and the following members of the single currency, Austria, Belgium, France, Germany and the Netherlands. This group of Euro Area countries had effectively fixed exchange rates over the period 1982–2000.

They can therefore be treated as the same location and aggregated together. For the sake of simplicity they will be denoted "Euro Area" throughout the paper. Seven two-digit manufacturing industries were considered, Food and Kindred Products, Chemicals and Allied Products, Primary and Fabricated Metals, Machinery, Electrical and Electronic Equipments, Transportation Equipment, Other Manufacturing. Data on direct investment include all foreign affiliates where US firms have direct or indirect ownership or control of more than 10 percent of voting securities. Year-to-year changes in the stock of FDI include net capital outflows between the U.S. parent and its affiliate, inter-company debt and reinvested earnings. Valuation adjustments, e.g. exchange rate adjustments, price changes and other capital gains and losses, are also included in year-to-year changes.

Net income reported by affiliates in year t divided by investment in the previous year was taken as a measure of the rate of return on investment in year t-1. Net income is gross profit net of local corporate taxes. Real data were obtained by deflating the original data by the U.S. Consumer Price Index. The sample period for estimation, however, was restricted to the period 1982–1998, since in 1999 a change in the industrial classification of Electrical Equipments, Appliances and Components created a break in the series. This data set naturally calls for panel data analysis by seven industries and over 17 time periods. We used the lagged dependent variable as a GMM-type instrument following Arrellano and Bond (1991).

3.2 Results

Our theoretical framework suggests that the change in FDI into a location will depend upon the profitability of that location and the risks associated with it.[2] Adjustment to long run changes in driving variables such as profitability is unlikely to be imm ediate, and hence any model we estimate has to take into account the dynamics of adjustment. Following the shareholder's perspective on investment adopted in our theoretical specification, the long-run relationship includes the rate of return, the cost of capital, the

---

[2] This can be seen by differentiating (24) with respect to time.

exchange rate risk and the correlation between exchange rates. We estimate the following equation:

$$\Delta FDI_{i,k,t} = \phi_1 FDI_{i,k,t-2} + a_1 FDI_{i,k,t-2} + a_2 RR_{i,k,t-2} + a_3 RR_{j,k,t-2} \tag{38}$$
$$+ a_4 USLR_{t-2} + a_5 RRX_{t-2} + a_6 \sigma_{i,t-2}^2 + a_7 \sigma_{i,t-2}^2 + a_8 \rho_{i,j,t-2}$$
$$+ \nabla(FDI_{i,t}, FDI_{j,t}, RR_{i,t}, RR_{j,t}, USLR_t, RRX_t, \sigma_{i,t}^2, \sigma_{j,t}^2, \rho_{i,j,t})$$
$$+ \gamma_{i,k} + u_{i,k,t}$$

for $i \neq j$ = UK, Euro Area. $FDI_{i,k,t}$ is the log of real US FDI in industry k in
location i, $RR_{i,k,t}$ the real rate of return reported by affiliates in industry k
in location i. $USLR_t$ is the U.S. ten years real interest rate and was included as a proxy for the cost of capital. RRX_t is the real sterling/euro exchange rate. $\sigma_{i,t-1}^2 \equiv Var[e_{i,t-1}]$ is the GARCH estimate of the variance in
location i. $\rho_{i,j,t-1} \equiv corr[e_{i,t-1}, e_{j,t-1}]$ is the GARCH estimate of the correlation between the exchange rate in location i and the exchange rate in an alternative location. $\gamma_{i,k}$ are individual effects. To simplify the notation of
(38), we use $\nabla(FDI_{i,t}, FDI_{j,t}, RR_{i,t}, RR_{j,t}, \sigma_{i,t}^2, \sigma_{j,t}^2)$ to represent the dynamics of the variables in brackets.

In (38) the lagged dependent variable also appears as explanatory
variable. In this case, it has been shown that the error terms are correlated with the values of the regressors. Maximum-likelihood and generalised least-square estimators are biased when the number of individuals N
is large and the number of time periods T short.[3] We thus adopt the Generalized Method of Moments (GMM) developed by Arrellano and Bond
(1991), who provide an efficient estimator of dynamic panels with large
N and short T. Estimation and hypotheses testing were conducted using
PcGive10.0.

We expect increases in the rate of return to have a positive impact on
FDI. The estimated coefficient of $RRR_{k,t}$ should be positive. Other things
equal, costlier capital tends to depress investment, so, the coefficient of
$USLR_t$ should be negative. Since we assume firms are risk-averse, the coefficient of the exchange rate variance should be negative. The implications of the sign of the coefficient of the correlation were presented in
Sect. 2 above. The sign of the real cross-exchange rate is expected to be
negative or not significant. In effect, over the period 1982–2000, total sales
of goods and services represented an average of 94 percent of the profits of

---

[3] See Hsiao (2003), Chap. 4.

U.K. affiliates in manufacturing industries, of which 60 percent were local sales. An average of 29 percent of total sales was exported to all countries excluding the U.S. Although the BEA does not specify which European countries U.K. affiliates export to, an average of 85 percent of exports by European affiliates was destined to the European Union. We can then infer that between 1982 and 2000, most of the exports of U.K. affiliates were bound to the European Union. If we assume that these exports amount to 85 percent, we can also infer that less than a quarter of the profits made by U.K. affiliates derive from their exports to the European Union affiliates.

For a general model, the results reported in Table 3, column [1], are generally poor. The coefficient of $FDI_{uk,t-2}$, is only significant at the 10 percent level, and the signs of several coefficients are not sensible. The rate of return in the U.K. should have a positive-rather than negative- impact on inward FDI in the U.K. Analogously, the coefficient of $\sigma_{uk,t-2}$ should be negative, and not positive as reported in column [1], whereas the coefficient of $\sigma_{eu,t-2}$ should be positive. An increase in the volatility of the euro dollar exchange rate would probably make the U.K. more attractive then the EU for outward U.S. investment. The results of column [1] indicate that the opposite would be more likely. The sign of the real cross-exchange rate in column [1] is positive, indicating that an increase in the sterling euro exchange rate should raise investment in the U.K.

$FDI_{eu,t-2}$ has a positive sign, suggesting that US firms may not regard Europe as a market segmented into Euro Area and non-Euro Area. A positive sign indicates that US firms increase their investment in the UK following a rise in FDI into the Euro Area. This result is consistent with the negative sign of the rate of return in the Euro Area ($RR_{eu,k,t-2}$), as it indicates that an increase in the rate of return in the Euro Area would relocate FDI from the UK to the Euro Zone. Finally, we note that the exchange rate correlation has a positive and significant sign. The positive coefficient indicates that US FDI in the UK increases as exchange rates become more correlated. A perfect positive correlation diminishes risk diversification opportunities as both rates move in the same direction. Investment location would then be determined by other factors, e.g. higher rate of return or more flexible labour market. This result is quite robust to changes in model specification, since correlation has a positive coefficient in column [1] and column [2].

Table 3. GMM estimates of US foreign direct investment in the UK

Variable	[1] Coefficient	t-value	[2] Coefficient	t-value
FDIuk(t-2)	-0.020739^b	-1.76		
FDIeu(t-2)	0.0577748^b	4.85		
RRuk(t-2)	-0.00036387^b	-4.40		
RReu(t-2)	-0.000305715^b	-3.43		
USLR(t-2)	0.0157985	1.51	-0.327862^b	-2.19
RRX(t-2)	0.0293338^b	2.54	0.0443337^b	1.77
σ_{uk}(t-2)	0.143071^b	4.02	-0.367782^b	-2.17
σ_{eu}(t-2)	-0.0103230^b	-4.11	0.696059^b	2.16
ρ(t-2)	0.00636854^b	3.91	0.213677^b	2.11
RFDI(-2)			-0.378010^b	-2.05
RRR(-2)			0.349345^b	2.26
ΔFDIuk(t-1)	-0.17649^b	-3.36		
ΔFDI$_{eu}$ (t)	0.0617439^b	3.76		
ΔFDIeu(t-1)	-0.0440503^b	-4.54		
ΔRRuk (t)	-0.000149372	-1.41	0.00194151^b	2.15
ΔRRuk(t-1)	0.0004093^b	3.03	-0.000454746^b	-2.02
ΔRRuk(t-2)			$6.81163e{-}005^b$	1.71
ΔRReu (t)	0.000197497^b	4.32		
ΔRReu(t-1)	$7.60663e{-}005^b$	2.20		
ΔRRX(t)	-0.0077929^b	-1.94		
ΔRRX(t-1)	-0.0653882^b	-2.64		
$\Delta\sigma_{uk}$ (t)	0.0253299^b	3.82	-0.0788412^b	-1.97
$\Delta\sigma_{uk}$ (t-1)	0.0429749^b	2.71	-0.203332^b	-2.23
$\Delta\sigma_{eu}$ (t)	0.0199979^b	1.74		
$\Delta\sigma_{eu}$ (t-1)	-0.00698858^b	-1.74		
$\Delta\rho$(t)	-0.00877742	-1.56		
$\Delta\rho$(t-1)	0.00210227	0.269		

Model 1: sigma=0.7242401, sigma^2=0.5245238, RSS=7.8678566788, TSS=3.207809963, no. of observations=58, no. of parameters=43. Transformation used: orthogonal deviations. Level instruments: Dummies, lrfdiuk(–), rcorr(–2), rvareu(–2), rvaruk(–2), rrruk(–2), rrreu(–2), ruslr(–2), lrfdieu(–2), dlfdiuk(–1), dlfdieu, drcorr, drvaruk, drvaruk(–1), drreu, drruk(–1), drreu(–1), drcorr(–1), drruk, dlfdieu(–1), lrukeurx(–2), dlrukeurx, dlrukeurx(–1), rvareu, drvareu(–1), druslr, druslr(–1), Gmm(dlfdiuk,3,99). Wald (joint): chi^2(2413)=1180 [0.000], Wald (dummy): Chi^2(19) =1180 [0.000]**, Wald (time): chi^2(13)=1180 [0.000], Sargan test: chi^2(107)=7.992e–016 [1.000], AR(1) test: N(0,1)=–1.837 [0.066], AR(2) test: N(0,1)=1.815 [0.069].

Model 2: sigma=1.696882, sigma^2=2.87941, RSS=80.623477618, TSS=3.3268586754, no. of observations=59, no. of parameters=31, Transformation used:none, Level instruments: Dummies, lfdiukeu(–2), rrukeu(–2), lrukeurx(–2), ruslr(–2), rcorr(–2), rvareu(–2), rvaruk(–2), drvaruk, drvaruk(–1), drruk, drruk(–1), drruk(–2), Gmm(dfdiukeu,3,99). Wald (joint): chi^2(12)=13.22 [0.353] Wald (dummy): chi^2(19)=13.22 [0.827], Wald (time):chi^2(13)=13.22 [0.431], Sargan test: chi^2(104)=–4.463e–014 [1.000], AR(1) test: N(0,1)=1.842 [0.066], AR(2) test: N(0,1)=1.483 [0.138].

^{b} denotes a diagnostic test significant at 5%. For Wald, Sargan, and AR(.) tests, the p-value is given.

A general to specific nested procedure produced the results presented in Table 3, column [2]. The opposite signs of $FDI_{uk, k, t-2}$ and $FDI_{eu, k, t-2}$, the negative sign of the Euro Area rate of return and the poor significance of some dynamic terms in the general model, lead us to estimate US FDI in the UK as a ratio of US FDI in the Euro Area. This specification not only generates the best results, but also emphasizes the role of location choice of US firms in Europe. We replaced the country specific rates of return $RR_{uk,k,t-2}$ and $RR_{eu,k,t-2}$ by the ratio of the former over the latter, $RRR_{k,t-2}$. Similarly, we replaced the dependent variable $\Delta FDI_{uk, k, t-2}$ by the log of the ratio of real US FDI in the UK industry k to real FDI in the Euro Area in industry k ($RFDI_{k,t}$).

All coefficients are significant and correctly signed, except the coefficient of RRX_{t-2}, which is positive but not significant at the five percent level. We expected the sterling euro exchange rate to have a negative impact on FDI or possibly no impact at all. As mentioned above, domestic sales rather than exports to the European Union are the main source of income of UK affiliates. Exports represented a larger share of total sales in some industries over the sample period. UK affiliates in Machinery and Chemicals, for instance, exported on average 40 and 28 percent of their total sales, respectively. However, in the remaining industries included in our sample, the average share of exports was less than the 23 percent average share of the manufacturing industry as a whole. Table 3 lends support to our theoretical assumptions about US firms' attitude to risk. U.S. firms investing in the U.K. tend to be risk-averse and decrease their investment when the relative volatility of the dollar-pound exchange rate increases. On the contrary, rises in the volatility of the euro/dollar exchange rate tend to divert US investment from the Euro Area to the UK. The coefficient of $\sigma_{uk}(t-2)=-0.37$ and the coefficient of $\sigma_{eu}(-2)=0.696$.

Finally, Table 4 corroborates our finding that increases in exchange rate correlation lead to a relocation of investment from the Euro Area to the UK. Table 4 presents the results of the estimation of (38) for US direct investment in the Euro Area. Two sets of results are shown. In column [1], the sterling euro exchange rate is included in the long-run relationship, following (38). However, it was not found significant, and equation (38) was subsequently re-estimated excluding RRX_{t-2}. Column [2] shows the results of this alternative estimation. In both cases the coefficient of the exchange rate correlation is negative. It is significant in column [2] but not in column [1]. Removing the sterling/euro exchange rate from the long-run relationship improves the significance of the correlation and of the rate of return on FDI in the Euro Area. The euro dollar exchange rate volatility and the U.S. interest rate have negative signs, as anticipated, and are significant at 5 percent.

Table 4. GMM estimates of US foreign direct investment in the Euro Area

Variable	[1] Coefficient	t-value	[2] Coefficient	t-value
FDI_{eu} (t-2)	-0.346331^{b}	-3.26	-0.340736^{b}	-3.24
RR_{eu} (t-2)	$5.96*10^{-5}$	1.28	$7.46334e-005^{a}$	1.81
RRX(t-2)	0.00784355	0.69		
USLR(t-2)	-0.122796^{b}	-3.05	-0.123328^{b}	-3.04
ρ(t-2)	-0.0338988	-1.52	-0.0438151^{a}	-1.80
σ_{eu}(t-2)	-0.0112264^{b}	-6.39	-0.0120693^{b}	-4.29
ΔFDI_{eu}(t-1)	0.0232151	0.79	0.0145616	0.357
ΔCPI_{eu} (t)	0.00491248	1.58	0.00501553^{a}	1.76
$\Delta USLR$ (t)	-0.0884616^{b}	-2.54	-0.0816780^{b}	-2.42
$\Delta\rho$ (t)	-0.0461836^{b}	-2.48	-0.0464129^{b}	-2.59

Model 1: sigma=0.5113763, sigma^2=0.2615057, TSS=8.3681814578, RSS=2.218376681, no. of observations=60, no. of parameters=28, Transformation used: orthogonal deviations. Level instruments:Dummies, dlfdieu(−1), lrfdieu(−2), ruslr(−2), rcorr(−2), rvareu(−2), rrreu(−2), dlcpieu, lcpieu, druslr, drcorr, Gmm(dlfdieu,3,99). Wald (joint): chi^2(9)=118.1 [0.000] , Wald (dummy): chi^2(19)=118.1 [0.000], Wald (time): chi^2(13)=118.1 [0.000], Sargan test: chi^2(105)=7.534e–015 [1.000], AR(1) test: N(0,1)=−1.614 [0.107], AR(2) test: N(0,1)=1.345 [0.179].

Model 2: sigma=0.5366653, sigma^2=0.2880097, RSS=8.9283005972, TSS=2.218376681, no. of observations=60, no. of parameters=29, Transformation used: orthogonal deviations, Level instruments:Dummies, dlfdieu(−1), lrfdieu(−2), ruslr(−2), rcorr(−2), rvareu(−2), rrreu(−2), dlcpieu, lcpieu, druslr, drcorr, lrukeurx(−2), Gmm(dlfdieu,3,99), Wald (joint): chi^2(10)=199.4 [0.000], Wald (dummy): chi^2(19)=199.4 [0.000], Wald (time): chi^2(13)=199.4 [0.000], Sargan test: chi^2(105)=1.176e–014 [1.000], AR(1) test: N(0,1)=−1.578 [0.115], AR(2) test:N(0,1)=1.239 [0.215].

[b] and [a] denote a diagnostic test significant at 5%, and 10%, respectively. For Wald, Sargan, and AR(.) tests, the p-value is given.

The econometric analysis of US FDI in the UK and the Euro Area presented above allows us to conclude that US firms investing in Europe tend to be risk-averse, and that their preferred location tends to be the U.K. As exchange rate correlation converges towards one, exchange rate risk diversification becomes a weaker determinant of location whilst other factors like rate of return become more relevant. There is ample evidence in the literature that market size and labour market flexibility, factor productivity, fiscal competitiveness, among others, are strong determinants in the choice of FDI location.

We compare these findings with Ricci (1997), who investigates agglomeration patterns in OECD countries, under different exchange rate regimes. A panel data analysis of net FDI flows for a group of small countries is estimated as a function of the volatility of the nominal effective exchange rate and the growth in real labour costs. An analogous panel is estimated for a group of large countries. Exchange rate volatility appears to contribute negatively to FDI flows to small countries, whilst increasing FDI to large countries. This positive relationship between FDI and exchange rate volatility implies that manufacturing production tends to agglomerate in large markets, with firms relocating production from small to large countries. Our results contrast with those of Ricci (1997), as we find that increased exchange rate correlation would divert US FDI from a larger market – the Euro Area – to a smaller market – the UK.

3.2.1 Market Power

Several articles proved that departures form perfect competition alter quite significantly the relationship between investment and uncertainty. Caballero (1991), for instance, demonstrates that the higher the mark-up less responsive investment levels to changes in price uncertainty. Simulating his model for several values of mark-up, Caballero (1991) found that investment can be practically independent of the level of uncertainty. There is also empirical evidence that US firms with market power tend to absorb exchange rate changes into their prices and their mark-up. Campa and Goldberg (1995) show that high mark-up firms are less responsive to changes in exchange rate volatility than low mark-up firms. We show in this section that these results may not be easily extended to foreign investment by US firms.

Our sample consists of two groups comprising low Herfindahl industries and high Herfindahl industries, respectively. In the U.K. the latter is composed by Food, Chemicals, Electrical Equipment, and Transportation Equipment. Primary Metals, Machinery and Equipment, and Other Manufacturing Industries form the group of low Herfindahl industries. In the Euro Area, Chemicals, Electrical Equipment and Transportation Equipment are high Herfindahl industries, whilst Food, Primary Metals, Machinery and Equipment, and Other Manufacturing Industries can be considered low Herfindahl industries. It should be noted that the Herfindahl Index of the Euro Area is an aggregate measure of concentration over the European Union, and thus covers more countries than the Euro Area, in particular it includes the United Kingdom.

The criterium used for splitting the sample is the higher benchmark value of the Herfindahl index published in the US Department of Justice Merger Guidelines. Two critical thresholds for measuring industrial concentration are considered in the guideline, $H=0.10$ and $H=0.18$. All the industries in our sample have Herfindahl indices greater than 0.10. We then split our sample into groups of industries with Herfindahl indices lower and greater than 0.18, respectively. To analyse the impact of market power on risk-aversion, we test the equality of the coefficients of the variances for the two groups of industries considered in this paper. We split the data on conditional variances in accordance to the level of the Herfindahl index. Equation (38) then becomes,

$$\Delta RFDI_{k,t} = \phi RFDI_{k,t-2} + a_1 RRR_{k,t-2} + a_2 USLR_{t-2} + a_3 \sigma^2_{uk,t-2,H}$$
$$+ a_4 \sigma^2_{uk,t-2,L} + a_5 \sigma^2_{eu,t-1} + a_6 \rho_{i,j,t-1} + a_7 RRX_{t-2} \qquad (39)$$
$$+ \nabla(RFDI_t, RRR_t, USLR_t, RRX_t, \sigma^2_{i,t}, \sigma^2_{j,t}, \rho_{i,j,t}) + \gamma_{i,k} + u_{i,k,t}$$

Where, $\sigma^2_{uk,t-2,H} = \sigma_{uk,t-1} * \delta_H$, $\sigma^2_{uk,t-2,L} = \sigma_{uk,t-1} * (1 - \delta_H)$ and

$\delta_H = \begin{cases} 1 & if \ H > 0.18 \\ 0 & otherwise \end{cases}$. *dynamics* are the sum of the lagged first differ-

ences of the variables in the long-run relationship. $\sigma^2_{uk,t-2,H}$ can be interpreted as the variance associated to high Herfindahl industries in the U.K. and $\sigma^2_{uk,t-2,L}$ as the variance associated to low Herfindahl industries in the UK. We then test the hypothesis that the two variances are equal. Results are reported in Table 5. All coefficients are significant at the five percent and six percent levels. The coefficients of the split variances are negative confirming our earlier results that the volatility of the sterling/dollar exchange rate has a negative impact on investment in all industries in the UK.

We expect the coefficient of $\sigma^2_{uk,t-2,H}$, $\sigma^2_{uk,t-2,L}$ and of their respective dynamic terms to be statistically different. The estimation is reported in Table 5. The test of equality of the coefficients of the two variances is accepted at the five percent level. We cannot then conclude that FDI into highly concentrated industries in the UK and FDI in less concentrated industries are distinctly affected by exchange risk. Moreover, we note that the coefficient of the variance associated with high Herfindahl industries is bigger than that associated with low Herfindahl industries. This suggests – unexpectedly – that the former are more sensitive to exchange rate risk than the latter. However, the risks inherent investment in foreign countries may be sufficiently strong to offset firms' market power.

Table 5. GMM estimates of investment in the UK.
Nested model

Variable	Coefficient	t-value
$RFDI_{t-2}$	-0.259772^a	-1.99
$USLR_{t-2}$	-0.344609^b	-2.19
RRR_{t-2}	0.325835^b	2.46
ρ_{t-2}	0.249420^b	2.17
$\sigma_{uk,t-2}$ High	-0.250678^b	-2.20
$\sigma_{uk,t-2}$ Low	-0.226249^b	-2.26
$\sigma_{eu,t-2}$	0.537189^b	2.19
$\Delta\sigma_{uk,t-1}$ High	-0.0899327^a	-1.98
$\Delta\sigma_{uk,t-1}$ Low	-0.0882757^b	-2.59
$\Delta RR_{t,uk}$	0.000958483^b	2.16
$\Delta RR_{t-1,uk}$	0.000421341^a	1.98
$\Delta RR_{t-2,uk}$	-0.000341463^a	-1.99

$\chi 2(1)=2.73004^c$

sigma=1.555853, sigma^2=2.420679, RSS=65.35833463, TSS=3.3268586754, no. of observations=59, no. of parameters=32, Transformation used: none. Level instruments: Dummies, drruk, drruk(-1), drruk(-2), rcorr(-2), ruslr(-2), rrukeu(-2), lrukeurx(-2), varuk1(-2), varuk2(-2), rvareu(-2), lfdiukeu(-2), dvaruk1(-1), dvaruk2(-2), Gmm(dfdiukeu,3,99). Wald (joint): chi^2(13)=18.47 [0.141], Wald (dummy): chi^2(19)=18.47 [0.491], Wald (time): chi^2(13)=18.47 [0.141], Sargan test: chi^2(104)=-3.363e-014 [1.000],AR(1) test:N(0,1)=2.280 [0.023], AR(2) test:N(0,1) =1.762 [0.078] .

[b] and [a] denote a diagnostic test significant at 5% and 6%, respectively. [c] denotes a diagnostic test significant at 10%. For Wald, Sargan, and AR(.) tests, the p-value is given.

4 Conclusion

In this paper we have sought to isolate the impact of exchange rate risk on US FDI in Europe, emphasizing the interaction between exchange rate uncertainty, exchange rate correlation and market power. We constructed a model based on the hypothesis that risk-averse firms would attempt to reduce the impact of uncertainty on their investment portfolio by exploiting correlations between exchange rates in alternative locations. We also showed that market power reduces the negative impact of uncertainty on investment. We test our theoretical model on US foreign direct investment in Europe, using a panel of seven two-digit industries. We find that exchange rate uncertainty in the Euro Area and in the UK has a strong negative effect on FDI. There is strong evidence that the correlation between the sterling dollar exchange rate and the euro dollar exchange rate influences location decisions of US firms in Europe. In particular, we found evidence that, as exchange rates become perfectly correlated, US firms tend to divert their investment from the Euro Area to the UK.

Finally, our results show that the degree of industrial concentration has little influence the impact of exchange rate volatility on US FDI in Europe. Using the degree of industrial concentration as a proxy for monopoly power, we found that FDI in industries with low monopoly power is not diversely affected by exchange rate volatility than FDI in highly concentrated industries.

5 Acknowledgements

We have benefited from discussions with Bettina Becker, Joe Byrne, Philip Davis and Ricardo Gottschalk. All remaining errors are ours. We gratefully acknowledge the support of the ESRC under Grant No. L138250122. Final responsibility for the contents of this paper rest solely with the authors.

6 References

Arrellano, M., Bond, S.R., (2001) Some tests of specification for panel data: Monte Carlo evidence and an application to employment equations, Review of Economic Studies, Vol.58, pp. 277-297.

Bénassy-Quéré, A., Fontagné, L., Lahrèche-Révil, A.(2001) Exchange-rate strategies in the competition for attracting foreign direct investment Journal of the Japanese and international Economies, vol.15, n° 2, pp. 178-198.

Bollerslev, T., R.F. Engle, J.M. Wooldridge, (1988) A capital asset pricing model with time varying covariances, Journal of Political Economy, Vol. 96, pp. 116-131.

Campa, J.M., Goldberg, L. (1995), Investment in manufacturing, exchange rates and external exposure, Journal of International Economics,Vol.38, pp. 297-320.

Cushman, D.O. (1985), Real exchange rate risk, expectations and the level of direct investment, Review of Economics and Statistics, Vol. 67, 297-307.

Cushman, D.O. (1988), Exchange rate uncertainty and foreign direct investment in the United States, Weltwirtschaftliches Archiv, Vol. 124, pp. 322-336.

Domowitz, I, Hubbard, R.G., Petersen, C. (1996),Business cycles and the relationship between concentration and profit margins, Rand Journal of Economics, vol.17, pp. 1-17.

Engle, R., Kroner, (1995), Multivariate simultaneous generalized ARCH, Econometric Theory, Vol. 11, pp. 122-150.

Hall, S.G., D.K. Miles, M.P. Taylor (1990), A multivariate GARCH in mean estimation of the capital asset pricing model, in K. Patterson and S.G. B. Henry
(eds.) Economic modelling at the Bank of England, Chapman and hall,
London.

Hall, S.G., D.K. Miles (1992), An empirical study of recent trends in world bond
markets, Oxford Economic Papers, Vol.44, pp. 559-625.

Hayashi, F. (1982), Tobin's marginal and average q: A noeclassical interpretation,
Econometrica, Vol. 50, pp. 213-224.

Hsiao, C. (2003) Analysis of panel data, Second edition, Cambridge University
Press.

Kraft, D.F., R.F. Engle (1982), Autoregressive conditional heteroskedasticity in
multiple time series, UCSD Manuscript.

Nucci, A., Pozzolo, A.F. (2001) Investment and the exchange rate: An analysis
with firm-level panel data, European Economic Review, vol.45, pp. 259-283.

7 Appendix

7.1 Data Appendix

The data on US outward direct investment and data on affiliates of US
firms abroad were obtained from the Survey of Current Business of the
Bureau of Economic Analysis, 1982–2001. These data include FDI at historical cost, the net income reported by affiliates, total, local sales, sales to
the US and sales to "other" countries. The sterling dollar exchange rate and
the US Consumer price Index were obtained from the OECD Main Economic Indicators and the euro dollar exchange rate from the IFS (1999
onwards). Prior to 1999, the euro dollar exchange rate was linked to ECU.
Data used for the construction of the Herfindahl Index were obtained from
Eurostat New Cronos database. The UK consumer price index is given by
the ONS, Economic Trends.

Foreign Direct Investment: Explaining the Regional Location Determinants in South-Eastern European Countries

Aikaterini Kokkinou[1,*] and Ioannis Psycharis[2]

[1] Aikaterini Kokkinou, PhD Candidate, Department of Geography, University of the Aegean, Greece, and Coordinator of Administration Office, Public Debt Management Agency, Ministry of Finance and National Economy, Greece
[2] Dr. Ioannis Psycharis, Assistant Professor, Department of Planning and Regional Development, University of Thessaly, Greece

1 Introduction

During last decades, regional development and convergence of the countries and regions of the enlarged European Union has been one of the main objectives of the European development strategy, focusing on achieving regionally balanced development levels. On the other hand, there are major differences in level of prosperity, economic performance, output, productivity and employment, reflecting continuing structural weaknesses among and within countries. Development problems are more intense in lagging regions which lack the necessary endowments to compete with others, such as South-Eastern European countries, which suffer from structural weaknesses, bounding their competitiveness and preventing them from achieving sustainable economic growth. In order to deal with this situation, lagging countries and regions pursue policies to promote economic development, using a variety of means, including assistance for technology and innovation, help for restructuring industries facing difficulties, support for entrepreneurial activities and incentives to inward investment.

The success of these political operations is linked to the ability of economic agents to support integration with appropriate levels of productive

* Email: kokkinou@pdma.gr

investments. Among others, emphasis was put on the ability of these countries to attract foreign direct investment. The importance of structural reforms leading to a stable and working market economy, the implementation of an appropriate and transparent legal framework for the business environment, the restructuring of the industrial base through privatisation programmes are all issues stressed by the enlarged European Union, since these factors are all likely to lead to an increased volume of foreign investments, and hence to development (Altomonte and Guagliano, 2003).

2 Importance of FDI

Foreign Direct Investment (FDI) is a category of international investment involving a long-term relationship and reflecting a lasting interest in and control by a resident entity in one economy (foreign direct investor or parent enterprise) of an enterprise resident in a different economy (FDI enterprise or affiliate enterprise or foreign affiliate).[1] Capital transferred from the parent firms adds to local stock and contributes to increase the host country's production base and productivity through a more efficient use of existing resources. Foreign investments promote the diffusion of new technologies, know-how and managerial and marketing skills through direct linkages or spillovers to domestic firms. Finally, FDI may also contribute to improve external imbalances due to their greater propensity to export with respect to domestic firms (Altomonte and Guagliano, 2003). The main aspects of the benefits that FDI confers on the recipient country can be summarised to the following points:[2]

- FDI brings in financial resources;
- FDI can attract and support the transfer of managerial skills and advanced technical expertise (know-how);
- FDI introduces improved and adaptable skills and new organisational techniques and management practices in the host economy;
- FDI brings in modern technologies, which could contribute in raising the efficiency;

---

[1] This definition is based on the F.D.I. concept as presented in the IMF Balance of Payments Manual (BPM 5, 1993).

[2] ECD, *Official development assistance and F.D.I.: Improving the synergies*, by Vangelis Vitalis, Global forum on International Investment, Attracting F.D.I. for development, Shangai, December 2002.

- FDI trans-national activities may provide improved access to export markets; and
- FDI causes spillovers of technologies, management experience and skills.

Foreign direct investment is considered to be an important feature of economic growth. This is because the internationalisation of production helps to better utilize the advantages of enterprises and stimulate technology transfer and innovative activity, raising a country's technological level. Furthermore, Foreign Direct Investment (FDI) can potentially play a key role in reducing regional disparities in economic performance not only as a source of income and jobs but as a means of transferring technology and know-how to lagging regions. It is particularly important for the accession countries, which are in need of substantial restructuring of their economies in order to increase their productivity and competitiveness. Moreover, a stable and capable inflow of FDI may strengthen the efficiency of related productive areas. Increasingly, FDI has been acknowledged as an influential and major medium to achieve development, growth and global cohesion process. Many countries have been therefore actively trying to attract foreign investors in order to advance their economic development (Markusen and Venables, 1998, Altomonte and Resmini, 2002).

FDI is considered to be one of the most important elements of the strategy of national economies regarding growth and development.[3] For this reason countries continuously try to attract foreign investment capital by adopting a favourable attitude towards FDI, as it may be seen in the following Table 1:

Table 1. Amendments to national legislations regarding FDI attraction in O.E.C.D. countries, 1991–2003

	1991	1994	1995	1996	1997	1998	1999	2000	2001	2002
Countries with amendments	35	49	64	65	76	60	63	69	71	70
Amendments, of which:	82	110	112	114	151	145	140	150	208	248
More favorable to FDI	80	108	106	98	135	136	131	147	194	236
Less favorable to FDI	2	2	6	16	16	9	9	3	14	12

Source: UNCTAD, World Investment Report, 2004.

[3] Balasubramanyam et al. (1996), Barrell and Pain (1997), Ramirez (2000), Buckley et al. (2002).

As it is demonstrated, compared to previous FDI attraction legislation, amendments more favourable to FDI represent the vast majority of the corresponding legislation amendments. During the last decades, most countries worldwide have adapted their corresponding policies so that they attract investment capital from multinational corporations, hoping that FDI will increase employment, exports, tax income and the transfer and diffusion of knowledge in the economy. Based on the argument that FDI may strengthen economic growth and development, a lot of countries have incorporated a spectrum of investment incentives in order to convince foreign enterprises to invest in their economy. During last decade, a lot of countries have limited the capital flows controls and the restrictions of foreign exchange have been reduced, while the cost of capital transfer has been decreased worldwide.[4] As a result of these changes, in combination with the continuously increasing perception regarding the importance of FDI in the economic growth of nations, a lot of national governments have incorporated aggressive policies of providing investment incentives so that they attract foreign investments (Simmons, 2003).

3 Attraction Incentives of FDI

Attraction incentives refer to economic advantages provided in certain enterprises by a government, so that these enterprisres are encouraged to locate in a specific country. A more general approach defines the provided incentives as government actions that have been planned aiming to affect the decision-making, to increase the rate of attribution of investment or to reduce the uncertainty of the potential investor.[5]

Attracting FDI is one of the more important development activities worldwide. National economies make a wide use of investment incentives so that they influence the decisions of location of foreign investors and the competition in national and regional level. According to Guisinger (1986), a general categorisation of investment incentives distinguishes in tax incentives, which refer to the profits of enterprise, its capital investment, the workforce, the raw material, the sales, the intermediary products, the financing incentives, subsidies, loans, guarantees, attendance in investments of high commercial danger, and other incentives, such as government owned attendance in the infrastructure, preferential prices of government

---

[4] Bosworth and Collins (1999) investigate the positive effects of the mobility of the investment capital to the economic growth level.

[5] O.E.C.D. (1989) Investment Incentives and Disincentives: Effects and International Direct Investment.

services, governmental contract of market of products in low prices, benefits of advisory services.

According to Basile (2004), the incentives to attract FDI may, may be categorized, depending on the form that they can have, in financing incentives, tax incentives, incentives of promotion of work indirect government contribution and government investments. The magnitude and the type of incentives vary and include tax exemptions, tax credits, advantages in enterprises installed in developmentally disgraced regions, subsidies of capital and infrastructure.

On the other hand, according to Crozet et al (2004), the factors of choosing a location can be categorized in four general categories: the expected demand in a certain region, the factors of cost, the number the domestic and foreigner enterprises in the same region, and the public policies of attracting investment capital. Moreover, the possibility for a firm to locate in an area according to classical location arguments asserts that the location decision is determined by considering the various local investment costs, such as those associated with the quality and availability of local labour, variations in efficiency wages and ease of labour acquisition, the level of local land prices and the distance-transactions costs (McCann et al. 2002).

The political, economic and legal environment is also identified as a key factor for foreign investors. Lankes and Venables (1996) and Bevan and Estrin (2000) confirm the importance of institutional determinants and suggest that announcement of progress towards EU membership has a positive and significant influence on FDI inflows. Stirboeck (2002) provided evidence on the importance of regional size, Gross Domestic Product, (GDP) population density, the number of patents, economic openness, capital market integration, and the peripheral or central location of the region in the explanation of the even or uneven allocation of investment.

More recently, Redding and Venables (2004) examine the conditions under which individual firms choose their location. This decision seems to be associated negatively with production costs and positively with market access. Moreover, according to Disdier and Mayer (2004), location decisions are influenced significantly and positively by the institutional quality of the host country. Disdier and Mayer (2004) assert that the location choice of individual firms is also determined by market access and production costs. Investors avoid areas in which the cost of production is high; they rather locate in central places that guarantee good access to the markets targeted. This market access effect is also summarized in the market potential of firms' profits presented by Head and Mayer (2004).

According to UNCTAD (2001), the main traditional factors driving FDI location – such as the large markets, natural resources and access to low-cost labour – have been diminishing in importance. Instead, other factors have increasingly been affecting the setting of trans-national corporations, such as policy liberalisation, favourable regulatory changes, technical progress, local conditions facilitating efficient operation of multinational corporations' technologies, managerial and organisational factors and efficient management practices.

Moreover, main location advantages are access to good information and communication technologies, an appropriate institutional infrastructure and the availability of productive and well-trained personnel at competitive costs. According to Cheng and Kwan (2000), there is a set of five variables: access to national and regional markets; wage costs adjusted for the quality of workers or labour productivity, and other labour market conditions such as unemployment and the degree of unionisation; policy toward FDI including tax rates; availability and quality of infrastructure, and economies of agglomeration.

The empirical studies regarding the incentives of attracting FDI propose that the foreign investors choose the region which has the probability of higher rate of profit. The rate of profit is considered as a result of the combination of the characteristics of each region, the cost of productive factors, the cost of transport, the size and the characteristics of local market, and the level of infrastructures (Basile 2004). Helpman and Krugman (1985), as well as Markusen and Venables (1998) provide the theoretical background for the undertaking of FDI and Dunning (1993) describes the incentives which lead to FDI undertaking and to the cross-border investment activity. Lucas (1993) and Jun and Singh (1996) support that the total stability and the general economic and social environment of a country determine to a large extent the attractiveness of a country as a host country. Haufler and Wooton (1999) focus on the size of market, the tax imposition of profits, the duties, and the indirect and direct taxation, while Bevan and Estrin (2000) support the importance of incentives, as the cost of labor, the size of market and the general investment dangers. Cheng and Kwan (2000) found that the large regional markets, the agglomeration effect, the level of infrastructure, and the preferential policy have a positive effect on the FDI, whereas the level of cost of work had a negative effect. The effect of level of education was positive, but no statistically important.

Globerman and Shapiro (2002) support that the economic success of a country depends to a large extent on its political, legal and institutional environment, namely the institutional infrastructure of a country. Furthermore, they examine the role of other forms of infrastructure, such as the natural environment and the human capital, and they assert that the institutional infrastructure is the main factor of influence of investment decisions in FDI (Dunning, 1981, Vickerman, 1990, Puga and Venables, 1996, Fujita et al, 1999, Head et al, 1999, Castellani and Zanfei, 2001, Basile, 2004).

Investments in institutional infrastructures not only attract investment capital, but also create the conditions under which the domestic enterprises are developed and invest in other markets and economies (Lucas, 1990). Moreover, the empirical approach tends to shows that the inter-country and inter-regional differences on the growth and productivity rates are related to various institutional infrastructures (Hall and Jones, 1999 Altomonte, 2000, Bevan and Estrin, 2000, Morisset, 2000, Stevens, 2000, Roll and Talbott, 2001, Lucas, 1993, Jun and Singh, 1996). Resmini (2000) focuses on the macroeconomic, institutional and the political stability. Coughlin, Terza and Arromdee (1991) consider incentives such as income per capita, wages and the geographic degree of concentration, while Woodward (1992) the force of market and the low force of working trade unions.

Dunning (1993) reports the importance of natural resources in low cost, the improvement of effectiveness with exploitation of comparative advantages, the growth of market and increase GNP, the strategic objectives, as the acquisition of share of market. Meyer (1995) focuses on the size of domestic market, the factors of cost, the purchasing force, the cost of work, the geographic proximity, the working force, the political and economic stability, and the lack of local competitors.

Respectively, Lankes and Venables (1996) determine as incentives the size of market, the political and economic stability, the geographic proximity, the natural resources, the regulating environment, the access to other markets, the low cost of specialized and unskilled work. Moreover, Chakrabarti (2003) develops a theory with regard to the territorial distribution of FDI and the relative location factors.

Among the main factors, Chakrabarti (2003) distinguishes the size of market and size of competitive markets, the cost of work, the duties, the height of interest-rates, the exchange parity, the political stability, the cost of transports, and political and economic characteristics of competitive host countries. Palaskas and Stoforos (2003) assert that rather important incentives are the size of market (GNP), the cost of work, and the FDI inflows in competitive host countries. Moreover, Palaskas, Pexlivanos, and Stoforos (2004) consider the political and economic stability, the dynamism of economy, the enterprising environment, the commercial completion, the cost of work, the privatizations, the geographic proximity, and the access and the most important incentives in new markets.

A lot of other studies have also analyzed the factors of location of FDI and have focused on the concentration of FDI in the most developed regions in a country (Glickman and Woodward, 1988, Bagchi-Sen and Wheeler, 1989, Coughlin et al., 1991, Hill and Munday, 1991, Freidman et al., 1992, O'huallachain and Reid, 1997, Devereux and Griffith, 1999, Wei et al., 1999).

4 FDI Trends in South-Eastern European Countries

The position towards inward Foreign Direct Investment (FDI) has changed significantly over the last decades, as most nations, including South-Eastern European countries – have liberalised their policies to attract investment capital from multinational corporations. Expecting that FDI will raise employment, exports, tax revenue, and knowledge spillovers in the host country, many South-Eastern European governments have introduced various forms of investment incentives to adopt an aggressive incentive policy to attract the investments (Simmons, 2003). According to the attraction incentives theory analysed in this paper, the fact that the South-Eastern European countries try to offer to potential investors a combination of relatively low wages, low corporate tax rates and access to EU market, make the accession countries attractive FDI locations.

As far as the last decade's South-Eastern European economic and development policy is concerned, it was characterized by a series of strategic plans, the aim of which was mainly the creation of business incentives in order to assist the economic reconstruction and the regional development of the countries. In order to deal with the arising changes and pursue the investment and regional development, states formed national development laws to attract foreign investment capital.

The investment laws posed, in fact, the regional development issue and helped the investors to extract capital through significant fiscal and financial provisions introduced by the government incentive policy. Reforms affecting world trade and the increasing pace of globalisation, affected South-Eastern European FDI since the mid-1980s. Expanded access to foreign markets resulted to increased flows of goods and services and capital across national borders, to the extent that, since the mid-1980s, FDI has experienced faster growth than world trade and the activities of foreign affiliates have continued to accelerate in recent years. During the last years the overall FDI performance is shown in the following Tables 2–5, presenting the low and high performers of the South-Eastern European region.

Table 2. Matrix of inward FDI performance and potential

	High FDI Performance	Low FDI Performance
	2000–2002	
High FDI potential	Front runners Bulgaria, Croatia, Cyprus, Czech Republic, Estonia, Hungary, Latvia, Lithuania, Malta, Poland, Portugal, Slovakia, Slovenia, Spain,	Below potential Greece, Italy,
Low FDI potential	Above potential	Under performers Romania,
	1993–1995	
High FDI potential	Front runners Czech Republic, Estonia, Hungary, Malta, Poland, Slovakia, Spain,	Below potential Bulgaria, Cyprus, Greece, Italy, Portugal, Slovenia,
Low FDI potential	Above potential Latvia,	Under performers Lithuania, Romania,
	1988–1990	
High FDI potential	Front runners Cyprus, Greece, Malta, Portugal, Spain,	Below potential Hungary, Italy, Poland,
Low FDI potential	Above potential	Under performers

Source: UNCTAD, World Investment Report, 2004.

During the last two decades there has been a major entrepreneurial activity in both trade and Foreign Direct Investment (FDI), in the countries of Central, Eastern and South-Eastern Europe. (Petrochilos, 1997, 1999; Salavrakos, 1997). In recent years an increasing number of neighbouring firms have acquired firm-specific advantages in the form of patents, own technology, etc. which have enabled them to upgrade their operations and enhance their productivity.

In addition, the rapid changes brought about by the end of the Cold War and the break-up of the former Soviet Union have helped to create the conditions for extending the influence of the free enterprise system throughout the former command economies.

As a consequence, the countries of south-eastern Europe welcomed the foreign presence as a useful means towards achieving their aims of a closer economic integration with Western economic structures (Salavrakos and Petrochilos, 2003). As a result, the FDI inflows in South-eastern European countries presented a significant increase, as it is illustrated in Table 3 below:

Table 3. F.D.I. Inflows in constant 1995 prices [% percentages per year]

	1994	1995	1996	1997	1998	1999	2000	2001	2002	2003
Czech Republic	31.90	10.0	6.0	5.0	10.0	14.0	6.0	8.0	11.0	4.0
Estonia	1.0	1.0	0.0	1.0	2.0	1.0	0.0	1.0	0.0	1.0
Greece	4.0	5.0	5.0	4.0	0.0	1.0	1.0	2.0	0.0	1.0
Spain	34.0	24.0	29.0	22.0	31.0	34.0	45.0	39.0	46.0	43.0
Italy	8.0	19.0	15.0	17.0	11.0	15.0	16.0	21.0	19.0	28.0
Cyprus	–	–	–	–	–	1.0	1.0	1.0	1.0	1.0
Latvia	1.0	1.0	2.0	2.0	1.0	1.0	0.0	0.0	0.0	1.0
Lithuania	1.0	0.0	1.0	1.0	2.0	1.0	0.0	1.0	1.0	0.0
Hungary	4.0	20.0	14.0	14.0	9.0	7.0	3.0	5.0	4.0	4.0
Malta	–	–	–	–	1.0	2.0	1.0	0.0	1.0	1.0
Poland	7.0	14.0	19.0	17.0	17.0	16.0	11.0	8.0	5.0	7.0
Portugal	5.0	3.0	6.0	9.0	8.0	3.0	8.0	8.0	2.0	2.0
Slovenia	0.0	1.0	1.0	1.0	1.0	1.0	0.0	1.0	2.0	0.0
Slovakia	1.0	1.0	2.0	1.0	2.0	1.0	3.0	2.0	5.0	1.0
Bulgaria	0.0	0.0	0.0	2.0	1.0	2.0	1.0	1.0	1.0	2.0
Romania	1.0	2.0	1.0	4.0	5.0	2.0	1.0	2.0	1.0	3.0

Source: Eurostat, 2004.

From mid-1990s to 2003, apart from Spain and Italy, almost 70% of FDI inflows to South-Eastern region flew into three countries, Poland, the Czech Republic and Hungary, which are by far the top FDI recipients in the area. At the same time, FDI inflows were relatively low in Slovenia, Estonia, Latvia and Slovakia. The same picture is also illustrated in Table 4 presenting the top 10 countries which received the highest level of FDI inflows in the years 2002 and 2003 with Poland, Czech Republic and Hungary being in the first three positions:

Table 4. CEE, top 10 recipients of FDI inflows, 2002–2003

Rating	Country	Inflows level in 2002 [bil. US Dollars]	Inflows level in 2003 [bil. US Dollars]
1	Poland	4.1	4.2
2	Czech Republic	8.5	2.6
3	Hungary	2.8	2.5
4	Croatia	1.1	1.7
5	Romania	1.1	1.6
6	Ukraine	0.7	1.4
7	Bulgaria	0.9	1.4
8	Serbia and Montenegro	0.5	1.4
9	Russian Federation	3.5	1.1
10	Estonia	0.3	0.9

Source: UNCTAD, World Investment Report, 2004.

Table 5. CEE: country distribution of FDI inflows by range, 2003

Range	Country
More than $ 1 billion	Bulgaria, Czech Republic, Hungary, Poland, Romania,
Less than $ 1 billion	Estonia, Latvia, Lithuania, Slovakia, Slovenia

Source: UNCTAD, World Investment Report, 2004.

The distribution of FDI inflows by range and country is shown in Table 5, which shows that, countries such as Bulgaria, Czech Republic, Hungary, Poland, Romania receive the largest foreign investment projects in 2003, compared to the rest of the neighbouring countries:

According to World Investment Report (2004) and the Third Report on Economic and Social Cohesion (2004), as far as the reasons for the FDI inflows increase are concerned, Czech Republic and Poland, together with Hungary, increased the level of FDI inflows because of large privatisation projects. More specifically, the Czech Republic improved the general economic environment, considering significant improvements in the inflation level, external trade flows and labour productivity rate. Poland experienced a rather significant increase in its GDP level (even though it was accompanied by a rather significant increase in the inflation rate) its openness improved and the trade flows increased. The labour productivity was also developed significantly. Furthermore, Hungary improved its macroeconomic situation, increased the GDP level, the trade flows and the labour productivity level. During 2002–2003, FDI inflows into South-eastern European countries declined, mainly due to the end of privatisation projects in the Czech Republic and Slovakia. FDI inflows in the rest of the region declined only marginally. On the other hand, there was no significant change in FDI flows from the older EU members to South-eastern European countries occurred at the time.

5 FDI Location Incentives and Attraction in South-Eastern European Countries

As it was mentioned above, the FDI attractiveness level depends on a wide range of factors – each of which is of special importance and of specific characteristics of the potential host country or region. In order to analyze the attraction incentives in South-Eastern European countries, we try to establish a relationship between the FDI level in each of these countries and the related determining factors, such as:

- Market size, proxied by the GDP growth level;
- Production factors cost, proxied by the employment rate;

- Macroeconomic stability, proxied by the inflation rate;
- The labor force quality, proxied by the total expenditure on Human Resources;
- The access to market, proxied by the trade openness;
- Externalities, proxied by the gross fixed capital formation rate and the total Research and Development expenditure.

Table 6 presents the rating of the FDI inflows level of South-eastern European countries and some of the above mentioned main macroeconomic situation indicators, such as GDP level, Research and Development level, employment rate, investment rate, trade openness and expenditures in human capital. The rating has been estimated by using the mean of each variable for the period 1994–2003 and then by comparing the means of each variable among different countries. As it may be seen, countries with high rating in determining factors, shows a relatively high level of FDI inflows, which illustrates the relationship between the variables.

Table 7 shows the growth level and all growth determining factors of the top five rating of the South-Eastern European countries. As in Table 6, the rating has been estimated by using the mean of each variable for the period 1994–2003 and then by comparing the means of each variable among different countries. As the Table presents, countries with top five high rating in determining factors represent a top five high level of FDI inflows, which also illustrates the existing relationship between the variables.

Table 6. South-Eastern European Countries rating

	FDI	GDP	R&D	Employment	Investment	Openness	Human Capital
Spain	1	2	3	10	5	2	8
Italy	2	1	2	11	13	1	7
Poland	3	8	8	9	11	3	5
Czech Republic	4	5	1	2	2	6	11
Hungary	5	6	4	10	7	7	6
Portugal	6	4	6	1	4	5	3
Slovakia	7	7	5	7	1	9	10
Romania	8	12	13	4	10	8	9
Greece	9	3	9	8	6	4	13
Bulgaria	10	13	10	13	12	10	12
Lithuania	11	10	11	5	8	11	4
Estonia	12	9	7	3	3	13	1
Latvia	13	11	12	6	9	12	2

Source: Our estimations.

Table 7. Top five rating of South-eastern European Countries

	1st position	2nd position	3rd position	4th position	5th position
FDI	Spain	Italy	Poland	Czech	Hungary
GDP	Italy	Spain	Greece	Portugal	Czech
R&D	Czech	Italy	Spain	Hungary	Slovakia
Employment	Portugal	Czech	Estonia	Romania	Lithuania
Investment	Slovakia	Czech	Estonia	Portugal	Spain
Openness	Italy	Spain	Poland	Greece	Portugal
Human Capital	Estonia	Latvia	Portugal	Lithuania	Poland

Source: Our estimations.

As it is inferred from the above Tables, countries experiencing a high degree of FDI inflows, also have a level of macroeconomic situation at a relatively high degree, as proxied by the above mentioned indicators. This descriptive relationship may assume that there is a tendency for the foreign investment capital to locate in countries with a high level of development FDI tend to locate in countries with high growth rate since these regions have consequently higher rate of infrastructure, business activity and market potential.

On the other hand, FDI inflows also tend to locate in countries with a low GDP per capita rate. This may happen due to the development prospects and dynamism that these countries present, because of their entry in the European Union and the access they can provide to European market, as well as their geographical proximity to some of the most developed members of the European Union in central Europe. More specifically, these countries present several general economic and social characteristics making them an FDI location which is assumed to be more attractive than the rival countries. Foreign investors try to exploit both these characteristics and the incentives provided by the corresponding national investment incentive legislations, which usually results to a significant amount of foreign investment capital located in a particular country.

6 Conclusion

To sum up, it may be assumed that, regardless the financial or other incentives and inducements, foreign investors are not necessarily attracted to places where there is a greater need, according to reports. It may be asserted that foreign investors tend to locate their activities either in countries which have already been developed, in order to take advantage of their economic features, exploit economies of scale and concentration and agglomeration effects of business, or in countries which are mainly characterised by high development prospects, either because of their entry into the European Union or because of their access to its large market FDI. Therefore, tends to go disproportionately to the stronger and more prominent rather than to the weaker and less prominent countries.

If South-Eastern European countries are to realize their economic potential, then all countries and regions need to be involved in the investment development process. The challenge for South-Eastern European countries could be to strengthen competitiveness in long-term in order to sustain high rates of economic growth by creating modern and adequate infrastructure, modernizing education and training systems and establishing a business environment favourable to investments. The incentive policies should incorporate measures in order to pursue macroeconomic, political and social stability, economic liberalisation, competition conditions, amenable investment environment, people, improved infrastructure, strategic location, strong competition, linkage creation, and technical networks, focusing on improving the micro- and macro-economic functioning of the economy and strengthening the factors which provide stability and benefits to investors. Strengthening regional attractiveness and competitiveness throughout the countries and helping them fulfil their potential will benefit the growth potential of the economies to the common benefit of the South-Eastern European region.

7 References

Altomonte, C. (2000) Economic determinants and institutional frameworks: F.D.I. in economies in transition, Transnational Corporations, 9(2), 75–106.

Altomonte, C., Guagliano, C. (2003) Comparative study of F.D.I. in Central and Eastern Europe and the Mediterranean, Economic Systems, 27, 223–246.

Altomonte, C., Resmini, L., (2002) Multinational corporations as a catalyst for industrial development: the case of Poland, Scienze Regionali 2, 29–58.

Bagchi-Sen, S., Wheeler, K.O. (1989) A spatial and temporal model of foreign direct investment in the United States. Economic Geography, 65, 113–129.

Balasubramanyam, V.N., Salishu, M., and Sapsford, D. (1996) Foreign Direct Investment and growth: New hypotheses and evidence, Discussion Paper Ec7-96, Department of Economics, Lancaster University.

Barrell, R., Pain, N. (1997) Foreign Direct Investment, technological change and economic growth within Europe, Economic Journal, 107, 1770–85.

Basile, R. (2004) Acquisition versus greenfield investment: the location of foreign manufacturers in Italy, Regional Science and Urban Economics 34, 3–25.

Bevan, A.A., Estrin, S. (2000) The determinants of Foreign Direct Investment in transition economies, CEPR Discussion Paper 2638, Centre for Economic Policy Research, London.

Bitzenis, A. (2003) The determinants of F.D.I. in Transition countries: Incentives and Barriers based on a Questionnaire Research in Case of Boulgaria, 1989–2000, in Petrakos, G., Kotios, A. and Chionis, D. (ed.) International Monetary Aspects of Transition in South-eastern Europe, Volos, University of Thessaly Press.

Bosworth, B.P., Collins, S.M. (1999) Capital flows to developing economies: Implications for saving and investment, Brookings Institution, Brookings Papers on Economic Activity, 1, 143–169.

Buckley, P.J., Clegg, J., Wang C. and Cross A.R., (2002) F.D.I., Regional differences and economic growth: panel data evidence from China, Transnational Corporations, 11, 1 1–28.

Castellani, D., Zanfei, A., (2001) Technology Gaps, Inward Investments and Productivity of European Firms, mimeo, University of Urbino.

Caves, R. E. (1996) Multinational Enterprise and Economic Analysis. Cambridge: Cambridge University Press.

Chakrabarti, A. (2003) A theory of the spatial distribution of foreign direct investment, International Review of Economics and Finance, 12, 149–169.

Cheng, L.K., Kwan, Y.K. (2000) What are the determinants of the location of foreign direct investment? The Chinese experience, Journal of International Economics, 51, 379–400.

Crozet, M., Mayer, T., Mucchielli, J. (2004) How do firms agglomerate? A study of F.D.I. in France, Regional Science and Urban Economics 34 (1), 27–54.

Coughlin, C.C., Terza, J.V., Arrondee, V. (1991) State characteristics and the location of foreign direct investment within the United States. Review of Economic Statistics, 73, 675– 683.

Devereux, M.P., Griffith, R., (1999) Taxes and location of production: evidence from a panel of US multinationals, Journal of Public Economics 68, 335–367.

Disdier, A.C., Mayer, T. (2004) How different is Eastern Europe? Structure and determinants of location choices by French firms in Eastern and Western Europe, Journal of Comparative Economics, 32, 280–296.

Dunning, J.H. (1998) Location and the multinational enterprise: a neglected factor? Journal of International Business Studies, 29, 45–66.

Dunning, J.H., (1993) Multinational Enterprises and the Global Economy. Addison Wesley.

Dunning, J.H., (1981) International Production and the Multinational Enterprise. Allen & Unwin, London.

European Union, (2004) 3rd Report on Economic and Social Cohesion.

Eurostat, http://www.europa.eu.int/eurostat.

Freidman, J., Gerlowski, D., Silberman, J. (1992) What attracts foreign multinational corporations? Evidence from branch plant location in the United States. Journal of Regional Sciences, 32, 403–418.

Fujita, M., Krugman, P. and Venables, A.J. (1999) The Spatial Economy: Cities, Regions, and International Trade, MIT Press, Cambridge, MA.

Glickman, N., Woodward, D. (1988) The location of foreign direct investment in the US: Patterns and determinants. International Regional Scence Review, 11, 137–154.

Globerman, S., Shapiro, D. (2002) Global Foreign Direct Investment flows: The role of governance infrastructure, World Development, 30 (11), 1899–1919.

Guisinger S. (1986) Host – country policies to attract and control foreign investment in T.H. Moran (ed.) Investing in development, New rules for private capital, New Brunswick: Translation Books, UN.

Hall, R., Jones, C. I. (1999) Why do some countries produce so much more output per worker than others, Quarterly Journal of Economics, 114(1), 83–86.

Haufler, A., Wooton, I. (1999) Country size and tax competition for foreign direct investment, Journal of Public Economics, 71, 121–139.

Head, K., Mayer, T. (2004) Market potential and the location of Japanese investment in the European Union, Review of Economics and Statistics, Mimeo, University of Paris, in press, available from http://team.univ-paris1.fr/trombi/mayer/Eu2.pdf.

Head, C.K., Ries, J.C., Swenson, D.L., (1999) Attracting foreign manufacturing: investment promotion and agglomeration. Regional Science of Urban Economics, 29, 197–218.

Helpman, E., Krugman, P.R. (1985) Market structure and foreign trade, Cambridge, MIT Press

Hill, S., Munday, M. (1991) The determinants of inward investment: a Welsh analysis. Applied Econometrics 23, 761–769.

International Monetary Fund (1993) Balance of Payments Manual, BPM 5, 1993.

Jun K.W. and Singh H. (1996) The determinants of Foreign Direct Investment: New empirical evidence, Transnational Corporations, 5, 67–106.

Lambrianidis, L. (2001) Geography matters in the orientation of F.D.I.: The case of Greek F.D.I. in the Balkans in Petrakos, G. and Totev, St. (ed.) The Development of the Balkan Region, Ashgate, London

Lankes, H. P. and Venables, A. J. (1996) Foreign direct investment in economic transition: the changing pattern of investments, Economics of Transition, 4 (2), 331–347.

Lucas, R. E. (1993) On the determinants of Foreign Direct Investment: Evidence from East and Southern Asia, World Development, 21 (3), 391–406.

Lucas, R. E. (1990) Why doesn't capital flow from rich to poor countries? The American Economic Review, 80(2), 92–96.

Meyer, Klaus E. (1995) Foreign direct investment in the early years of economic transition: a survey. Economics of Transition 3 (3), 301–320.

Markusen, J.R., Venables A.J. (1998) Multinational firms and the new trade theory, Journal of International Economics, 4, 183–203.

McCann, P. (1995) Rethinking the Economics of Location and Agglomeration, Urban Studies, 32(3), 563–577.

McCann, P., Arita, T. and Gordon, I.R.C. (2002) Industrial Clusters, transactions costs and the institutional determinants of MNE location behaviour, International Business Review, 11(6), 647–663.

McCann, P. (2002) Urban and Regional Economics, Oxford University Press, Oxford

Morisset, J. (2000) F.D.I. in Africa: policies also matter. Transnational Corporations, 9(2), 107–126.

OECD (1989) Investment incentives and disincentives: Effects and International Direct Investment, Paris

O'Huallachain, B., Reid, N., (1997) Acquisition versus greenfield investment: the location and growth of Japanese manufacturers in the United States, Regional Studies 31, 403–416.

Palaskas, T., Pexlivanos, L., Stoforos, C., (2004) Greece in the International Investment Market, Athens, IOBE, (in Greek)

Palalskas, T., Stoforos, C. (2003) Financial Sources of Investments and Development: Attraction determinants of Foreign Direct Investment in Greece, IOBE, (in Greek)

Petrakos, G., Totev, St. (ed.) (2001) The Development of the Balkan Region, Ashgate, London

Petrochilos, G.A. (1999) Explaining Greek outward foreign direct investment: a case of regional economic integration, Economics Research Paper Series, Coventry University

Petrochilos, G.A., (1997) Theory, policy and practice of Greek outward foreign direct investment, in: Kantarelis, D. (Ed.), Business and Economics for the 21st Century. Anthology of 1997 B.E.S.I. Conference Papers. Worcester, MA 01605, USA, pp. 117–127.

Puga, D., Venables, A., (1996) The spread of industry: spatial agglomeration in economic development. Journal of Japanese and International Economics 10, 440– 464.

Ramirez, M.D. (2000) Foreign Direct Investment in Mexico: A Cointegration Analysis, Journal of Development Studies, 37,1, 132–162.

Redding, S., Venables, A. J. (2004) Economic geography and international inequality, Journal of International Economics, 62 (1), 53–82.

Resmini, L., (2000) The determinants of foreign direct investment in the CEECs: new evidence from sectoral patterns. Economics of Transition 8, 665–689.

Roll, R., Talbott, J. (2001) Why many developing countries just aren't, San Diego: Mimeo: World Development Inc.

Salavrakos, I.D., Petrochilos, G.A. (2003) An assessment of the Greek entrepreneurial activity in the Black Sea area (1989–2000): causes and prospects, Journal of Socio-Economics, 32, 331–349.

Salavrakos, I.D., (1997) The Black Sea Economic Co-operation (BSEC): problems and prospects of integration with the global economy. Occasional Paper No. 10. Institute of International Economic Relations, Athens

Simmons, R.S. (2003) An empirical study of the impact of corporate taxation on the global allocation of foreign direct investment: a broad tax attractiveness index approach, Journal of International Accounting, Auditing & Taxation, 12, 105–120.

Stevens, G. V. G. (2000) Politics, economics and investment: explaining plant and equipment spending by US direct investors in Argentina, Brazil and Mexico, Journal of International Money and Finance, 19(2), 115–135.

Stirboeck, C. (2002) Relative Specialisation of EU Regions: An Econometric Analysis of Sectoral Gross Fixed Capital Formation, ZEW Discussion Paper No.02-36.

UNCTAD (2004) World Investment Report

UNCTAD (2004) World Development Report

UNCTAD (2001) World Investment Report, 2001. Promoting Linkages. UN, New York.

Vickerman, R.W. (1990) Infrastructure and Regional Development, European Research in Regional Science, Pion, London.

Vitalis, V. (2002) Official Development assistance and F.D.I.: Improving the synergies, Global Forum on International Investment, Attracting F.D.I. for Development, OECD

Wei, Y., Liu, X., Parker, D., Vaidya, K., (1999) The regional distribution of foreign direct investment in China, Regional Studies 33, 857–867.

Woodward, D.P. (1992) Locational determinants of Japanese manufacturing start-ups in the United States, Southern Economics Journal 53, 690–708.

Starting with the Local - a Knowledge-Based Approach to Economic Integration

Parminder Singh Sahota*, Paul Jeffrey and Mark Lemon

The School of Water Sciences and International Ecotechnology Centre, Cranfield University, United Kingdom

1 Introduction – Locality and Mess Encouraging "Wickedness" into Integration

The value of "local studies" has often been contested, firstly in terms of their contribution to theory and, secondly, in terms of their relevance to policy. These concerns are based upon the correct assumption that the "local" is invariably heterogeneous and the false one that this assumption prevents them from providing data that advances theory or supports policy development. Indeed the application of policy or theory to different localities often results in a poor fit which is explained by the "uniqueness" of that locality rather than deficiencies in the theory or policy. Langley et al (1995 p. 261) argue that no decisions can be understood "de novo or in vitro, apart from the perceptions of the actors and the mindsets and cultures of the contexts in which they are embedded".

This paper will argue that an improved description and understanding of these "unique" localities, which occur at all levels of organisation, is necessary for advances in theory building and policy formation (Murdoch, 1995). Regionalisation and economic integration should be understood and studied in toto and in vivo assimilating insights about integration as a whole, about geographically and organisationally distinctive local contexts and about the interactions between them. Processes of local change are seldom restricted to the locality concerned and are also subject to multiple and continuously evolving interpretations (Green and Lemon, 1996). It is only through the raised awareness about these perspectives that a description of process can be obtained

* Email: psahota@iscom.nl

which represents a "systemic" picture and places local changes in the context of non-local (systemic) restructuring (Lemon et.al., 2004). The following paper will explore the range of knowledge-based factors that can help improve our understanding of economic restructuring and will discuss how such insights might translate into policy and theoretically relevant formats.

The failure to explain the range of complex social processes using a priori accounts of structural transformation is often attributed to local idiosyncrasy and relates to the levels of abstraction adopted by the researcher(s) or policy makers (Cox and Mair, 1989). More specifically, in the policy environment it has to do with the assumption of a top down approach that fails to pay sufficient attention to local differences either in the definition of policy or in the manner of its implementation. In both cases the local is seen as "wicked" (Rittel and Webber, 1988) where variety and unpredictability can only be managed by "stabilizing" and simplifying local systems using various generic models. Elsewhere this simplification process has been interpreted as a way of exercising power over the consumer through the establishment of prescribed rules and procedures which effectively restrict participation from the "bottom up" (Bachrach and Baratz, 1970; Lemon et.al., 2004; Robinson and Bond, 2003).

Therefore, the control of the flow of information is an important lever affecting the type of change that occurs, the authority exercised over it and thereby the inclusiveness and equity associated with it. This is equally applicable to the process of scientific enquiry as it is to policy formulation and implementation. Indeed, local description is the basis for, and not the product of, an improved understanding (see Latour, 1993). Three initial points will be developed relating to use of the term 'local' in the context of the following paper. Firstly, it does not necessarily relate to the lowest hierarchical level. "Local" studies can focus on the company boardroom or the political cabinet as well as the street corner, farmers collective or village (Law, 1994). It is the interactions between actors operating within and across different localities, including hierarchically distinctive localities that need to be focused upon to establish a clearer understanding of how knowledge emerges and behaviours are informed. Secondly, the description of process inevitably moves towards a broad systemic picture which covers a range of spatio-temporal scales, rates of change and descriptive sub-systems or themes. For example Ehrenfeld (2004) talks in terms of sustainable development as human, natural and ethical interaction, whereas Botchway et.al. (2002) conceptualise local economic problems as being defined by the complex interactions between technological, natural and social systems across time and geographical and organisational space.

Thirdly, we need to elicit the multiple perspectives from local actors because, broadly speaking, decisions are made and behaviours undertaken on the basis of the world as it is perceived. This latter point can be modified by Giddens (1984) concept of discursive consciousness whereby individuals have a varying ability to articulate the world they perceive and also a differential propensity to act upon those perceptions (Miller, 1980).

The ability of policy to influence local behaviour is therefore indicative of how effective, if not necessarily appropriate, that policy and its delivery mechanism may be. Has it been defined and introduced with a clear "sense of audience" (Stubbs and Lemon, 2001). The impact of collective local decisions will also affect the environmental "landscape" upon which policy is determined. Such a process, however, often fails to "learn" from the local cultural context relating to those decisions (Hollings and Gunderson, 2002); for example, by being restricted to the condition of physical, natural and economic resources rather than the underlying social mechanisms that impact upon, and are impacted by, those conditions (Lemon et.al., 2004).

The paper will draw upon this case study to highlight different types of knowledge and knowledge conversion. These will then be considered in the context of what barriers and enablers affect the "learning" capability of an integrated economy. In order to make this leap we will argue that economic integration should manifest some of the characteristics associated with organisational learning and, by extension, should be interpreted as an organisational form that is defined by the level of integration sought after. Organisations are effectively defined by purpose with fuzzy boundaries separating them from the environment that determines their need to adapt in order to survive (Gunderson and Holling, 2002). In the same way that organisations need to develop adaptive capability and absorptive capacity (Cohen and Levinthal, 1990), then the process of economic integration needs to nurture those attributes that underpin resilience and adaptivity. Central to these is the ability to recognise, assimilate and develop knowledge at different economic levels and scales (knowledge management) and to put in place mechanisms that will support knowledge management as the basis of organisational learning.

The next section of the paper will introduce the case study used to exemplify how knowledge management and organisational learning should be key to improved economic integration. The role of knowledge management will then be considered and different forms and areas of knowledge discussed and characterised through a range of knowledge archetypes. The final sections of the paper will explore how knowledge might be converted and the potential barriers to that conversion before concluding with a discussion about how organisational learning might be conceptualised in the context of economic integration.

2 Technological Change and Economic Integration, Water Management and Agriculture in the Argolid Valley, Greece

The case study used in this paper was undertaken throughout the 1990's and is well documented elsewhere (Lemon, 1999; Lemon, Jeffrey and Seaton, 1998; Oxley and Lemon, 2003; Oxley, Jeffrey and Lemon, 2002, 2003). It was carried out as part of an extensive research project into desertification[1] and highlighted the inter-relatedness and emergent properties of economic, cultural, natural and technological systems and the policies relating to them. The studies also clearly indicated the importance of temporal, spatial and organisational scale, and situational knowledge, to these processes and our understanding of them. The purpose of presenting the case for this paper is to provide a practical example about how different forms of knowledge and knowledge transfer processes can significantly affect the ability to move towards more effective and adaptive economic integration.

We will firstly present a brief and descriptive sketch of the Argolid Plain in Southern Greece as defined by agricultural production, water quality and availability and related technologies in the 1990's. This provides a background for the examples relating to knowledge management and economic integration that are used to populate the rest of the paper.

Records of the Argolid Valley in the Peloponnese, Greece, convey a picture of rain-fed farming and grazing with salt marshes along some of the coastal strips. The contemporary visitor to the coastal Argolid Plain, however, will drop from the surrounding foothills into a carpet of lush green vegetation. It is a physical landscape that has been transformed through the access to, and use of, irrigation water. This transformation has taken place above ground with the expansion of irrigated agriculture and is represented, in its physical form, both through vegetation, with a profusion of citrus trees, and the sight and sounds of the water technologies that have been introduced to support their production.

The area is laced with water infrastructure in the form of concrete irrigation canals ranging from six metres in diameter to small channels which skirt individual fields with metal sluice gates for supplying 'flood' irrigation to the crops. Elsewhere irrigation pipes snake through the orchards taking water from the crudely built brick bore-hole housings to the sprinkler irrigation systems that are also used in winter to protect the crops

---

[1] The case study used in this paper was undertaken for the European Commission as part of the ARCHAEOMEDES (ENV4-CT95-0159) project.

*against frost. Adjacent to some of these housings can be found the old sur-
face wells that were animal driven.*

*In the coastal plain the level carpet of trees is broken by the presence of
air-mixers, a form of inverted wind mill, which are also used to protect the
crops against frost by disturbing the cold air. Not only do the mixers stand
above the orchards, when they are operating in the winter evenings they
make a distinctive sound which re-emphasises the dominance of agricultural production in the area. Similarly as the demand for water has increased, and the ready access to it has become problematic, the Argolid
Valley has become dotted with 'exploratory' irrigation rigs.*

*Agricultural production, and in particular citrus production, dominates
the senses throughout the year with the powerful scent of the orange blos-
som and the shrill grinding of chain saws cutting trees for splicing in the
spring and the muffled accents of the migrant pickers as they walk to work
early in the winter mornings.*

*Throughout the valley, but especially in the peripheral villages where
more diverse cropping takes place, transportation is dominated by small
pick-ups trucks. A continuous stream of these can be observed on the Ar-
gos-Athens road (approximately 150 kms) in the early morning and late af-
ternoon as farmers take their products to market in the capital or to the
premises of the agricultural co-operatives which sell directly through the
European Union.*

What this brief description has attempted to convey is, firstly, that a
surface landscape has been constructed around agricultural production in
the Argolid Valley. This is emphasised by the fact 50% of the work force
in the area were registered in the census as being employed within the agricultural industry although, as will be seen, this was distorted by the number of part-time farmers with distinctive cultural characteristics. Secondly,
it is clear that the economic activity, as represented by agricultural production operates at multiple levels of organisation (individual, collective, centralised etc.) and, thirdly, that issues of knowledge underpin the decision
making and behavioural competence at each level and between levels. The
first two factors provide a background to the third observation which is the
focus of this paper, the potential role of knowledge management as a key
component of flexible economic integration.

2.1 Knowledge Management and Integration

The idea that the process of regional economic integration can be seen as a
systemic and organisational response to a continually changing external
environment raises questions about the competencies that are required to

deal with that uncertainty in an adaptive and appropriate manner. If we define knowledge management as the ability to harness and build upon an organisation's intellectual capital and we bound the organisation according to the agencies and processes that are to be integrated then an awareness of what knowledge exists, what knowledge is and might be necessary, and how to close the gap between the two becomes a fundamental requirement. It is a requirement, not only through the need to provide a systemic response to ongoing and recognised external influences such as the shape of changing labour markets etc. but through the generation of redundant knowledge capability that will provide a buffer against 'unknowable' futures (Jeffrey, 1997). The harnessing and generation of knowledge as a dynamic (Lemon and Sahota, 2004) response to external uncertainty is the central objective of knowledge management that can be facilitated through:

- a faster reaction to changing markets (opportunities) and an improved understanding of customer perceptions alongside improved internal communication;
- reductions in wasted effort and resources resulting from improved internal communication and understanding;
- the combination of tacit and explicit knowledge in the pursuit of innovative responses to organisational needs;
- the instigation of meaningful bottom up as well as top down information transfer leading to the empowerment of stakeholders (Lemon et.al., 2004).

It is important to state that "internal" as used above, in common with the use of the term environment, relates to organisation as defined systemically by the, admittedly somewhat, fuzzy boundaries of economic integration. Within those boundaries there are multiple forms of data, information and knowledge that need to be differentiated before considering how they might be transferred through the use and development of internal networks.

2.2 Data, Information and Knowledge

Knowledge is the basis for action and is generated through action (Schon, 1983); it is invariably dynamic context specific and intangible (Sahota and Lemon, 2004). As such it is necessary to differentiate between data which arrives on our desks as dispersed elements (Saint-Onge, 1996) with no inherent order or rationale (500 mm rain, 50 kgs oranges, Market Street etc.). It is messy, unstructured and unique, whereas information is data that has been compiled into meaningful patterns, although the meaning attached to those patterns will often remain context specific (five hundred millimetres of rain in the Argolid; fifty kilos of oranges cost twenty five euros in the local market; Market Street is adjacent to the market between the cathedral and the police station). There is some cross over here between information as structured data which can inform action (e.g. is there enough rain to grow citrus; should we sell or purchase oranges at the local market or through the co-operative; how can I get to the market) and explicit knowledge which can express that information in formal and systematic language.

Explicit knowledge is articulated and as such can be stored, shared, communicated and diffused in the form of data, formulae, procedures, manuals, specifications etc. Tacit knowledge by comparison is the implicit knowledge used by organisational members to perform their work and to make sense of their worlds. It is unarticulated knowledge and as such is hard to verbalise because it is expressed through action – based skills and cannot be reduced to rules and recipes or easily captured, stored and dis-tributed. Such knowledge is embedded in individual experience and in-volves intangible factors such as personal belief, perspective and values.

The difficulty in articulating tacit knowledge means that the individual who possesses it may be unable to express it in a formal and structured way (e.g. empathic skills; recognizing potential market trends; generating greater crop productivity in a sustainable way). This knowledge is sometimes cate-gorized through the use of a general label that perpetuates the "mystery" of the related skills or wisdom associated with them (Fig. 1); for example in the latter case (s)he has "green fingers". Such tacit skills are also evident in the underlying message of this paper, namely that we need to look at

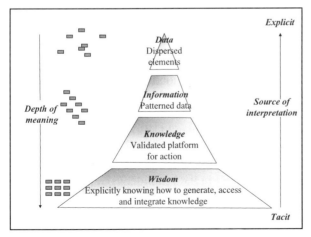

Fig. 1. From data to wisdom (after St-Onge, 1996)

economic integration from a systemic and organizational perspective. Within that perspective and related "fuzzy organisational' boundary", we need to consider how to identify, acquire, share and exploit the internal competencies or intellectual capital of stakeholders as the basis for increasing adaptive capability and thereby generating new knowledge. We can then make a link to knowledge management as the capture, creation, distillation, sharing and use of know-how (Collison and Parcell, 2001) both individually and collectively at all organizational levels. It is the ability of an organization to embody this cumulative knowledge and create a culture that is sympathetic to knowledge creation and transfer as an ongoing process that will be seen to form the basis of organizational learning, represented through the pursuit of economic integration for the purpose of this paper.

3 Social Networks as Attributes of Knowledge Integration

Before looking at how different knowledge archetypes might be expressed we need to consider the way that knowledge is generated and expressed at different scales and particularly how this might underpin adaptive capability. In a recent paper on technological transitions Geels, argues for a multi-level perspective whereby changes at the landscape level (e.g. regional policy or macro in Fig. 2) can put pressure on the regime (e.g. area government, village groupings, co-operatives) or meso level and thereby the opportunities or constraints at the micro or local level of individual and small group decisions (Geels, 2002). While it is not the purpose of this paper to delve into the extensive literature on innovation and technology pathways (Madu, 1990; Tidd and Bessant, 1991), we will briefly consider how organisational scale determines and is determined by the available knowledge and competencies.

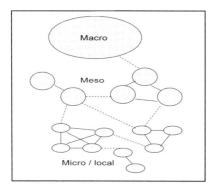

Fig. 2. Strong and weak ties at differing organisational levels (adapted from Granovetter, 1973)

In a seminal paper on social networks, Granovetter (1973) argues that the ability to draw upon different social networks is fundamental to enlarging the knowledge base of a system (community, company, family etc.) and thereby its adaptive capability. Where only strong ties exist – the sold linkages in Fig. 2 – then the network is restricted to the capabilities within the network. As discussed earlier, it is only by engaging with the external environment that organisations can 'learn' and one feature of this engagement is the ability to identify and create 'bridges' – dotted lines – with other networks.

The "weak ties" described by Granovetter are purely functional and are only initiated or drawn upon when a specific need arises, the rest of the time they lay dormant. They also provide an example of how contemporary knowledge management tools might enhance economic integration (e.g. through the use of data management techniques such as (inter and intra) organisational 'Yellow Pages', and support the allocation of resources into the generation of adaptive capability or the potential to respond under conditions of uncertainty. Figure 2 also suggests the importance of information being transferred between, and knowledge existing about, the activities and characteristics of other functions and groupings within the organisation of economic integration. One example of this would be the ability and willingness to access different levels of economic organisation (e.g. farmers grouping to purchase expensive technologies; access to co-operative ventures; stakeholder knowledge of relevant government departments and or specific individuals within local and regional government).

Let us return to the case study and consider how some of these organisational scale issues affect influence the decisions relating to agricultural production and natural resources. The case conveys a landscape that is constructed around agricultural production and an agricultural production that is constructed through agencies operating at a number of different scales (Table 1).

Table 1. Case study agencies and their multiple levels of operation

Level	Agency
Individual	Farmers, Private agronomists, Drillers, Geologists etc.
Collective	Informal farmer groupings (e.g. to purchase pumping technology), Farmer associations (young farmers), Self and local consumption of produce
Area	Agricultural Co-operatives, Water distributers, Electricity company, Local agricultural and land improvement services, Local market.
National	Agricultural Bank, Central Government (Departments of Agriculture and Public works), Universities (Athens and Patras), National market.
European	European Union, External market/Dealers (within and outside of the EU), European research programmes, Migrant labour.

Table 1 shows that a multi-tiered technological hierarchy has emerged with technologies introduced at the level of individual farmers (e.g. self financed shallow bore holes and sprinkler systems), at the collective level (collectively financed air mixers and deep bore holes) at national level (reduced electricity costs, central government support for large scale infrastructure and other agricultural technologies) and at the European level through subsidy and support for infrastructure and research into aquifer replenishment.

Similarly the marketing of agricultural products has emerged at the level of the individual farm with a reduction in the amount produced for family or local consumption (e.g. cereals and vines) and the sale of produce, particularly vegetables, at the local markets (Athens, Argos and Nafplion). At a collective level the co-operatives were developed to market selected crops through the price guarantee system of the European Union. The majority of these crops (citrus), with the exception of olives, are heavy water users and even where additional capital support has been provided it tended to relate to the processing of water intensive crops (e.g. juicing and canning factories).

Information was transferred between individual farmers or between groupings such as the Young Farmers organisation with their intra and international contacts. At the local level the Service of Agriculture, private agronomists, geologists and drillers all offered services to the agricultural community and the central agricultural service was responsible for interpreting and communicating information about policy instruments from the European Union to its "local" offices.

In consequence much of the agricultural practice in the area was not locally determined. Rather it was defined primarily by the price guarantees of the European Union and a local reluctance to change existing crops. The water intensive nature of this agriculture was supported by the introduction and increased accessibility of irrigation technologies and their subsequent adaptation to ameliorate the effects of increasingly degraded natural resources. This meant that the landscape was no longer seen as the product of individual endeavour and the perception of it became increasingly dependent upon the ability of "external" scientific and technological innovation to triumph over nature, (Green and Lemon, 1996).

The information flows surrounding the issue of water could be seen to have emerged in a number of forms. Those which related to the scientific agenda could be distinguished between scientific debates within the scientific community and the perceived desire to control information and the way that science was subsequently imparted to the 'community' (see also Gibbons, 1994). This form of technological determinism was reinforced by the positive, and on occasions unquestioning, attitude of sections within the agricultural community to scientific and technological solutions as a means of ensuring a short / medium term income (e.g. while price support lasted).

A second set of information flows were grounded in the three way relationship between the farming community, the public administration and local political representation. This was manifest through a perceived change in the relationship between farmers and agronomists employed by the public service, whereby they were seen to be more office based and less active in the community, as well as a belief that political allegiance had influenced decisions about infrastructural development and the (re)placement of public servants.

A final knowledge related issue that related to the flow of information between the European Union (Macro) the regional and local administration and co-operatives (Meso) and the individual farmers was considered to be the greatest source of uncertainty for many within the farming community. This failure to ensure an effective flow of information was in part due to inadequate knowledge about the receptivity (willingness and ability to take on board information) of different stakeholders and a failure to fully understand the audience to which that information was directed. It is important to realise that this failure was not restricted to the (in)ability of higher organisational levels to communicate from the top – down and of "local" agencies to make use of information when it was provided. It also related to the (in)ability of more centralised (higher) organisational levels to access information about local contexts and of local actors' (in)ability to establish how to influence decisions at those higher levels. These constraints are in themselves knowledge based and in particular grounded in inadequate cultural knowledge. It is to this that we will now focus our attention.

4 Knowledge Archetypes and Culture as Indicators of Integrative Capability

Having discussed the differences between data, information and knowledge and briefly considered some of the knowledge related network issues that are implicit in multi-level organisations we will draw upon Blackler's (1995) knowledge archetypes to convey how different types of knowledge and organisational arrangement might affect the decision space within which different stakeholders can operate. Blackler builds upon the work of Colilns (1993) to suggest five knowledge archetypes that are based upon explicit to tacit and individual to collective dimensions. These will be introduced in turn and related to examples derived from the case study.

1. Embrained knowledge *(individual-explicit)* is of particular importance for this paper because it recognises the value of, and is based upon, conceptual skills and cognitive abilities. Other writers have identified this form of knowledge as 'higher level' abilities (Fiol and Lyles, 1985) that support systems thinking (Senge, 1990) in the identification and interpretation of complex causal relations. One manifestation of this type of knowledge is the ability to question the existing way of doing things and to suggest radical rather than incremental change. This is consistent with both Argyris and Schon's (1978) double-loop learning and radical rather than incremental approaches to innovation.

> The unwillingness of farmers to adopt water reduction sprinkler systems for irrigation and protection against frost was less to do with the effectiveness of the technologies or even their cost. By looking at the problem from a different perspective the agronomists responsible for encouraging the take-up of the technologies mapped out a series of possible related causes including the observations that water was not charged for although electricity was and frost protection required the farmer to leave home or the café to visit the farm at night and turn on the sprinklers.

2. Embodied knowledge *(individual-tacit)* is action oriented and practical knowledge that is often difficult to articulate (Polanyi, 1962; 1966). It is knowledge about behaving in specific contexts, the how (Lam, 2000), and is not necessarily formalised or shared although the related behaviours might be imitated. Embodied knowledge requires problem-solving techniques which depend on an intimate knowledge of a situation rather than abstract rules as is the case with embrained knowledge (Barley, 1996).

3. Encultured knowledge *(collective-tacit)* is expressed by Blackler (1995) as the process of achieving shared understandings. These are

> The young farmers group in the area were predominantly well educated locals, often the children of traditional farmers, with a common engagement in the pursuit of ideas and approaches that were new to the area and environmentally and economically sustainable (alternative crops, farming practice, market opportunities etc.). They actively scanned for opportunities (e.g. using the internet, attending conferences) and developed new ways to share knowledge both among themselves and the wider, less innovative farming community

established through socialization (see Nonaka, 1991; 1994) and are open to negotiation (Srivastva and Barrett, 1988). The willingness and ability to experiment with new ways to communicate these insights and understandings (e.g. through story telling and the use of metaphors) is central to encultured knowledge.

> The pruning of citrus trees is perceived to be a skill that can only be communicated in part. It is seen to be primarily dependent upon the ability to 'feel' what is required and as such is not attempted by many of the farmers. An alternative example of embodied knowledge would be a personal appreciation of who to contact, and more important, how to make contact, with individuals in order to instigate local political change.

4. Embedded knowledge *(collective-tacit)* is knowledge that resides in organisational routines and shared norms and is often affected by networks of social relations (Granovetter, 1985) that in turn are influenced by a complex mix of technologies, formal and informal roles and socio-structural factors. Such knowledge is dynamic, contextual and dispersed; it is also capable of supporting complex patterns of interaction in the absence of written rules.

5. Encoded knowledge *(collective-explicit)* is similar to the definition of explicit knowledge provided above and is conveyed by signs and symbols such as books, manuals and codes of practice. As such it

> Agronomy texts and EU policies and related grant documentation provide clear examples of encoded knowledge as would crop prices and geographical and organisational routes to market. With such 'general' information farmers might then question their existing practice and identify alternative behaviours as modifications of what they are currently doing or as radical departures from it. This might tie in with the existence and availability of encultured knowledge as suggested above with the example of the Young Farmers group.

tends to generate unified and predictable patterns of behaviour, however clarity in encoded knowledge can form the basis for embrained knowledge by providing a bench-mark against which new conceptual interpretations – theories – can be developed and related questions asked.

If we look back to the stakeholders and agencies that have been identified in the previous sections it is possible to identify not only clearly defined generic identities e.g. farmers, public administrators, scientists, but more confusingly, heterogeneity within many of those groupings. This is a significant point for policies directed at economic integration because it counsels against making assumptions about uniformity within stakeholders. Cultural knowledge, or an awareness of what underpins cultural difference, is a key factor in establishing how that integration might be facilitated and perpetuated.

5 Culture and Knowledge and Knowledge About Culture

Culture is the means by which people communicate, perpetuate, and develop their knowledge about attitudes towards life. It provides the fabric of meaning through which human beings interpret their experience and guide their action (Geertz, 1973). Schein (1985) states that culture is the way in which a group of people solves problems and reconciles dilemmas and cultural knowledge refers to the assumptions and beliefs that are used to describe and explain reality as well as the conventions and expectations that are used to assign value and significance to new information.

We need to think about culture on a number of levels. The *explicit* reality of culture can be observed and directly experienced through language, logos, uniforms, food, buildings, transport, dress etc. Even culturally important actions such as bowing, shaking hands and opening doors are initially explicit and observed but may be devoid of meaning to the uninitiated.

> Herzfeld (1992) discusses the (dys) functional role allocated to the Greek bureaucracy by the community who defer responsibility for their actions to the bureaucracy while collectively allocating them high status. The political affiliations of particular communities were also seen to affect the level of influence that they had in the initiation of political change. These constraints were recognised but not formally recorded and were radically altered with electoral change.

To develop an earlier example from the case study, the retrenchment of agricultural extension staff into the office and away from the field was perceived to coincide with firstly, an emphasis upon academically trained and often younger personnel who had limited practical experience and did not feel comfortable away from their own cultural environment. Secondly, there was an increasingly tight control on these staff with regard to time-keeping and this was felt to discourage a more flexible regime, which combined working "out of hours" when the farmers were able to meet with them, with "clocking on and off" which was far less convenient for full time farmers in particular. These potential cultural barriers were also evident in reverse with some farmers, particularly the less educated ones, feeling uncomfortable entering the offices of the Agricultural Service and dealing with the formal protocols necessary to arrange and carry out a meeting or complete specific documentation. These are practical cultural issues that reside within any attempt at communication and integration.

Norms are the sense of right and wrong that help to define a particular cultural group. They may be explicit and formal through written rules or laws or informal expressions of social control e.g. preventing children from pushing in front of a queue or informal and implicit such as the likelihood of a farmer's children continuing to work in the industry. In the Argolid the full time farmers of the foothills tended to expect their children to carry on with the farm and the children were sympathetic to this expectation. The part time mono-croppers in the Valley were far less likely to encourage their offspring to farm and may well have put the proceeds of their agricultural activity towards the education of their children either directly through the payment of university fees and maintenance or indirectly through the purchase of property in which they could reside while undertaking their studies.

The Young Farmers group pursued a third form of normative behaviour with many having returned from full time tertiary education intent on farming in an innovative manner with a clear orientation towards natural, social and economic sustainability. Economic policies that are unable to reflect or to differentiate between such cultural groups are likely to have unintended and potentially negative consequences not dissimilar to those that encouraged the rapid and unsustainable mono-cropping of citrus by land-owners many of whose life-style and commitments would have prevented them growing the more time-consuming crops (in terms of production and marketing) that required greater agronomic expertise (e.g. vegetables).

If we accept that cultural knowledge is necessary for planning and managing economic integration it is important to consider the attributes that can help us define cultural difference and identify common traits? The ability to understand how a particular section of a community (as defined by common interest) might respond to different conditions entails a clear vision of how they are constrained and what their cultural drivers are. We do not have the space to explore cultural attributes in the current paper but the work of Hofstede (1984, 1991) provides a useful introduction and Lemon (1999) locates cultural variation in the context of the case study presented here.

6 From Know-Why to Know-When: Locating Areas of Knowledge

Having established a number of different knowledge types, and the importance of recognising the cultural attributes that might contribute to their profile, we need to consider how knowledge can be transferred or constrained within the organisation of economic integration. Prior to this, however, we will quickly outline a number of general areas to which these different forms of knowledge might refer. Collison and Parcell (2001) provide a practical example of these in the context of the oil industry and it is important to recognise that they exist at all levels of economic integration.

1. The conceptual understanding of how a decision option relates to its environment (i.e. that which influences a system but over which it has little influence) is fundamental to making an informed decision. Knowledge about why a particular option is preferable has to be based on a perception of the whole which might be clearly articulated (explicit) or remain in its tacit form and thereby difficult to communicate or transfer. The importance of seeing the big picture is central to economic integration and the message of this paper. It implies the existence of experience, paradigms, perspectives, assumptions etc. as the basis of decisions and behaviours at all levels of organisation. An important feature of such knowledge is that any understanding of the "big picture" must include an appreciation of what drives other stakeholders, their "**know-whys**". This raises an important consideration in terms of adaptivity and learning. We have already considered the role of strong and weak ties and networks for expanding the learning and adaptive capability of an organisation through the expansion of the knowledge base upon which it can draw, and this is pertinent to each of the following knowledge areas.

    Such collective responses can also fundamentally change the reasoning behind specific behaviours by providing a broader perspective and opening up new potential opportunities albeit often with attached costs. The concept of knowing why a particular behaviour or decision option is appropriate raises a number of dilemmas. Firstly, as we have already seen, the willingness and ability to look at a decision issue systemically, the receptivity to the approach, raises a number of questions. Firstly the "know-why" might be constrained by a reductionist perspective that determines the nature of a problem through a disciplinary or functional lens. Secondly, there is not a consistent environment and as such perceptions of it will alter considerably within

and between formal and informal organisations and at different hierarchical levels (e.g within and between farming communities and at
different layers of government). This also highlights the importance
of networks and the emergent nature of insight about why a particular
response might be (in)appropriate under various circumstances and at
different organisational scales (e.g. the options available to single
farmers will vary considerably to those who are engaged in collaborative or co-operative activity). The combination of these two factors
mean that initially economic integration and other forms of collaborative enterprise cannot be based upon the pursuit of consensus in the
sense of agreement over common features but in the sense of agree-
ing over, and recognising difference. The need to agree over common
features can serve to obfuscate the very differences that are the drivers of a system and thereby force any response into a "clear" but inappropriate decision frame.

2. The acquisition of skill or *know-how* implies the physical ability to
   produce some action. This is captured in routines, techniques and
   tools and draws upon both tacit and explicit knowledge. In practical
   terms, at the level of the farm, this might relate to the ability to install,
   use and maintain irrigation equipment or to negotiate the procedures
   for applying for grant aid. From the top down this knowledge might
   be exemplified by a clear understanding of how to establish an
   integrated and collaborative supply chain network of producers,
   distributors and retailers.

3. There is not necessarily a direct correlation between knowing how to
   do something and *knowing what* is necessary to undertake a task.
   Using the supply-chain example from above, the ability to instigate a
   network may well be dependent on an extensive number of diverse
   contacts and the ability to facilitate interest and commitment from
   them. The realisation that the livelihood of local producers might be
   protected through the establishment of supply chains oriented toward
   sustainable development as defined in economic, ecological and
   ethical terms does not necessarily equate with the ability to instigate
   the process.

4. We can identify a fourth area of knowledge by continuing with the
   same example and focusing upon the need to *know-who* has
   knowledge about the different actors within the supply chain and who
   has the ability to access and negotiate with them. The field work for
   the Argolid Case study was undertaken by a local agronomist with
   extensive contacts in the farming and administrative communities and
   the ability to engage with farmers of different political persuasions.
   This highlights both the value of gatekeepers who can facilitate

access to stakeholders, and the potential problems associated with them whereby that access is perceived in the context of the gatekeeper and as such can have a negative impact upon the outcome where they are seen to have an unsympathetic agenda.

5. In much the same way that knowledge exists about who has particular competencies we need to *know-where* explicit data and information and information are located and how to navigate through it. The Argolid Young Farmers had established a network that was able to scan the web for information about agronomic and technological innovations and to distribute that information to its members and thereby the wider farming community. Alternatively, decisions about where to target a specific policy innovation are dependant upon knowledge of the socio-economic and cultural characteristics of different locations and how well these align with the stated aims of the policy.

6. The concept of alignment also suggests the ability to *know-when* to instigate a particular change. Knowing when to uproot one crop and replace it with another was in part based upon agronomic knowledge and in part economic knowledge relating to market and policy changes that might affect price support conditions. Alternatively the degree of trust that exists between stakeholders in the supply chain example will in part determine the appropriate time to suggest collaborative ventures as opposed to instigating exploratory negotiations designed to build trust.

Having considered some of the broad knowledge areas we can focus our attention on the processes for and barriers to transferring that knowledge and by extension the ability of organisations, as represented by the process of economic integration in this case, to learn.

6.1 Knowledge Conversion and Organisational Learning

The processes by which knowledge can be shared often involves the conversion of that knowledge from one form to another (e.g. from tacit to explicit) and as requires different modes and mechanisms of conversion according to the context and requirements of that transfer. For example the need to transfer knowledge about farmers with an expertise in growing a delicate crop may well involve a relatively straight forward transfer of information. Understanding and communicating whether those farmers would be receptive to sharing that insight would be a more subtle process involving the transfer of tacit knowledge about the characteristics of the farmers concerned and their willingness and ability to share tacit knowledge,

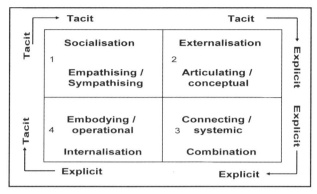

Fig. 3. Modes of knowledge conversion

namely their ability to grow a difficult crop. It is important to consider the following generic framework of knowledge conversion and transfer as potentially occurring at and between all levels and agencies of economic integration. The following discussion will draw heavily upon Nonaka's SECI model of knowledge conversion (Nonaka and Teece, 2001; Nonaka and Takeuchi, 1995) which is presented in Fig. 3. While this is outlined as a cycle we will concentrate upon each stage as indicative of specific types of knowledge transfer within the context of economic integration in general and the case study specifically.

1. The ability to transfer tacit knowledge and convert it into new tacit knowledge is essentially undertaken through shared social experience (e.g. mentoring, apprenticeship, observation). This is increasingly evident with attempts to harness and retain traditional skills (e.g. local building techniques, tree pruning) but is equally apposite in the transfer and acquisition of the social skills necessary to generate trust. In the context of economic integration the ability to acquire an understanding and "feel" of the roles performed by other agencies and how they contribute to the process as a whole is very different from a descriptive and formalised understanding of the activities they undertake.

2. Externalisation is the process of converting new explicit knowledge from shared experiences and is often based upon the development of creative dialogue to extract and "communicate" tacit knowledge – e.g. through the use of metaphors and story telling (Morgan, 1997). Examples of this might be the bottom-up harnessing of shop-floor, operational expertise to improve manufacturing processes or the top down transfer of insight about the setting up of an agricultural co-operative to the local farming community.

3. The conversion of explicit knowledge into more systematic and potentially complicated formats (combination) might involve the translation and communication of a high level concept such as a mission statement or vision (e.g. integration) into specific operational procedures. It can also take the form of knowledge re-use, for example through the adoption of computerised networks and data-bases for forecasting or the identification and collection of information in order to generate a specific report (e.g. farm sizes, production levels, market potential as the basis for evaluating the viability of a local co-operative).

4. The structured, and supported, sharing and acquisition of tacit knowledge from clearly defined explicit knowledge is a process of internalisation facilitated through training and may coincide with the socialisation process whereby tacit skills are also transferred. The ability to articulate and capture a particular competence may well support the development of tacit knowledge when it is linked to repeated action e.g. being taught how to manage a meeting with multiple and potentially confrontational stakeholders and practicing this through role play. That knowledge might emerge differently through 'in-situ' non-verbal socialisation with individuals in possession of those attributes. The two forms of knowledge conversion would appear to be complementary and return us to the cycle that Nonaka indicates in his model. Having presented some of the areas of knowledge that might underpin, or at least contribute to, improved economic integration and how knowledge might be converted within the process we will now consider what factors might constrain that conversion or transfer and thereby the capacity for organisational learning.

7 Barriers to Organisational Learning

Figure 4 locates a number of potential barriers to organisational learning. These are grounded in an organisational hierarchy from individual beliefs and actions, that might occur at any level within economic integration (i.e. they are not restricted to 'bottom-up' knowledge transfer) and affect the ability of the organisation to impact on and respond to its external environment (i.e. the source of change that economic integration is seeking to manage). This direct impact upon the environment may well be limited, as discussed above, but is a contributory factor to overall responses that affect individual beliefs as the basis for action. There are potential barriers at each of these stages of interaction.

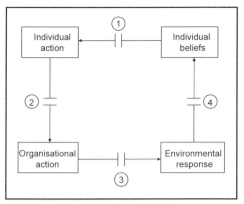

Fig. 4. The barriers to organisational learning
(adapted from March and Olsen 1975)

The perception of the environment and the beliefs relating to acceptable and "productive" behaviour, in the context of individual, collective and systemic contribution and learning are often constrained by the role(s) of the individual. The existence of a primary non-farming occupation will restrict the crop choice options available to a part-time farmer to those that require relatively little personal commitment in terms of time. As suggested above, this may be reinforced by the belief that heavy manual farm work is low status and not an option.

We have already considered the changing role of agronomists within the Agricultural Services from one that is extension and farm-based to one that is primarily office based. Alternatively, the role played by centralised administrators and auditors within the European Union may be restricted to matching the measures and targets associated with the implementation of a policy to behaviours on the ground (i.e. does it meet with the stated agricultural, environmental, economic criteria) rather than establishing whether those behaviours contributed to a more sustainable agriculture in social, ecological and ethical terms. In each of the above examples the beliefs about how individual roles are formally and/or informally defined bounded, have restricted the ability to learn, and thereby to transfer learning, about the impact of alternative behaviours. A second set of barriers can be located between the actions of individuals and their influence on the organisation as a whole. The failure to learn about how each of the above behaviours affect the delivery of an integrated and more sustainable agriculture is a pertinent example here and coincides with a form of normative behaviour where individuals act in the way that they are expected to. Herzfeld's (1992) argument about the role played by the public administration in offsetting responsibility also provides a relevant example. A number of more specific learning barriers can be suggested that relate to the failure of individual learning to be converted into an organisational context (March and Olsen, 1975).

Much learning is situation specific whereby individuals solve a problem on the spot but fail to codify the process. This failure may occur because of the role constraints discussed above where the acquisition and communication of insight outside of the individual's direct role is either not recognised by the individual or no mechanisms are in place within the organisation to collect, codify and assimilate such information. Poor situational learning may also occur as the result of time constraints on the individual. Fragmented learning occurs when individuals learn but the organisation does not. For example, the process of establishing a useful contact within the public administration and the subsequent benefit accrued from that relationship may not be shared with other members of the farming community – possibly through the desire to "control" the knowledge or through the lack of formal mechanisms for recording and sharing such contacts.

A final example of learning that is not always codified or made available to the organisation concerns opportunistic knowledge that occurs in small groups because it is impractical to wait for the organisation to change. The role played by the young farmers was to some extent opportunistic in that the need for information about more sustainable farming was considered to be necessary and in advance of any formal policy or administrative mechanisms to ensure changed farming and market behaviours. The learning acquired and shared by the group was not readily assimilated into the wider regional context of integrated agro-economic and environmental organisation. Much of this paper has argued the need to ensure that local context forms the basis for organisational change. This requirement has two key aspects to it that coincide with barriers 3 and 4 in Fig. 4. Firstly, assumptions about the link between organisational action and environmental response are questionable and attention needs to be paid to the generation of adaptive rather than predictive capability. Secondly, and linked to the above point is a recognition that learning takes place under conditions of ambiguity and the failure to accept the "noise" in the system tends to emphasise operational rather than conceptual learning at the individual and group level. We will finish the paper by considering how some of these conceptual capabilities are fundamental to organisational learning as exemplified by economic integration.

8 Summary – Enabling Organisational Learning

Economic integration is a complex process operating within an emergent and thereby uncertain environment. In consequence we need to look at the nature of the relationships within and between the organisation of economic integration and the multiple systems (social, economic, technological,

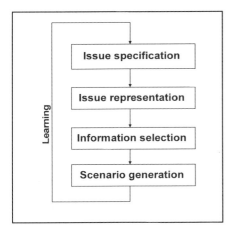

Fig. 5. Systems thinking cycle (after Lemon and Longhurst 1996)

ecological etc.) that interact to generate the environment to which it is responding. It is this appreciation of systemic properties that Senge (1992) considers to be the key to managing knowledge and generating adaptive capability as the basis for organisational change. Figure 5 suggests how learning might be conceptualised in systemic terms as a cycle moving from the need to understand about multiple localities, and how issues are defined by the stakeholders within them, through the identification of the information necessary to "deepen" and "broaden" this understanding in the context of the internal and external environments. By recognising that history is invariably a poor guide to the future and most economic integration will relate to unique circumstances in terms of systemic (re)configurations at different organisational levels we argue that meaningful learning is ultimately facilitated through the generation of, and learning from, potential futures and the identification of the attributes and competencies that *might* be needed to adapt and respond appropriately.

The appreciation of systemic properties is, therefore, directly linked to the recognition that there are inevitably going to be different views and competencies within and between the layers of an organisation and that these will change through time. Accepting that these multiple perspectives will often lead to conflict and increase complexity should not lead to their control or "averaging out". Consensus and creativity do not necessarily sit easily together, with the former orienting us towards what is already known rather than learning from new experiences and or failure i.e. what we do not know. The acquisition of meaningful and ongoing insight about these multiple perspectives is essential for making informed judgements about how different areas (geographic, cultural and sectoral) and levels of integration might be facilitated e.g. through a better understanding about the receptivity (ability and willingness) of different stakeholders to change in particular ways and the resulting sense of audience about how to elicit from, and communicate with, those agencies for specific purposes. For economic integration to develop this appreciation of systemic properties a number of cultural attributes need to be taken into consideration. The acceptance of uncertainty and the meaningful engagement with stakeholders at all levels is necessary to make informed and inclusive judgements about how to manage change in the context of "local" difference. While ignoring these differences may well reduce the "messiness" of the process, it also means that the basis for judgements about the strategic shape of integration will be devoid of insight about the agendas that have to be responded to, if not concurred with. In cultural terms the organisation of economic integration, and the agencies who assume responsibility for it in strategic terms, must *learn to learn* as an ongoing and dynamic process. Eden and Ackermann (1998) argue that this cultural change should be underpinned by a need to communicate the core assumptions of economic integration to the agencies and stakeholders concerned and to continually question them and to learn from that process. In the Argolid case study policies directed at economic support for agricultural communities resulted in the degradation of natural resources and a disjointed and potentially inequitable agricultural economy. The failure to acquire ongoing, grounded information about these impacts meant that farmers and related agencies became entrenched in "playing the system" rather than focusing upon sustainable economic and ecological development. This chapter has argued that the same danger exists for the process of economic integration if it forces diverse localities, at all stages and levels of integration, into generic boxes defined by economic models and criteria. The failure to develop a culture that has systemic thinking at its centre and within this an appreciation that understanding and managing local difference, accepting messiness, is fundamental to integrative capability means that the organisation of economic integration will fail to learn on an ongoing basis. It is this facility for organisational learning that holds the key to adaptive and flexible responses to uncertain operating environments.

9 References

Argyris, C., D. Schon (1978) Organizational Learning: A theory of action perspective. Reading, MA, Addison Wiley.

Barley S (1996) Technicians in the workplace: ethnographic evidence for bringing work into organization studies. Administrative Science Quarterly 41 (3) pp 404-441.

Bachrach, P., M. Baratz (1970) Power and Poverty: Theory and Practice, New York: Oxford University Press.

Blackler F (1995) Knowledge, Knowledge Work and Organizations: An Overview and Interpretation Organizational Studies, 16 (6) pp 1021-1046.

Botchway, Q. Goodhall, G. Noon, D., Lemon, M. (2002) An Emergence-based local Economic Development Model: a way forward in responding to turbulent operating environments, Entrepreneurship and Regional Development 14 (2) pp. 155-174.

Cohen, W., D. Levinthal (1990) Absorptive Capacity: A new perspective on learning and innovation, Administrative Science Quarterly, 35 pp. 128-152.

Colilns, H. (1993).The structure of knowledge, Social Research 60 pp. 95-116.

Collison, C., G. Parcell (2001) Learning to Fly. Oxford, Capstone.

Cox, K., A. Mair (1989). Levels of Abstraction in Locality Studies, Antipode, 21(2), 121-132.

Eden, C., F. Ackerman (1998), Making strategy: The Journey of Strategic Management. London, Sage.

Ehrenfeld, J. R. (2004) Searching for Sustainability: No Quick Fix Society for Organizational Learning. All Rights Reserved.

Fiol C M, Lyles M A (1985) Organizational Learning. Academy of Management Review, 10 (4) pp. 803-13.

Geels, F. (2002) Technological transitions as evolutionary reconfiguration processes: a multi-level perspective and a case study, Research Policy, 31 pp. 1257-1274

Geertz, C. (1973) The Interpretation of Cultures, Basic Books, New York

Gibbons, M. Limoges, C. Nowotny, H. Schwartzman, S. Scott, P & Trow, M. (1994) The New Production of Knowledge: The Dynamics of Science & Research in Contemporary Societies. London, Sage

Giddens, A. (1984) The Constitution of Society, Cambridge, Polity Press.

Granovetter, M. (1973) The Strength of Weak Ties, American Journal of Sociology, 78, 1360-1380.

Granovetter M (1985) Economic action and social structure: the problem of embeddedness. American Journal of Sociology 91 pp. 481-510.

Green, S., Lemon, M. (1996) Perceptual Landscapes in Agrarian systems: Degradation processes in North-western Epirus and the Argolid Valley, Greece, Ecumene, 3(2). pp. 181-199.

Herzfeld, M. (1992) The Social Production of Indifference: Exploring the Symbolic Roots of Western Bureaucracy. Oxford, Berg.

Holling, C., L. Gunderson (2002) Panarchy: Understanding Transformations in Human and Natural Systems. Washington, Island Press.

Hofstede G (1984) Culture's Consequences Abridged edition, Sage PublicationsNewbury Park California.

Hofstede G (1991) Multilevel Research of Human Systems: Flowers, Bouquets and Gardens, Human Systems Management 14 pp. 207-217.

Jeffrey, P. (1997) Management strategies in turbulent operating environments: A case study of managers and decision support practitioners in Israel, Israel Affairs, 4 (2) pp. 94 –111.

Langley, A. Mintzberg, H. Pitcher, P. Posada, E.and Saint-Macary, J. (1995) Opening up Decision Making: The View from the Black Stool Organization Science Vol. 6, No. 3, May-June 1995

Lam A (2000) Tacit Knowledge, Organizational learning and Societal Institutions: An Integrated Framework, Organizational Studies, 2000, 21 (3) pp. 487-513.

Latour, B. (1993). We have never been Modern, Hemel Hempstead, Harvester Wheatsheaf.

Law, J. (1994). Organizing Modernity, Oxford, Blackwell.

Lemon, M. and Sahota, P. (2004) Organizational culture as a knowledge repository for increased innovative capacity, Technovation 6 June pp 483-498

Lemon, M., Sahota, P. (2004) Organizational culture as a knowledge repository for increased innovative capacity, Technovation 6 June pp. 483-498

Lemon, M. ed. (1999) Exploring environmental change using an Integrative Method, Gordon and Breach, Reading.

Lemon, M. Jeffrey, P., Seaton, R. (1998) Deconstructing the orange: The evolution of an agricultural milieu in Southern Greece, International Journal of Sustainable Development, Vol 1 (1) pp. 9-23.

Lemon, M. Jeffrey, P. McIntosh, B, Oxley, T. (2004) Agenda setting for participation: A process oriented approach to mapping personal perceptions of change, JEAPM 6 (2) pp. 1-23

Lemon, M., Longhurst, P. (1996) Towards a Conceptual Framework for Environmental Education, Proceedings of 3rd International Conference on Environmental Impact Assessment, 3, pp. 613-621

Madu, C. N. (1990). Prescriptive Framework for Transfer of Appropriate Technology. Futures 9, 932-950.

March, J., J. Olsen (1975) Organizational learning and the ambiguity of the past, European Journal of Political Research 3: 147-171.

Miller, G. (1980). Afterword', in Message, Attitude, Behaviour Relationship, Cushman, D.P. & R.D. McPhee (eds) 319-328, London, Academic Press.

Morgan, G. (1997) Images of Organization, (2nd edition). Newbury Park, CA: Sage Publications.

Murdoch, J. (1995). Actor networks and the evolution of economic forms: combining description and explanation in theories of regulation, flexible specialization, and networks, Environment and Planning A, 27, 731-757.

Nonaka I (1991) The knowledge creating company. Harvard Business Review (Nov.-Dec) pp. 96-104.

Nonaka I (1994) A dynamic theory of organizational knowledge creation. Organizational Science 5 pp. 14-37.

Nonaka, I., Treece, D. (2001) Managing Industrial Knowledge. London, Sage.

Nonaka, I., H. Takeuchi (1995) The Knowledge Creating Company. New York, OUP.

Oxley, T., Lemon, M. (2003) From Social enquiry to decision support tools: A Synthesis of an Integrative Method, Journal of the Arid Environment 53 (3) pp. 595-617

Oxley, T. Jeffrey, P., Lemon, M. (2002) Policy relevant modelling: relationships between water, land use, and farmer decision processes. Integrated Assessment. 3 (1) pp. 30-49

Oxley, T. Lemon, M., Jeffrey, P. (2003) Indicators of socio-natural change: scientific meaning and contextual interpretation, JEAPM 5 (1) pp. 1-26.

Polanyi M (1966) The Tacit Dimension. Rotledge and Kegan Paul, London

Polanyi M (1973) Personal Knowledge towards a Post-Critical Philosophy. Chicago, IL: University of Chicago Press.

Rittel, H., M. Webber (1981). Perspectives in Systems Thinking and Systems Analysis, in Systems Thinking, F.E. Emery (ed) Harmondsworth, Penguin, 81-102.

Robinson, M., Bond, A. (2003) Investigation of Different Stakeholder views of Local Resident Involvement During Environmental Impact Assessments in the UK, Journal of Environmental Assessment Policy and Management, 5(1) 45-82.

Saint-Onge, H. (1996) Tacit Knowledge: The Key to the Strategic Alignment of Intellectual Capital. Strategy and Leadership, March/April: 10-14.

Schein, E. (1985) Organisational Culture and Leadership, Jossey-Bass, San Francisco.

Schon, D. (1983) The reflective practitioner: How professionals think in action, New York, Basic books.

Senge, P. (1990) The Fifth Discipline: The art and practice of the learning organisation. London, Random House.

Srivastva S, Barrett F (1988) The transforming nature of metaphors in group development: a study in group theory. Human Relations 41 pp. 31-34.

Stubbs, M. and Lemon, M. (2001) Learning to Network and Networking to Learn: Facilitating the Process of Adaptive Management in a Local Response to the UK's Air Quality Strategy, Environmental Management 27, (8) pp. 321-334.

Tidd, J., J. Bessant (2001) Managing Innovation, Wiley, Chichester.

Part III

Policies and Institutions of Regional Integration

Education, Research and Regional Economic Disparities in the European Union After 2004 Enlargement: Econometric Models and Policy Challenges

Maria-Carmen Guisan* and Eva Aguayo

University of Santiago de Compostela, Spain.
They have published many articles on interregional econometric models
and participated in several European Congresses of Regional Development
and Employment

1 Introduction

In comparison with the USA the European Union (EU) shows more regional disparities in income per inhabitant and in many variables related
with socio-economic development, as the educational level of population
and the expenditure on education and research.

The need to improve EU policies to answer the citizens' concerns is of
uppermost importance. Changes to be developed in European Institutions
to correct their divorce with the majority of public opinion, should include,
in our view, an improvement in development policies focused to increase
democratic rights, employment and income per inhabitant in all the regions. The policies aimed to share low levels of employment and income is
clearly rejected by the majority of citizens. European citizens give support
to policies aimed to improve the quality of life of all citizens and regions,
but not those policies focused on diminishing the standard of living of the
average citizen in many regions in the name of solidarity.

Here, we present a general view of economic disparities in 151 regions
of the 15 countries included in the EU in year 2005. Our main concern is
the incapability shown for the last decades (1986–2005) of EU institutions
to develop more effective policies to foster employment, increase real income per inhabitant, and rise the levels of expenditure on Education and

* Email: eccgs@usc.es.

Research, in comparison with those in the USA, and to promote a higher level of proximity between EU institutions and public opinion concerns in all European regions. So we think that EU policies should be more focused to get these aims instead to develop a high level of bureaucratic power far beyond citizen's concerns. The Forum on the Future of Europe which has been promoted In Aguayo and Guisan (2004) and Guisan (2005), we present a more detailed study of some complementary questions related to regional development and employment policies in Europe, as well as references to another interesting studies related to regional development in the EU and other areas.

In Sect. 2, we summarise the economic literature related to human capital and regional development with particular reference to EU, and we compare the main features of EU regions, based on Eurostat statistics, national statistics of several EU countries and our own provisional estimations for many unavailable data; these data seem to be worthly examining, in spite of the hundreds of hours of extra work the estimation has implied for us. In Sect. 3 we present an interregional econometric model which shows the important positive impact that the expenditure on Education and Research has on regional development. This model represents a new approach developed by the authors after some previous works on inter-sector relationships. Finally, in Sect. 4 we concludes present some of the main conclusions.

2 Education, Research and Development (R&D), Industry and Development in 151 EU Regions

During the last decades, some interesting studies have shown the positive role of Education and Research expenditure on economic development. Some interesting and pioneering studies on this topic are those by Denison, Barro, North, Goldin and Katz, and other relevant researchers specialized in international development. At regional level, some interesting studies have been published in the last years, and they are related to the role of education and research expenditure on regional development. In this regard some outstanding studies are those published by Schubert (1982), Jaffe (1989), Mayes (1997), Schmitt (1999), Newlands (2003), Korres, Chionis and Staikouras (2004), Guisan (2004) and Caruso and Palano (2005) among others.

In this Section we present a general view of the positive correlation between human capital and development, and industry and development. We measure the degree of economic development by means of real Gross Domestic Product (GDP) per inhabitant at Purchasing Power Parities (PPPs), due to the general difficulties to get data for income per inhabitant at regional level. In many regions GDP per inhabitant is a good proxy for income per inhabitant although in some particular regions, where primary factors of production (physical capital and labour) from outside the region have an important role on GDP, the values of GDP per inhabitant could overestimate the value of income per inhabitant.

Figures 1–3 show the important positive correlation between human capital and real GDP per inhabitant in year 2000 for the 151 European regions listed in Tables 1 and 2. All the variables are expressed in thousand dollars. Real GDP is expressed in thousand dollars at 2000 prices and PPPs.

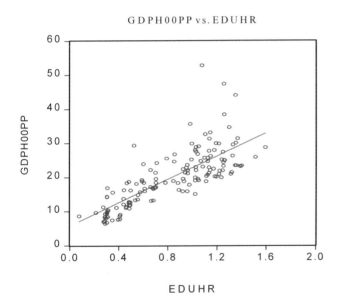

Fig. 1. Education Expenditure & Gdph

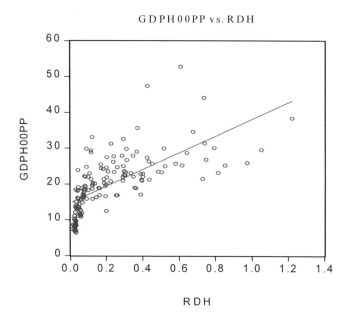

Fig. 2. RD Expenditure & Gdph

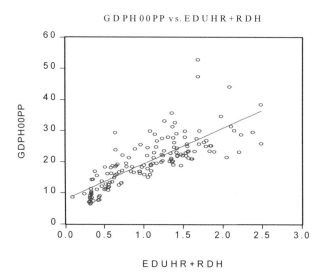

Fig. 3. Education+RD expenditure and Gdph

Table 1. Regions classified by gdp per inhabitant in year 2000 [thousand dollars at PPPs]

Group:Income	Countries	Regions
G1: 29.6 to 52.9	Belgium, Luxembourg, Germany, France, UK, Italy, Netherlands, Austria	Bruxelles, Luxembourg, Hamburg, Ile de France, London, Bremen, Trentino-Alt Adige, Lombardia, Hessen, Emilia Romagna, Bayern, West Nederland, Valle d'Aosta, Ost Osterreich, Baden-Württemberg
G2: 25.8 to 29.4	Czech R., Italy, Denmark, Ireland, Austria, UK, Spain, Germany, Sweden, Belgium	Praha, Piemonte, Veneto, Denmark, Ireland, West Osterreich, Friuli-Venezia Giulia, Toscana, Lazio, South East, Madrid, Nordrhein-Westalia, Liguria, Sweden, Vlaams
G3: 23.4 to 25.7	Netherlands, Spain, Finland, UK, France, Italy, Germany	Zuid Nederland, Navarra, Finland, Eastern(UK), Rhône-Alps, Alsace, Marche, Noord Nederland, Pais Vasco, Umbria, Cataluña, Baleares, Scotland, Saarland, Rheinland-Pfalz
G4: 22.1 to 23.4	Germany, Austria, France, Netherlands, UK, Spain, Portugal	Schleswig-Holtstein, Nieder Sachen, Sud Osterreich, Berlin, Haute Normandie, Champagne-Ardenne, Oost Nederland, East Midlands, Bourgogne, West Midlands, Rioja, South West, Lisboa e Val do Tejo, Centre (France), Provence-Alps-Côte d'Azur
G5: 19.9 to 21.9	France, UK, Spain, Italy	Aquitaine, Pays de Loire, Midi-Pyrennees, Yorkshire Humberside, Aragon, Franche-Comté, North West, Auvergne, Bretagne, Basse Normandie, Abruzzo, Lorraine, Poitou-Charentes. Picardie, Limousin
G6: 18.4 to 19.6	France, UK, Spain, Italy, Belgium, Greece, Cyprus, Hungary	Nord-Pas-de-Calais, Wales, Cantabria, C.Valenciana, Molise, Wallone, Northern Ireland, Languedoc-Rousillon, Canarias, North East(UK), Attiki, Corse, Castilla y Leon, Cyprus, Kozep-Magyarorszag
G7: 16.0 to 18.3	France, Portugal, Italy, Spain, Germany, Greece, Slovenia	Sardegna, Madeira, Basilicata, Asturias, Sachsen, Nisia A-Kriti, Thüringen, Brandeburg, Mecklenburg-Vorpommern, Murcia, Sachsnen Anhalt, Slovenia, Puglia, Castilla-La Mancha, Algarve

Table 1. (continued)

Group:Income	Countries	Regions
G8: 12.7 to 15.9	Italy, Spain, Greece, Poland, Hungary, Portugal, Malta, Czech R.	Sicilia, Campania, Galicia, Voreia, Calabria, Andalucia, Kentriki, Mazowieckie, Nyugat-Dunantul, Norte (Portugal), Malta, Alentejo, Centro (Portugal), Extremadura, Jihozapad
G9: 9.3 to 12.5	Portugal, Hungary, Czech R., Slovakia, Poland, Estonia	Açores, Kozep-Dunantul, Jihovychod, Severovychod, Stredny Cechi, Moravskoslezko, Slovakia, Severozapad, Stredni Morava, Slaskie, Wielkopolskie, Dolnoslaskie, Estonia, Promorskie, Zachodniopomorskie
G10: 6.4 to 9.0	Hungary, Lithuania, Poland, Latvia	Del-Dunantul, Del-Alfold, Lithuania, Lubuskie, Kujawsko-Pomorskie, Malopolskie, Lodzkie, Opolskie, Eszak-Magyarorszag, Eszak-Alfold, Latvia, Swietokrzyskie, Warminsko-Mazurskie, Podlaskie, Podkarpackie, Lubelskie

Source: Elaborated from the tables by Guisan and Aguayo (2005), based on Eurostat statistics and other complementary sources.

Table 2. Expenditure on Education and Research per inhabitant and per year [thousand $ 2000]

Eduhr+rdh	Countries	Regions
G1: 1.79 to 2.48	Sweden, France, Germany, Denmark, Finland, UK	Sweden, Ille de France, Baden-Württemberg, Denmark, Berlin, Bayern, Hessen, Hamburg, Midi-Pyrennes, Bremen, Nieder Sachen, Finland, Eastern, Rheinland-Pfalz, South East
G2: 1.55 to 1.78	France, Germany, Netherlands, Belgium, Luxembourg, Italy, Austria	Rhône-Alps, Nordhrhein-Westfalia, West Nederland, Zuid Nederland, Bruxelles, Luxembourg, Lazio, Schleswig-Holstein, Auvergne, Bretagne, Saarland, Franche-Comte, Sud Osterreich, Alsace, Vlaams
G3: 1.38 to 1.54	France, Netherlands, Austria, UK, Italy	Aquitaine, Oost Nederland, Ost Osterreich, West Osterreich, Provence-Alps-C.Azur, Languedoc-Rousillon, Bourgogne, South West, Pays de Loire, Umbria, Haute Normandie, Piemonte, Lombardia, Liguria, Noord Nederland

Table 2. (continued)

Eduhr+rdh	Countries	Regions
G4: 1.23 to 1.37	Belgium, Italy, France, UK, Ireland	Wallone, Friuli-Venezia Giulia. Lorraine, Emilia-Romagna, Limousin, London, North West, Basse Normandie, East Midlands, Poitou-Charentes Ireland, Trentino-Alt Adige, Scotland, Centre, Abruzzo
G5: 1.08 to 1.23	Italy, UK, France, Spain, Germany	Toscana, West Midlands, Picardie, Madrid, Nord-Pas-de-Calais, Marche, Veneto, Cham- pagne-Ardenne, Yorkshire Humberside, Wales, Sachsen, North East, Molise, Valle d´Aosta, Campania
G6: 0.84 to 1.05	Italy, Spain, Portugal, UK, Germany, France	Calabria, Pais Vasco, Basilicata, Lisboa e Val Tejo, Sicilia, Northern Ireland, Sardegna, Navarra, Puglia Brandeburg, Thüringen, Cataluña, Sachnsen Anhalt, Corse, Mecklenburg-Vorpommern
G7: 0.64 to 0.81	Spain, Portugal, Czech Republic, Cyprus	Aragon, Castilla y León, Cantabria, Rioja, Asturias, Alentejo, Centro, Murcia, Açores, C.Valenciana, Algarve, Canarias, Baleares, Praha, Cyprus
G8: 0.51 to 0.63	Spain, Greece, Slovenia, Portugal, Malta, Czech R., Hungary	Galicia, Andalucia, Attiki, Norte, Slovenia, Madeira, Malta, Jihovychod, Jihozapad, Stredni Morava, Severovychod, Castilla-La Mancha, Extremadura, Stredni Cechy, Kozep-Magyarorszag
G9: 0.34 to 0.50	Czech R., Hungary, Slovakia, Greece, Latvia, Poland	Severozapad, Nyugat-Dunantul, Kozep- Dunantul, Del-Dunantul, Eszak- Magyarorszag, Del-Alfold, Eszak-Alfold, Slovakia, Voreia, Nisia A.-Kriti, Latvia, Kentriki, Malopolskie, Mazowieckie, Lubuskie
G10: 0.16 to 0.33	Poland, Estonia, Lithuania	Slaskie, Dolnoslaskie, Promorskie, Podkar- packie, Wielkopolskie, Moravskoslezko, Opolskie, Lubelskie, Zachodniopomorskie, Lodzkie, Kujawsko-Pomorskie, Swietokrzyskie, Podlaskie,Warminsko- Mazurskie, Estonia, Lithuania

Source: Elaborated from the tables by Guisan and Aguayo (2005), based on Eurostat statistics and other complementary sources.

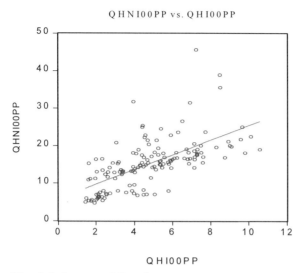

QHI00PP

Fig. 4. Industry and Development

Figure 1 uses as indicator of human capital the estimated value of Educational Expenditure per inhabitant in EU regions (Eduhr) around 1995, expressed in thousand dollars at 2000 prices and PPPs, while Fig. 2 relates Gdp per inhabitant with the expenditure on Research and Development per inhabitant (Rdh) around 1999, expressed in thousand dollars at 2000 prices and Exchange Rates, and Fig. 3 uses the sum of both variables (Eduhr and Rdh) as indicator of human capital. Figure 4 shows the existing positive and important relationship that exists between Industry and Non-industrial sectors at regional level for the same 151 regions in year 2000.

The variables utilized for the interregional comparisons and for the estimation of the econometric model of industrial and non-industrial Gross Domestic Product at regional level, presented in the next section, are the following ones:

1. GDPh00pp: Gross Domestic Product per inhabitant in year 2000, in thousand dollars at current prices and Purchasing Power Parities, PPPs, calculated applying the regional percentage on EU15 from Eurostat to the average of EU15 in OECD statistics.

2. ps200: percentage of population with secondary studies second cycle or more in year 2000, from Eurostat Main Regional Indicators.

3. eduhr: regional expenditure on public education per inhabitant of year 1995 in thousand dollars at current prices and PPPs, elaborated having into account the percentages of public expenditure on education at national level and the values of ps2 at regional level.

4. rdh: expenditure on research and development per inhabitant in 1999, in thousand dollars at 2000 prices, elaborated from statistics of Eurostat (2005) and own estimations based on several sources for distribution of national figures at regional level.
5. path: number of patents per one million inhabitants in 2000.
6. onsh: thousand of overnights stays in hotels per one thousand inhabitants. This variable is an indicator of hotel tourism. In some regions we have found that there is also an important positive impact of non-hotel tourism with a high degree of development of secondary residences.
7. qhi00pp: Industrial GDP per inhabitant in year 2000, in thousand dollars at current prices and PPPs. Elaborated from Eurostat, OCDE and UK statistics.
8. qhni00pp: Non Industrial GDP per inhabitant in year 2000, in thousand dollars at current prices and PPPs.

Table 1 shows ten groups of regions according to their levels of GDP per inhabitant. We can notice that there are some important differences within the same country as well as a diversity among different countries. The differences in average GDP per inhabitant in European Union are higher than in the USA, partly due to a less degree of mobility of citizens across regions and partly due to the lack of enough general policies to foster economic development in all regions. Table 2 illustrates ten groups of regions classified according to their expenditure on Education and Research per inhabitant. We can note the lack of enough support to these important activities in some countries, particularly in Spain, which is a country that has a level of this kind expenditure clearly below the expected value and which should correspond to its level of real Gdp per inhabitant. EU policies for the period 1986–2005 did not help much in diminishing the uneven distribution of R&D expenditure among Spanish regions.

In comparison with the USA, European Union presents lower levels of employment, wages and income per inhabitant. One important cause of the EU difficulties to attain this is the lack of support to Research and Development activities per inHabitant (RDH) in comparison with the high level of support in the USA. RD has a positive role in development not only at regional level but also at national and European level. Figures 5 and 6 illustrate the low levels of RDH and the low levels of the percentage of RDH on GDP per inhabitant (%R) in many EU15 regions. The order of the regions in these graphs is shown in the Table 3.

Table 3: Number of order of EU15 regions in graphs 5 and 6

Country	Regions
Belgium	1Bruxelles, 2 Vlaams, 3 Wallone
Denmark	4 Denmark
Germany	5 Baden-Württemberg, 6 Bayern, 7 Berlin, 8 Brandeburg, 9 Bremen, 10 Hamburg, 11 Hessen, 12 Mecklenburg-Vorpommern, 13 Nieder Sachen, 14 Nordhrhein-Westfalia, 15 Rheninland-Pfalz, 16 Saarland, 17 Sachsen, 18 Sachnsen Anhalt, 19 Schleswig-Holtstein, 20 Thüringen
Greece	21Voreia, 22 Kentriki, 23 Attiki, 24 Nisia A.-Kriti
Spain	25 Galicia, 26 Asturias, 27 Cantabria, 28 Pais Vasco, 29 Navarra, 30 Rioja 31 Aragon, 32 Madrid, 33 Castilla y León, 34 Castilla-La Mancha, 35 Extremadura, 36Cataluña,37 C.Valenciana, 38 Baleares, 39 Andalucia, 40 Murcia,41 Canarias
France	42 Ille de France,43 Champagne-Ardenne, 44 Picardie, 45 Haute Normandie 46 Centre,47Basse Normandie,48 Bourgogne, 49 Nord-Pas-de-Calais, 50 Lorraine, 51 Alsace, 52 Franche-Comte, 53 Pays de Loire, 54 Bretagne 55 Poitou-Charentes, 56 Aquitaine,57 Midi-Pyrennees, 58 Limousin, 59 Rhône-Alps, 60 Auvergne, 61 Languedoc-Rousillon, 62 Provence-Alps-Côte d´Azur, 63 Corse
Ireland	64 Ireland
Italy	65 Piemonte, 66 Valle d´Aosta, 67 Liguria, 68 Lombardia, 69 Trentino-Alt Adige, 70 Veneto, 71 Friuli-Venezia Giulia, 72 Emilia-Romagna, 73 Toscana, 74 Umbria, 75 Marche, 76 Lazio, 77 Abruzzo, 78 Molise, 79 Campania, 80 Puglia, 81 Basilicata, 82 Calabria, 83 Sicilia, 84 Sardegna
Luxembourg	85 Luxembourg
Netherlands	86Noord Nederland, 87 Oost Nederland, 88 West Nederland, 89 Zuid Nederland
Austria	90 Ost Osterreich, 91 Sud Osterreich, 92 West Osterreich
Portugal	93 Norte, 94 Centro, 95 Lisboa e Val Tejo, 96 Alentejo, 97 Algarve, 98 Açores, 99 Madeira
Finland	100 Finland
Sweden	101 Sweden
UK	102 North East, 103 North West, 104 Yorkshire Humberside,105 East Midlands, 106 West Midlands, 107 Eastern, 108 London, 109 South East, 110 South West, 111 Wales, 112 Scotland, 113 Northern Ireland

Source: Elaborated from Eurostat regional statistics and some complementary sources.

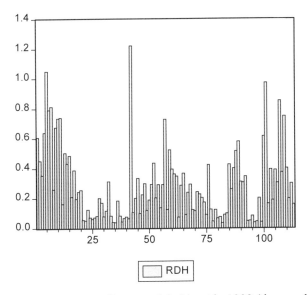

Fig. 5. RD expenditure per inhabitant in 1999 (thousand dollars)

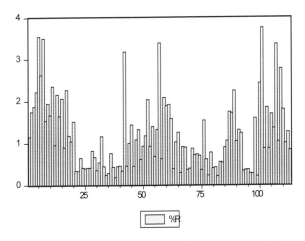

Fig. 6: Percentage of RD expenditure on regional GDP

These graphs show the important disparities that exist among EU regions as well as the low general values of the majority of EU regions in comparison with the USA. According to Korres, Chionis and Staikouras (2004) and OECD (2002), the average expenditure on RD in EU15 was $458 in year 2000, far below the value of 963 dollars in the USA. Besides that, we have found that in the USA there are smaller discrepancies among regions and that all of then receive support for research both from state and federal institutions. Very few EU regions have a level of Rdh similar to the average of the USA, being the most outstanding: Denmark, Ile de France and Sweden. As mentioned above Spain is one of the countries with the lowest levels of expenditure on RD per inhabitant.

3 Estimation of an Interregional Econometric Model for 151 European Regions

Here, we present an small model which has taken into account inter-sector relationship between industrial and non industrial sectors, as well as human capital and other variables which have a positive impact on regional development. Data definitions and sources have already been presented in Sect. 2. We have estimated Tables 4 and 5 for non-industrial GDP per inhabitant (qhni00pp): without and with dummies for special effects in some regions. In both cases all the coefficients were positive and significantly different from zero, so the result support that industrial production, tourism and human capital (measured by the sum of past expenditure on education and research) have an important positive impact on non industrial sectors. If we consider separately the variables Eduhr and Rdh, the highest impact corresponds to Educational expenditure, which seems to be more important than R&D expenditure, although both have a positive impact on development.

Table 4. GDP per inhabitant in non-industrial sectors: without dummies

Dependent Variable: QHNI00PP				
	Method: Least Squares. Sample: 1 151			
Variable	Coefficient	Std. Error	t-Statistic	Prob.
QHI00PP	1.156034	0.201996	5.723069	0.0000
ONSH	0.279486	0.043020	6.496697	0.0000
EDUHR+RDH	7.578228	0.880025	8.611380	0.0000
R-squared	0.586985	Mean dependent var		15.19466
Adjusted R-squared	0.581403	S.D. dependent var		6.593187
S.E. of regression	4.265729	Akaike info criterion		5.758771
Sum squared resid	2693.074	Schwarz criterion		5.818717
Log likelihood	−431.7872	Durbin-Watson stat		1.435557

Table 5. GDP per inhabitant in non-industrial sectors: with dummies

Dependent Variable: QHNI00PP				
Method: Least Squares. Sample: 1 151				
Variable	Coefficient	Std. Error	t-Statistic	Prob.
QHI00PP	1.085512	0.146399	7.414727	0.0000
ONSH	0.280978	0.030947	9.079373	0.0000
EDUHR+RDH	7.300276	0.637950	11.44333	0.0000
D1.Bruxelles	24.22521	3.084581	7.853646	0.0000
D10. Hamburg	10.38521	3.097498	3.352773	0.0010
D85. Luxembourg	16.71011	3.093908	5.400973	0.0000
D108. London	16.00863	3.086276	5.187037	0.0000
D115. Praha	13.85103	3.078657	4.499049	0.0000
R-squared	0.794273	Mean dependent var		15.19466
Adjusted R-squared	0.784203	S.D. dependent var		6.593187
S.E. of regression	3.062798	Akaike info criterion		5.128060
Sum squared resid	1341.444	Schwarz criterion		5.287916
Log likelihood	–379.1685	Durbin-Watson stat		1.353710

Table 6. GDP per inhabitant in industry: with dummies and path

Dependent Variable: QHI00PP				
Method: Least Squares. Sample: 1 151				
Variable	Coefficient	Std. Error	t-Statistic	Prob.
C	1.473094	0.252515	5.833684	0.0000
EDUHR	3.230794	0.350773	9.210496	0.0000
ONSH	–0.007877	0.011564	–0.681198	0.4970
PATH/1000	7.345726	1.360963	5.397446	0.0000
R-squared	0.780877	Mean dependent var		4.731387
Adjusted R-squared	0.747166	S.D. dependent var		2.172757
S.E. of regression	1.092518	Akaike info criterion		3.143248
Sum squared resid	155.1675	Schwarz criterion		3.562870
Log likelihood	–216.3152	F-statistic		23.16377
Durbin-Watson stat	1.206657	Prob(F-statistic)		0.000000

Note: The estimated coefficients for regional dummies where:
D4 –1.87, D7 –2.96, D61 –2.27, D62 –1.89, D63 –1.95, D82 –2.75, D83 –2.17,
D108 –1.31, D28 3.15, D29 4.27, D30 3.20, D36 3.06, D64 4.57, D65 3.33,
D68 4.01, D125 2.08, D126 2.79

Tables 6 and 7 related industry to the variables Eduh, Onsh, Path and Rdh. Both Rdh and Path seems to have a positive impact when included separately. Regarding educational expenditure per inhabitant, its effect is positive and significant in both tables. We have included and intercepted some dummies which have into account industrial background and other circumstances of some regions. The variable onsh could have in some regions a negative impact on industrial development, indicating that some regions specialized in the development of tourism do not foster industrial development well due to the fact that there is some degree of incompatibility with tourism development.

Figures 7 and 8 show a good relationship between actual values of the dependent variables and their fitted values in Tables 5 and 7. Forecasted values are indicated with the letter F at the end of the name of the variable.

Table 7. GDP per inhabitant in industry: with dummies and Rdh

Dependent Variable: QHI00PP				
Method: Least Squares. Sample: 1 151				
Variable	Coefficient	Std. Error	t-Statistic	Prob.
C	1.188145	0.264325	4.495009	0.0000
EDUHR	3.784008	0.383320	9.871661	0.0000
ONSH	−0.010180	0.012451	−0.817610	0.4151
RDH	1.680458	0.601800	2.792384	0.0060
R-squared	0.746951	Mean dependent var		4.731387
Adjusted R-squared	0.708020	S.D. dependent var		2.172757
S.E. of regression	1.174053	Akaike info criterion		3.287200
Sum squared resid	179.1919	Schwarz criterion		3.706822
Log likelihood	−227.1836	F-statistic		19.18672
Durbin-Watson stat	1.254728	Prob(F-statistic)		0.000000

Note: The estimated coefficients for regional dummies where:
D4 –2.36, D7 –3.57, D61 –2.77, D62 –2.10, D63 –2.15, D82 –3.03, D83 –2.43,
D108 –1.51, D28 2.88, D29 4.29, D30– 3.07, D36 3.03, D64 4.34, D65–3.24,
D68 4.28, D125 2.18, D126 2.90

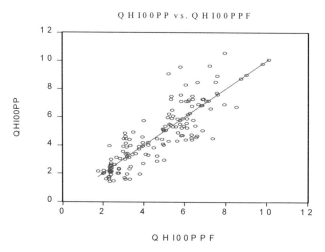

Fig. 7. Industry: actual & forecast-Graph

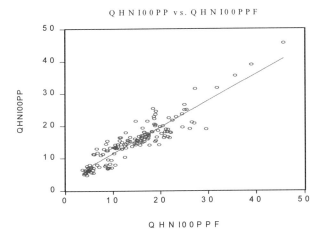

QHNI00PP vs. QHNI00PPF

Fig. 8. Non-Industrial: actual & forecast

On the other hand Employment and population depend greatly on the territorial distribution of real value added, as shown in Aguayo and Guisan (2004), Guisan and Aguayo (2005) and other studies. Table 8 from the last article shows the share of each region in total EU employment, as a function of the lagged value of the share, and the increase in the shares of GDP and Population during the period 1995–2000. The goodness of the fit is very high, and the coefficients are positive and significantly different from zero. The increase in the share of employment has at the same time a positive impact on the population

Table 8. LS estimation: Employment Share

Dependent Variable: SLT00				
Method: Least Squares. Sample 1 151				
Variable	Coefficient	Std. Error	t-Statistic	Prob.
SLT95	0.995046	0.003681	270.3331	0.0000
D(SGDP)	0.158964	0.065848	2.414097	0.0170
D(SPOP00)	1.325356	0.253123	5.236017	0.0000
R-squared	0.995901	Mean dependent var		0.662252
Adjusted R-squared	0.995845	S.D. dependent var		0.618050
S.E. of regression	0.039837	Akaike info criterion		–3.588360
Sum squared resid	0.234877	Schwarz criterion		–3.528414
Log likelihood	273.9212	Durbin-Watson stat		1.281764

Source: Guisan and Aguayo (2005).

Table 9. Coefficients of different kinds of RDH in EU regions, 1995

Variable	Coef.	SD	t-stat	R^2
RDHB	0.4176	0.1014	4.12	0.9697
RDHG	1.8466	0.3694	5.00	0.9695
RDHU-SSH	7.7413	1.4313	5.41	0.9708
RDHU-NSE	2.0556	0.4024	5.11	0.9698

Note: Regression coefficients of Gdph on RD expenditure.
Source: Guisan et al(2001).

Finally, in Table 9 we show the different coefficient estimated for different kinds of research expenditure, with European regional data of Research Expenditure for the period 1990–1994 and its impact on GDP in the year of 1995, corresponding to the following sectors: Business (B), Government (G) and Higher Education (Universities, U). The research performed in Higher Education institutions is split into two groups: Social Sciences and Humanities (U-SSH) and Natural Sciences and Engineering (U-NSE)

From these results as well as, from those takenfrom another studies, it seems that there is a higher impact of Universities research on economic development, on average, in comparison with research developed in another organisations. It is particularly striking, and opposite to many common beliefs, that Research expenditure on Social Sciences and Humanities does have a higher impact on economic development than that Research expenditure on Natural Sciences and Engineering.

Although the high coefficient of Rdhu-ssh overestimated due to the effect of some missing variables in the regression, might have been similar results have been reached in another studies such as in Guisan, Cancelo and Diaz (1998) where several of those variables were not excluded from the regression. Of course, both types of research are needed to contribute to economic development and, in the case of many European regions, it is very likely to get an increase of financial support to university research, from regional, national and European institutions, particularly in the case of Social Sciences and Humanities which sometimes receive only an small budget, between 10% and 20% of total research expenditure of universities.

4 Conclusions

We have presented a general view of education, research and development of 151 European regions during the last years, based on European and national statistical sources as well as on our own provisional estimations for the cases of data unavailability. The analysis of data and the econometric models show the important positive role of education expenditure on economic development, which is outstanding both in industrial and non-industrial sectors.

In some cases, EU policies have financed "training courses", under the perspective that only some "technical knowledge" is needed to improve workers' productivity, but the positive effects of education on development are not only linked to the educational levels of workers and business staff, but also they act through many indirect ways, improving the quality of public and private institutions, which in turn contribute to the creation of a socio-economic environment which encourages initiatives for research, investment and development. Even the electoral systems and the results of political elections are positively influenced very often by the level and quality of the educational level of citizens. In many cases of EU regions, the levels of expenditure on education are low in comparison with the USA, although the average level of expenditure has shown a clear tendency to increase in many regions during the last years.

Another variable which has a significant positive effect on economic development of industrial and non-industrial sectors is the expenditure per inhabitant on Research and Development, and in this case of that of European regions is very much below that it is in the USA. It is of uppermost importance to foster RD expenditure in EU not only in technological fields but also in other disciplines that play an important role in fostering socio-economic development.

The above illustrated econometric models show that RD expenditure on universities both in of Social Sciences and Humanities as well as in Natural Sciences and Engineering, have a very important and positive role to play in economic development and employment at regional level. This issue should be emphasised this question because the general approach of many European governments and EU institutions seems to be a "technological bias". Many people thinks that only "technology" is useful for development, but this is not true because many important initiatives to improve economic development and employment depend more on economic and social research than on technology.

On the other hand, low levels of expenditure on R&D in many EU regions need to be increased from several financing sources. Generally, researchers do not complain about which institution is in charge of giving support to R&D activities, but they think that economic policies should take this issue into account for budgets distribution (regional, national or European). Thus, those institutions should experience increases of their budgets depending on if they give or do not give adequate support to RD activities, according to researchers' opinion. At the same time, it is important to increase financial support, diminish bureaucratic barriers which create particular difficulties to many researchers, as well as to design good channels for R&D financing decisions and supervision, in order to avoid that pressure groups with decisions that various committees are to made, thus altering those decisions in favour of their interests and with unfair refusals of support to other groups. As there have been many complains about some negative experiences in this regard in some countries, and many researchers have shown concern about the future organization of European committees for research grants, this question should be properly analysed and organized.

On the other hand, EU economic policies should –in our opinion- foster both employment and income per inhabitant in all regions, if they are to promote higher levels of economic activity. Less bureaucracy, fewer taxes and a very good dialogue with non-governmental organizations and researchers could be of great help. A favourable role of EU to promote research and development in all regions should not mean intromission in the national or regional policies; it should rather support research activities, particularly in universities, and other initiatives which contribute to foster economic development.

We agree with Fertig and Scmidt (2002) when claiming that regional development research in EU *"has to be conducted from a pronounced European perspective... Such an ambitions task can hardly be performed by a handful of researchers alone. Instead, it is necessary to co-ordinate these endeavours on an European basis. In the light of the overwhelming relevance of these topics, it is hoped that representatives and institutions of the European Union will spend more effort in supporting the development of more and better knowledge on issues decisive to the future development of European societies"*.

During the last years, the citizen's opinions in Euro-Barometer and other surveys have shown a clear concern about wrong policies of EU institutions regarding the promotion of employment, well-being and prosperity of many regions and countries. The dissatisfaction with those policies has had indeed a role to play in the lack of affirmative support to the project of European Constitution presented to referendum in several EU countries during the first semester of year 2005. Now, it is time to see some positive changes in European policies, and the new economic policies should take into account the important role of human capital and industry the development of non-industrial sectors and to reach higher levels of employment and income per inhabitant.

5 References

Aguayo, E., Guisan, M.C. (2004) Employment and Population in European Union: Econometric Models and Causality Tests. Working Paper No. 80, Economic Development, USC.

Caruso, R. and Palano, D. (2005) Regioni e istitutzioni nello spazio europeo della ricerca. Brevi note sulla territorializzazione delle politiche di R&S. Regional and Sectoral Economic Studies, Vol. 5–2.[1]

Eurostat (2005) Main Regional Indicators and other regional statistics.

Fertig, Schmidt (2000) Aggregate-Level Migration Studies as a Tool for Forecasting Future Migration Streams.

Fertig, Schmidt (2002) Mobility within Europe. What do we (still not) know?. IZA, document No. 447.

Fidrmuc, J. (2002) Migration and Regional Adjustment and Assymetric Shocks in Transition Economices. William Davidson Institute, working paper no. 441.

Guisan, M.C. (2004) Education, Research and Manufacturing in EU25: An Intersectoral Econometric Model of 151 European Regions, 1995-2000. Regional and Sectoral Economic Studies, Vol. 4-2, pp. 22–32.

Guisan, M.C. (2005) Employment, Wages, Investment and Human Capital in European Union: Econometric Models and Comparisons with the USA, 1960-2003. Working Paper no. 83 of the series Economic Development, on line.[1]

Guisan, M.C., Aguayo, E. (2005) A general view of economic development and employment in European regions. Working Paper no. 84 of the series Economic Development, on line.[1]

Korres, G., Chionis, D.P. and Staikouras, C. (2004) Regional Systems of Innovation and Regional Policy in Europe. Regional and Sectoral Economic Studies, Vol.4-1, pp. 25–44.[1,2]

Jaffee, A.B. (1989) Real Effect of Academic Research.[2]

Mayes, D.G. (1997) The Evolution of the Single European Market. Edward Elgar Publishing.

Newlands, D. (2003) The Role of Universities in Learning Regions. ERSA Conference Papers, no 398.[2]

OECD (1995) Basic Science and Technology Statistics.

OECD (1996) National Accounts. Main Aggregates.

Schmidtt, B. (1999) Economic Geography and Contemporary Rural Dynamics: An Empirical Test on Some French Regions. Regional Studies, Vol. 33–8, pp. 697–711.

Schubert, U. (1982) REMO: An interregional labor market model of Austria. Environment and Planning A 14: 1233–1249

[1] articles available at: http://www.usc.es/economet/welcomei.htm
[2] articles available at: http://ideas.repec.org

European Regional Convergence: Some Evidence for the Role of Information Communication Technologies

Federico Biagi [1,*] and Massimiliano R. Riggi [2]

[1] Università di Padova, Econpubblica and SDA, Bocconi, via Gobbi, 5, 20136 Milano, Italy. Financial support from SDA-Research Division is gratefully acknowledged.
[2] CERTeT, IEP, and SDA, Università Bocconi, piazza Sraffa, 11, 20136 Milano, Italy

1 Introduction

The Third Cohesion Report of the EU (European Commission, 2004) highlights that regional disparities are striking within the European Union, and observes that "In the absence of corrective policies, the diversity of territories may easily lead to important disparities, often cumulative, in the physical and human capital endowment of those territories, ultimately resulting in significant divergences in terms of relative wealth, population densities and demographic flows which exacerbate the already divergent economic growth trends". (p. 8). On the basis of the Lisbon and Gothenburg strategy, the Commission assigns to the dissemination of knowledge an important tool for achieving social and economic cohesion.

This consideration recognises the pivotal role of knowledge and its diffusion in the process of regional convergence across European regions. Knowledge is embedded and transmitted across individuals, regions, countries, but the main feature is its relational dimension: knowledge diffusion increases its value and role in fostering regional growth. Innovation is only one part of the process of knowledge diffusion, since new ideas, developed in private firms, public institutions or simply by individuals, need to get circulated and become part of social, physical or human capital.

This is why institutions are very important in the process of knowledge diffusion, and in this process a particular relevance should be given to

* Email: federico.biagi@unipd.it.

knowledge diffusion at the regional level, because of the relational nature of knowledge. The availability of new technologies, and of ICT in particular, can be an engine for knowledge diffusion and hence for growth. The diffusion of ICT can have both direct and indirect effects on productivity, and these effects are likely to be more visible at the regional level. This is because ICT are a complex phenomenon. On the one hand, these are technologies that could be produced on one side of the world and be adopted by the other side, so that the link between ICT production and overall productivity might be tenuous, for lagging regions. On the other hand, ICT become fully usable only when they interact productively with the resources locally available. Hence, they might give rise to rapid knowledge diffusion, providing room for reducing regional disparities through their promotion.

2 The Regional Dimension of Growth

In the 20th century, a new paradigm explaining the dynamics of economic systems has emerged characterised by a sharp shift from the relevance of physical elements to the relational dimension (Castells, 2000), which is an important ingredient especially for regional development (Riggi, Bramanti, and Maggioni, 2002). It is currently recognised that disparities in productivity and growth have to do with both the abundance of natural resources and the ability to improve the quality of human capital and factors of production, to create new knowledge and ideas and incorporate them in equipment and people (David and Foray, 2002).

This contributes to the definition of the "knowledge society", to enrich and complement the "information society" typically dealt with within the framework of the Internet (Castells, 1996). This distinction allows us to stress the importance of relational factors and the difference between information and knowledge stemming from the cognitive filière (Campanelli, 1998). When people supported by ICT interact to create and exchange new knowledge, a knowledge-based society emerges. This perspective stresses the fact that the most valuable asset is intangible investment (human and social capital) and that the key factors are knowledge and creativity. Along the cognitive filière, as defined below, the process goes from information to knowledge through ICT and is filtered by territorial factors, which are regionally produced and transmitted.

The main point here is that the most valuable assets are intangible investments (human and social capital) and that knowledge and creativity are key factors. The rise of the "Knowledge Economy" lies in the observation that knowledge, skills or information-based activities have been playing an increasingly significant role in economic growth. Capital, labour, technology and natural resources are essential ingredients for firms, but economists have come to recognise the increasing role of information, innovation, and creativity, in expanding economic potential. Two reasons can be hereby accounted for regions to become the central entity to cope with growth issues.

On the one hand, the process of globalisation, requires a strengthening of the local dimensions of growth. On the other hand, the rise of the new economy (Bramanti and Maggioni, 1997) stresses the need to find an equilibrium between the global and the local dimensions for regions to be competing successfully. In a global world, individuals, regions and countries are tightly connected with exchanges and communication; the success of nations mainly relies on factors that are embedded in regions, such as innovation, stemming from relations, inter-connections among regional actors as a main source of regional competitiveness (Porter, 2003). Moreover, the importance of regions in economic growth is a striking feature of successful economic performances. This new paradigm implies a sharp shift from the relevance of physical elements to the relational dimension of the structure and dynamics of economic systems.

The relational elements of development are those stressed in the literature as regional factors of development. As long as the relational factors of development are embedded in the regional dimension (according to our definition of "Knowledge Society" as a relational-relevant version of the information society), ICT are economically successful when they are internalised in the production system, and their introduction is able to spur a structural change.

This perspective implies that ICT diffusion is likely to lead to a resurgence of the importance of regions. The economic relevant definition of "regions" ranges from the city level, to the supranational level, and the adoption of either definition depends on data availability and on the issue to be investigated; this implies the identification of the economic ties and inter-dependences that define self-contained and self-sufficient entities. In empirical studies, often, no concern rises about the aggregation level at which regional units of analysis should be studied. However, the level of resolution and aggregation of basic units are important parts of the analysis itself: there exists an optimal dimension that best describes the phenomenon under study, but being endogenous, no recipe can a priori be provided. This issue is particularly relevant when studying transnational borders or territories that are integrated.

The starting point is the distinction between administrative and functional regions. Administrative regions are exogenously defined for mainly data collection purposes by the policy maker, and they usually account for just spatial contiguities among units. Functional regions account for economic ties, encompassing an economic dimension in the definition of the basic unit under analysis. It is not possible to uniquely define each region as a basic unit for applied research. Administrative regions are defined as standard size box spaces, whereas functional regions also take into account economic flows directions, thus giving the territory a relational relevance.

Whilst it is probably not appropriate to produce statistical information based on functional as opposed to administratively defined regions, it is however possible to think in terms of analytical methods which can be used to aggregate lower levels of territorial analysis based on some structural and/or behavioural similarities. Often, a compromise between administrative and functional regions is found, giving rise to an optimal definition of region given both research objectives and data availability constraints. In this way, it is possible to detect economically interesting sources of disparities and divergence, which may be hidden under the administrative level.

3 On Convergence

When gauging with European regions a relevant policy question is whether or not interregional disparities increase or decrease over time. From an economic point of view this question does not clearly distinguish clearly between endogenous (per-capita GDP) and exogenous variables (the determinants of per-capita GDP) variables. The issue can be better disentangled looking at the difference between conditional and unconditional convergence. The traditional Solow (1956) growth model predicts that, for a given country or region, there is a negative relationship between the initial per-capita GDP level and its growth rate over a given period.

For country/regions sharing the same steady state, this implies that poorer regions will grow faster. For regions that do not share the same steady states we have no clear predictions regarding a general cross-region relationship between initial per-capita GDP level and growth rates (that is we no longer predict that poorer regions growth at higher rates).

The main policy implication from this discussion is that, if we are worried about distributional issues, finding unconditional convergence is reassuring because it implies that cross-country (or cross-region) differences in well-being (as measured by per-capita GDP) are reduced with time. On the contrary, the finding of just conditional convergence (which is what the original Solow model predicts[1]) simply means that countries or regions tend to converge (more or less rapidly) towards their steady state, but has no implication whatsoever for the overall distribution of per-capita GDP: a reduction in its dispersion could be achieved only by reducing the dispersion in steady-state determinants.[2]

Based on these theories of assumptions, researchers have started to test whether or not countries and regions converge over time. Barro and Sala-i-Martin (1992b) as well as Mankiw, Weil, and Romer (1992a) are paramount examples of the test of neo-classical growth models. The dominant approach in the early empirical literature is regression of income growth rates on initial income in order to test whether poor countries grow faster than rich ones[3] as in the following equation:

$$\frac{1}{T}\ln\left(\frac{gdp_{t+T}^i}{gdp_t^i}\right) = \alpha + \gamma \ln(gdp_t^i) + \varepsilon \tag{1}$$

where $gdp_{i;t+T}$ is per-capita GDP in region (i) at the end of the time span considered (whose length is T) and $gdp_{i;t+T}$ is its initial value.

This specification implicitly assumes that all countries share the same steady state determinants (which would be reflected in the constant term). From the coefficient on the log of initial per-capita GDP it is possible to get an estimate of the convergence parameter, which measures how fast countries approach their steady state. Empirical estimates have often found no sign of absolute convergence (i.e. positive or not significant values for (γ). This approach fails to properly represent the intuition behind the original Solow model, that countries tend to converge towards their own steady state and that countries that are further away from their steady state tend to grow at a higher rate (which does not imply that poorer countries grow at higher rates than the richer). To account for different steady states, Sala-i-Martin (1996) proposes the estimation of models of the following form (test for conditional convergence):

---

[1]In contrast, endogenous growth models can generate patterns of growth that do not necessarily exhibit conditional convergence (Romer, 1986).
[2]The term σ-convergence has been created to describe how the overall distribution of per-capita GDP changes with time. Sala-i-Martin (1996) argues that both concepts of convergence are interesting and should be analysed empirically.
[3]Several authors, and in particular Quah (1993) argued that although these regressions may detect mobility within a distribution they tell us little about convergence in the sense of a reduction in income dispersion across countries.

$$\frac{1}{T}\ln\left(\frac{gdp^i_{t+T}}{gdp^i_t}\right) = \alpha + \beta\ln(gdp^i_t) + \gamma X^i_t + \varepsilon \tag{2}$$

To grasp the difference between the two convergence concepts, consider two economies, with the same technologies, and with the same values of the parameters representing savings, technological progress, population growth, capital depreciation and so on (the parameters which drive the dynamics of a Solow growth model and characterise the steady state). Hence, these two countries share the same values for the X's, but they differ only in the initial level of per-capita GDP.

In such a case the model in (2) would be identical to the model in equation (the X's and their coefficients would collapse in the intercept). Then, if the Solow model (or other models that predict conditional convergence) is correct, we expect a negative value for β; i.e. lower per-capita values for GDP tend to be associated to higher average growth rates. But if the two countries do not share the same values the X's, we need to control for these differences before we can draw any conclusion about convergence. Once we control for the X's, the Solow model still predicts a negative value for β, but the interpretation of this value (which could even be country/region specific if we allow the convergence rate to change across countries/regions) would be very different, since it would simply mean that the further away is each country/region from its steady state (captured by the X's) the higher it is its growth rate. Obviously, this does not allow us to make any inference on the relative growth performance of rich and low-income countries (this inference should be based on steady state determinants). Notice that there would be no tendency towards convergence in per-capita GDP if the countries had different steady states. For example, one country might have a higher initial level of output per person, because of some historical accident, and yet the lower steady state level because of a low saving rate.

Though not uniquely recognised, Barro and Sala-i-Martin (1992b); Barro and Sala-i-Martin (1992a) and Sala-i-Martin (1996) are probably the first relevant contributions to extend the convergence framework to regional data. A different perspective (see for example Quah (1996a); Quah (1996b)) discusses the problems that such an approach encounters in gauging distributional properties of income, well beyond the idea of σ convergence. A recent and complete review on regional convergence can be found in Magrini (2003), in which it is argued that a vast number of studies have reported unconditional or conditional β convergence across groups of regional economies worldwide; in particular, at E.U. level, the hypothesis of unconditional convergence is confirmed, but wide variations are found in the estimated values of the rate of convergence across different countries. Shifting the attention to the whole Europe, member States dummy variables (as proxies for different steady states) are generally considered and conditional convergence across various groupings of European NUTS regions is again found.

A striking result is that there have been profound changes in the pattern of convergence over time (weaker in the 1980's and stronger in the 1990's). Results are sensitive to the choice of countries, the level of NUTS regions used and the choice of additional explanatory variables. In general, β convergence is much weaker in Europe than in other areas and is governed by a country specific component (some authors record convergence within selected homogeneous groups of countries, limiting the phenomenon to restricted 'clubs' (Fagerberg and Verspagen, 1996)).

The main contribution from our work is to verify how ICT related variables (the share of the population with tertiary education or more and the share of the population in high tech employment-EHT) affect the growth performance of various regions. Our priors are that the proxy for human capital investment should have a positive effect on the steady state growth rate (if the augmented Solow model proposed by Mankiw, Romer, and Weil (1992b) is appropriate) and that both the log of EHT and the growth rate of EHT should positively affect the growth rate in a neighbourhood of the steady state (which is where we assume to be when estimating this type of models). In the reminder of the paper, we will discuss these points.

4 Data Issues

The main constraint that empirical analyses have to cope with is the unavailability of census or survey data. This issue is particularly relevant when looking at European Data sets at the regional level that contain data on technology in general and ICT in particular. Direct indicators of ICT diffusion are available only at national level. Given these constraints, we choose to proxy ICT diffusion with the share of the population Employed in High-Tech (EHT).

Hence we interpret EHT as a proxy for one of the determinants of the level of technology (so that its rate of change captures technological trajectories that regions undertake). In other words, we believe that TFP depends positively on ICT diffusion proxied by the share of the population in high-tech employment. We are quite aware that the latter is an endogenous variable, but, for our purposes, its behaviour is driven by the available technology, and in particular by the available Information and Communication

Technologies (ICT), which troughs ICT producing sectors and indirectly (through ICT using sectors) the overall level of Total Factor Productivity. The complete list and description of the variable used in this paper is the following:

- regional per-capita Gross Domestic Product (GDP) in purchasing parity standards and its growth rate. This time series spans 1977 to 2000, but earlier values display many missing values. The farthest cross section without significant gaps is 1988, whereas, for the sake of comparability with other ICT related variables, 1996 is assumed as the starting year;
- employment in high technology and knowledge intensive sectors[4], as a percentage of the working population is the raw data; within this paper, EHT is defined as the share of individuals employed in high-tech over the whole population. This is preferred to the alternative definition of EHT as the share of high-tech employment over total employment because it incorporates both labour force participation and unemployment. Otherwise, we would have the undesirable result that regions characterised by low labour force participation and high unemployment appear as 'high-tech' regions just because a larger portion of the limited number of available jobs is in high-tech. This time series spans from 1994 to 2002 for European regions, with many missing data for 1994. Notice that this variable captures the importance of ICT producing sectors (almost all jobs would be qualified as employment in high technology) but clearly under-estimates the diffusion of ICT in ICT using sectors. Considering the many missing values reported, we choose 1996 as the starting year;
- educational attainment of working population at time period t ($ISCED_t$)

  Extracted from the European Labour Force Survey, this variable accounts for the percentage of individuals aged 25–59 with a given level of education.

The International Standard Classification of Education (ISCED) is elaborated by UNESCO and encompasses eight categories (0 to 7) from primary education to postgraduate university degree or equivalent. More in detail, these are the ISCED categories:

- *ISCED*-0 Pre-primary education, mainly school or centre-based, aimed at providing educational properties;

---

[4] Several authors, and in particular Quah (1993), argued that, although these regressions may detect mobility within a distributions they tell us little about convergence in the sense of a reduction in income dispersion across countries.

- *ISCED*-1 Primary education and first stage of basic education, providing the beginning of systematic apprenticeship of reading, writing and mathematics;
- *ISCED*-2 Lower secondary education and second stage of basic education, providing full implementation of basic skills and foundation for lifelong learning;
- *ISCED*-3 (Upper) secondary education, providing typical entrance qualification and a minimum entrance requirement;
- *ISCED*-4 Post-secondary non tertiary education;
- *ISCED*-5 First stage of tertiary education (not leading directly to an advanced research qualification), providing National degree and qualification structure;
- *ISCED*-6 Second stage of tertiary education, providing research oriented content;
- *ISCED*-7 Advanced research qualification, preparing graduates for faculty and research posts.

These categories are then classified in four groups in order to proxy skill levels (the so called ISCO skill levels). Data used in the present paper considers categories 0 to 2, 3 and 5 to 7 (category 4, post-secondary non-tertiary education, is left without content); the percentage of workers with educational attainment *ISCED*5-7 is considered the most suited proxy for the purposes of this paper. This data are only available for 1996–1997.

This implies that we have almost complete observations (since missing values are still present) from 1996 to 2000, with the exception of the education variable, which is reported only for 1996 and 1997. Data availability also reduces dramatically our degrees of freedom in the choice of the appropriate definition of economic regions. Available data are collected at regional level, with the standard European statistical units (NUTS).

The *Nomenclature of Territorial Units for Statistics* (NUTS) is a geo-code standard for referencing to administrative division of countries for statistical purposes. The standard was developed by the European Union, and thus only covers the member states of the EU in detail; Eurostat also devised a hierarchy for the ten countries which joined the EU in 2004, but these are subject to minor changes. The NUTS divisions do not necessarily correspond to administrative divisions within the country. The label is derived from the French name for the scheme, *Nomenclature des Unités Territoriales Statistiques*.

A NUTS code begins with a two letter code referencing the country. The subdivision of countries is then referred to with one number, corresponding to NUTS first level regions. A second (NUTS 2) or third (NUTS 3) subdivision level is referred to with another number each. Each numbering starts with one, as zero is used for the upper national level. In the case it has more than nine entities capital letters are used to continue the numbering. Within our sample, the most detailed information available refers to NUTS 2 regions.

This aggregation level also seems suitable in terms of economic meaningfulness: NUTS 3 regions are too disaggregated to account for economic ties behind the role that technological development and ICT diffusion can play in boosting growth, while wider aggregations become too similar to county level analyses, changing the scope of the study. When data for NUTS 2 regions are unavailable, the upper level (NUTS 1) is used. As a result, the territorial units analysed are a sort of composition trying to exploit at best all available information; the *best* units used are referenced in Table 1 in italic (see Sect. 7); country level units are indicated in bold.

Table 2 (see Sect. 7) groups European regions according to two dimensions: growth rates of GDP and Employment in High Tech sectors (EHT) between 1996 and 2000, each expressed relative to the average value for the relevant series. Notice that, if growth in EHT is a proxy for technological progress, then we should expect higher frequencies in the columns that correspond to positive correlation between per-capita GDP growth rates and EHT growth rates (i.e. Columns 1 and 4). This is only partially true since columns 2 and 3 are quite numerous as well.

Figure 1 plots EHT and per-capita GDP levels. We notice that there is a clear positive correlation between the two variables. It is worthnoting that high levels of per-capita GDP tend to be strongly and positively associated with high levels of EHT. In Fig. 2 we notice that the positive correlation that we have found for the levels extends only partially to growth rates.[5]

We observe a group of regions (the ones in the lower part of the graph) for which a positive correlation is quite evident and this could be interpreted as evidence for the hypothesis that technological progress leads to GDP growth. We cannot be more specific unless we are ready to clarify the channels through which technological growth affects GDP and the potential feedback from GDP growth to technology. One step ahead towards this direction can be done by looking at Fig. 3, in which we report on the Y-axis the growth rate of per-capita GDP between 1996 and 2000 and, on the X-axis, the log of EHT in 1996. If the latter is a proxy for the level of ICT diffusion, we expect a positive correlation between the two variables. The picture that emerges is not clear cut: UK regions are characterised by higher rates of growth in per-capita GDP and higher levels for EHT, but we cannot make any additional inference unless we properly control other

---

[5] Notice that this should be complemented with the evidence reported in Table 2.

covariates, such that country fixed effects, which would capture institutional common features.

In fact, country fixed effect would affect the intercept of the relationship between the variables here considered and hence the estimated correlation between the two.[6] Figure 4 reports the relationship between the rate of change in EHT between 1996 and 2000 and the log of per-capita GDP in 1996. The intuition for this graph is that countries that have a high per-capita GDP level might be keen to invest in ICT.

Coming now to the relationship between per-capita GDP and the proxy for human capital (i.e. the share of population with tertiary education or more), in Fig. 5 we notice immediately a very strong positive correlation, which seems to be confirmed when looking at rates of change between 1996 and 1997 (Fig. 6).

Since the paramount focus of the paper is on the determinants of growth, in Fig. 7 we plot the relationship between the rate of change of per-capita GDP (in the 1996–2000 interval) and the initial level for the proxy for human capital. Once again, the picture cannot be read unambiguously.

Both positive and negative correlations are consistent with this simple graph, and hence it is necessary to control other covariates (especially country fixed effect) that might affect the intercepts for different regions; in section this point will be discussed in detail. In this case controlling country-fixed effects is even more important since usually education systems are usually quite similar within countries, while varying much across-countries.

From Fig. 8 that we do not find a clear relationship between the log of per-capita GDP in 1996 and the rate of change of the share of population with more than tertiary education between 1996 and 2000. Once again covariates and country fixed effects might be responsible for this (on the importance of such variables, see, for example, Rodriguez-Pose and Fratesi (2004)).

Finally, Fig. 9 illustrates the relationship between the rate of change of per-capita GDP (between 1996 and 2000) and the level of per-capita GDP in 1996. Under the absolute convergence hypothesis, we expect a negative relationship (compatible with the data-plot if we separate between two groups[7]), whereas we cannot say much about the conditional convergence

---

[6] Country fixed effects are less relevant, when relationships between rates of change are looked at, since they get differenntiated away when computing the latter ones.

[7] This may be consistent with the findings by Fagerberg and Verspagen (1996) and the existence of convergence only of a club of wealthier regions in Europe.

hypothesis, which states that regions converge to their region-specific steady state. If European regions shared a common technology and common values for the conditioning variables (human capital, technological development, investment, capital depreciation etc.), we would expect absolute or unconditional convergence, but we know that these territorial units are quite heterogeneous, so that our prior does not support unconditional convergence.

To give complete picture we mention the time-path for the standard deviation of per-capita GDP among the European regions per the period 1988–2000. Fig. 10 confirms the view that regions are characterised by high and persistent GDP inequalities and club convergence:[8] within some countries income dispersion decreases, whereas in others (mainly newly industrialised counties in the EU) we observe an increase in dispersion. Overall, the values for the standard deviations show persistent regional inequalities over the time span analysed.

5 Estimation

We test for both absolute and conditional convergence. The conditioning variables are country fixed effects, the log of EHT, its rate of change and the log of human capital investment, defined as the share of the population with tertiary education or more. A major issue in cross-section region growth models over time is the choice of the appropriate estimation strategy. One option is to estimate absolute (equation) and conditional (equation) convergence using cross sections. This implies taking a given time interval (sometimes 20 or 30 years long) and regress the (average) growth rate for per-capita GDP over the initial level of per-capita GDP and a set of covariates. As more thoroughly discussed in Islam (1995), Caselli, Esquivel and Lefort (1996) this approach is basically affected by omitted variable bias, because the initial level of technology – which is, together with its rate of change, one of the determinants of per capita GDP growth in a neighbourhood of the steady state – is not observable and is hence incorporated in the error terms.

This results in inconsistent parameter estimates and, particularly, in a downward bias for the estimate of the parameter representing the speed of convergence only if the level of technology is likely to be (positively) correlated with the conditioning variables. The problem can be solved (if we

---

[8] Values refer to the standard deviation of GDP distribution across regions (mostly NUTS 2 regions). Computations are implemented on natural base logarithms values to avoid scale effects.

assume log linearity) with the use of panel data, since fixed effects can be differenced away without having to make any assumptions about the covariance between observables and unobservables. In our framework, the omitted variable problem is partly solved, by the fact that we actually have a proxy for both the initial level of technology and its rate of change.

Moreover, even in a cross section, we are able to control country fixed effects, and this allows us to control many cross-region within country common factors. This implies that the likely positive correlation between unobservables and observables is much smaller than in typical OLS estimation of cross-country growth models. Given the very short number of years available and that we have values for the human capital proxy only for years 1996 and 1997, we only implement Least Squares Dummy variables, being aware that our estimates might be downward biased because of inconsistency.

In Table 4 (the full description of the variables is provided in Table 3) we notice a strong evidence of absolute convergence if we do not control country fixed effects (strong version of absolute convergence), while the evidence weakens once we introduce control variables (weak version of absolute convergence). This is quite puzzling, since it goes contrary to our expectations (i.e. once controlled common country effects, if regions are similar among themselves we would find weak absolute convergence). This outcome can be attributed to either downward biased estimates of absolute convergence which are mitigated through country dummy variables or to country specific variables as being the main source for regional convergence, as some authors argue (see Rodriguez-Pose and Fratesi (2004)). Given that all the country dummies are highly significant and given that, as previously documented, the conditioning variables show quite relevant cross-region variations, we turn to a test of conditional convergence where control variables are ICT related proxies for the steady state. Our results show that our proxies for ICT diffusion (EHT) and its rate of change enter with positive and significant coefficients.

Obviously, these results should be interpreted with care. Yet, if we are ready to assume that what drives EHT are mainly fundamental developments in ICT, then our results indicate the importance of these technologies in determining regional growth performances. As for the proxy of investment in human capital, we find a negative and significant coefficient. Though puzzling, this is not new, since many studies prior to ours have found similar results.

The reasons for this might be various: our proxy could poorly perform or it could be that effective human capital, once controlling technology, ceases to be significant; for instance, agents might over-react to skill-biased technological changes creating an excess of over-qualified workforce which finds no room in the labour market and ends up depressing growth in the short or medium run. This effect should properly work in the long run, when skilled workers and technologies set up a virtuous circle for growth (for a similar argument see Acemoglu (1998)).

6 Conclusion and Policy Implications

With the Lisbon and Gothenburg strategy "Making of Europe the first knowledge economy in the world", the Commission views the dissemination of knowledge as an important tool to achieve social and economic cohesion. ICT diffusion is considered, together with human capital, one of the two pillars of the knowledge economy: technological progress, embedded in new machines and products that can be more efficiently used by a more skilled and educated workforce, is considered the growth engine for an ageing and enlarged Europe. Given that technology adoption and the skill composition of the workforce depend upon conditions determined at the regional level, the previous considerations have immediate consequences for regional unbalances: regions endowed with a more skilled and educated workforce would tend to adopt and utilise ICT technology faster and more productively and this will ultimately have the effect of amplifying regional disparities.

In our paper, we have examined and tested whether differences in proxies for human capital and ICT diffusion tend to be positively associated with growth rates so that a convergence process can be triggered within a diverse and unified EU. On the other hand, we have documented the existence of wide regional disparities in terms of both human capital investment (proxied by the share of the population with at least tertiary education) and ICT diffusion (proxied by the share of the population employed in high-tech jobs), and we have estimated a growth equation in which the per-capita GDP growth rate over the relevant period (1996–2000) is regressed over the log of its initial value, the log of human capital investment, the log of ICT diffusion and its growth rate (following an extended version of the basic Solow model). Our results indicate that proxies for the initial level of the technology (the log of ICT diffusion) and for technological progress (the growth rate of ICT diffusion) are positively and significantly correlated with per-capita GDP growth rates.

On the other hand, we find that once controlling for technological variables, human capital enters with a negative and significant coefficient.

This result is puzzling, especially if we think that there might exist technology-human capital complementarities, but is not new to some relevant empirical findings, such as the case of southern Italy. There is a large literature trying to verify the robustness of estimates of the effects of human capital to changes in the variable that proxies human capital (in our case we have only one potential candidate for human capital and hence we could not try alternative specifications).

We interpret our results as an indication that ICT diffusion has indeed a positive effect on growth. At the same time, we realise that the growth-regression approach adopted in this paper is not fully suitable to grasp the determinants of cross-regional differences in technology diffusion and human capital investment. Hence, we believe that the issues of ICT production and ICT adoption should constitute a priority in the regional policy agenda: ICT as an important part of technology has a high potential in the process of catching up for European regions and more widely on the ground of regional cohesion if social features of ICT applications are considered.

This tool needs to be handled with care: physical investments cannot boost such an important process by themselves; this tool should rather be properly combined with human investment, the basic ingredient for growth in the knowledge economy and society. Further empirical and theoretical investigations of the determinants of ICT adoption, at sectorial or firm level, are needed, so that to get a clearer picture of the factors that are at the roots of the regional disparities and the opportunity to narrow them with the help of ICT would be delineated. Data availability is the main constraint at the present time.

7 Appendix: Tables and Figures

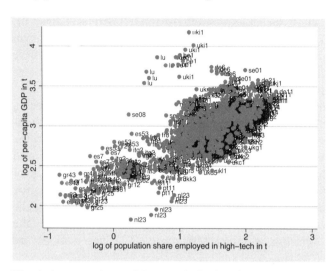

Fig. 1. A comparison of GDP and ICT levels across EU regions

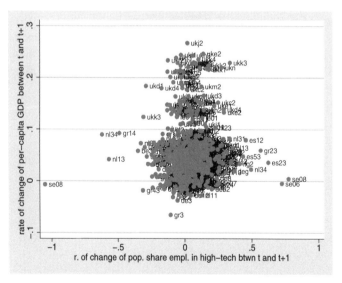

Fig. 2. A comparison of GDP and ICT growth rates across EU regions

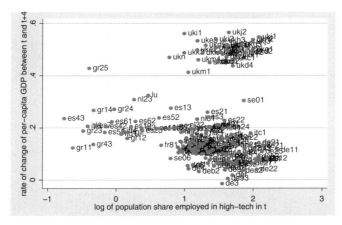

Fig. 3. A comparison of GDP growth rates and ICT levels across EU regions

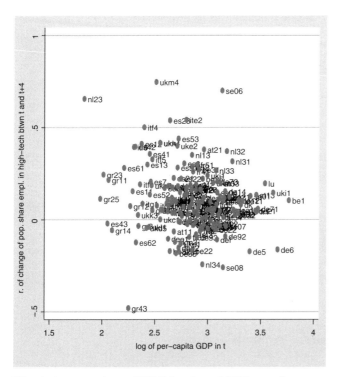

Fig. 4. A comparison of GDP levels and ICT growth rates across EU regions

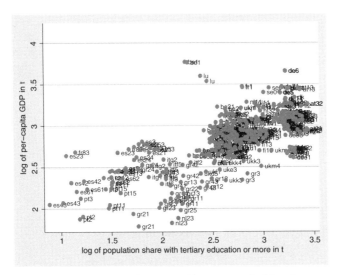

Fig. 5. A comparison of GDP and human capital levels across EU regions

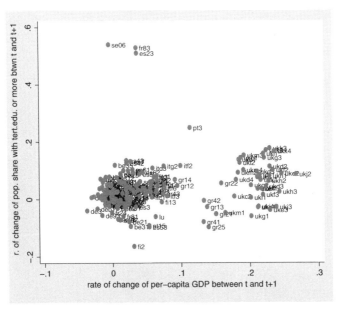

Fig. 6. A comparison of GDP and human capital growth rates across EU regions

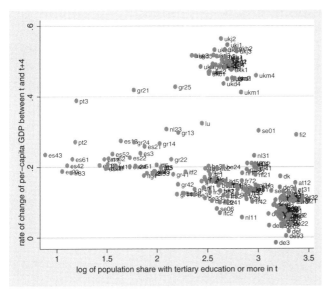

Fig. 7. A comparison of GDP growth rates and human capital levels across EU regions

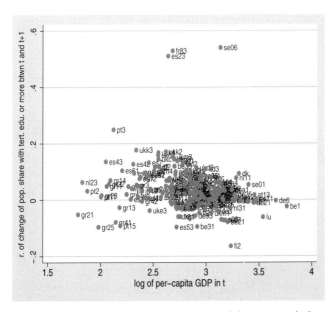

Fig. 8. A comparison of GDP levels and human capital growth rates across EU regions

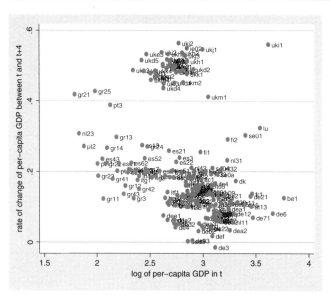

Fig. 9. A comparison of GDP growth rates and GDP levels across EU regions

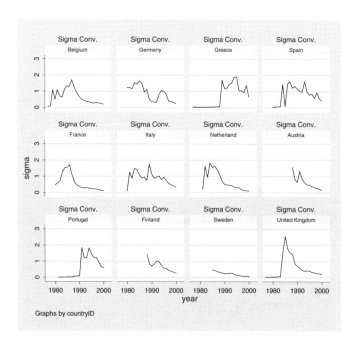

Fig. 10. Sigma convergence: inequality across regions over time and by State

Table 1. The NUTS considered in the analysis are in *italic*, usually NUTS 2 level, unless data availability constraints to higher aggregations

European NUTS labels		
be Belgium	Fr France	es Spain
Be1 Region de Bxl-Capitale	fr1 Île de France	es1 Noroeste
be2 Vlaams Gewest	fr2 Bassin Parisien	es11 Galicia
be21 Prov. Antwerpen	fr21 Champagne-Ardenne	es12 Principado de Asturias
be22 Prov. Limburg (B)	fr22 Picardie	es13 Cantabria
Be23 Prov. Oost-Vlaanderen	fr23 Haute-Normandie	es2 Noreste
be24 Prov. Vlaams Brabant	fr24 Centre	es21 Pais Vasco
be25 Prov. West-Vlaanderen	fr25 Basse-Normandie	es22 Comunidad Foral de Navarra
be3 Region Wallonne	fr26 Bourgogne	es23 La Rioja
be31 Prov. Brabant Wallon	fr3 Nord - Pas-de-Calais	es24 Aragon
be32 Prov. Hainaut	fr4 Est	es3 Comunidad de Madrid
be33 Prov. Liege	fr41 Lorraine	es4 Centro (ES)
be34 Prov. Luxem-bourg (B)	fr42 Alsace	es41 Castilla y Leon
be35 Prov. Namur	fr43 Franche-Comte	es42 Castilla-la Mancha
dk Denmark	fr5 Ouest	es43 Extremadura
de Germany	fr51 Pays de la Loire	es5 Este
de1 Baden-Wurttemberg	fr52 Bretagne	es51 Cataluna
de11 Stuttgart	fr53 Poitou-Charentes	es52 Comunidad Valenciana
de12 Karlsruhe	fr6 Sud-Ouest	es53 Illes Balears
de13 Freiburg	fr61 Aquitaine	es6 Sur
de14 Tubingen	fr62 Midi-Pyrenees	es61 Andalucia
de2 Bayern	fr63 Limousin	es62 Region de Murcia
de21 Oberbayern	fr7 Centre-Est	es7 Canarias (ES)
de22 Niederbayern	fr71 Rhone-Alpes	pt Portugal
de23 Oberpfalz	fr72 Auvergne	pt1 Continente (PT)
de24 Oberfranken	fr8 Mediterranee	pt11 Norte
de25 Mittelfranken	fr81 Languedoc-Roussillon	pt15 Algarve
de26 Unterfranken	fr82 Provence-Alpes-Cote d'Azur	pt2 Regiao Autonoma dos Acores (PT)
de27 Schwaben	fr83 Corse	pt3 Regiao Autonoma da Madeira (PT)

Table 1. (continued)

European NUTS labels		
be Belgium	Fr France	es Spain
de3 Berlin	ie Ireland	fi Finland
de4 Brandenburg	ie01 Border, Midlands and Western	fi1 Manner-Suomi
de5 Bremen	ie02 Southern and Eastern	fi13 Ita-Suomi
de6 Hamburg	uk United Kingdom	fi2 Aland
de7 Hessen	ukc North East	at Austria
de71 Darmstadt	ukc1 Tees Valley and Durham	at1 Ostosterreich
de72 Giessen	ukc2 Northumberland, Tyne and Wear	at11 Burgenland
de73 Kassel	ukd North West (including Merseyside)	at12 Niederosterreich
de8 Mecklenburg-Vorpommern	ukd1 Cumbria	at13 Wien
de9 Niedersachsen	ukd2 Cheshire	at2 Sudosterreich
de91 Braunschweig	ukd3 Greater Manchester	at21 Karnten
de92 Hannover	ukd4 Lancashire	at22 Steiermark
de93 Luneburg	ukd5 Merseyside	at3 Westosterreich
de94 Weser-Ems	uke Yorkshire and The Humber	at31 Oberosterreich
dea Nordrhein-Westfalen	uke1 East Riding and North Lincolnshire	at32 Salzburg
dea1 Dusseldorf	uke2 North Yorkshire	at33 Tirol
dea2 Koln	uke3 South Yorkshire	at34 Vorarlberg
dea3 Munster	uke4 West Yorkshire	it Italy
dea4 Detmold	ukf East Midlands	itc1 Piemonte
dea5 Arnsberg	ukf1 Derbyshire and Notting-hamshire	itc2 Valle d'Aosta
deb Rheinland-Pfalz	ukf2 Leicestershire, Rutland and Northants	itc3 Liguria
deb1 Koblenz	ukf3 Lincolnshire	itc4 Lombardia
deb2 Trier	ukg West Midlands	itc5 Trentino-Alto Adige
deb3 Rheinhessen-Pfalz	ukg1 Herefordshire, Worcestershire and Warks	itd3 Veneto
dec Saarland	ukg2 Shropshire and Staffordshire	itd4 Friuli-Venezia Giulia
ded Sachsen	ukg3 West Midlands	itd5 Emilia-Romagna
ded1 Chemnitz	ukh Eastern	ite1 Toscana
ded2 Dresden	ukh1 East Anglia	ite2 Umbria
ded3 Leipzig	ukh2 Bedfordshire, Hertfordshire	ite3 Marche
dee Sachsen-Anhalt	ukh3 Essex	ite4 Lazio
dee1 Dessau	uki London	itf1 Abruzzo
dee2 Halle	uki1 Inner London	itf2 Molise
dee3 Magdeburg	uki2 Outer London	itf3 Campania
def Schleswig-Holstein	ukj South East	itf4 Puglia

Table 1. (continued)

European NUTS labels		
be Belgium	Fr France	es Spain
deg Thuringen	ukj1 Berkshire, Bucks and Oxfordshire	itf5 Basilicata
gr Greece	ukj2 Surrey, East and West Sussex	itf6 Calabria
gr1 Voreia Ellada	ukj3 Hampshire and Isle of Wight	itg1 Sicilia
gr11 Anatoliki Makedonia, Thraki	ukj4 Kent	itg2 Sardegna
gr12 Kentriki Makedonia	ukk South West	lu Luxembourg (Grand-Duche)
gr13 Dytiki Makedonia	ukk1 Gloucestershire, Wiltshire and North Somerset	nl Netherlands
gr14 Thessalia	ukk2 Dorset and Somerset	nl1 Noord-Nederland
gr2 Kentriki Ellada	ukk3 Cornwall and Isles of Scilly	nl11 Groningen
gr21 Ipeiros	ukk4 Devon	nl12 Friesland
gr22 Ionia Nisia	ukl Wales	nl13 Drenthe
gr23 Dytiki Ellada	ukl1 West Wales and The Valleys	nl2 Oost-Nederland
gr24 Sterea Ellada	ukl2 East Wales	nl21 Overijssel
gr25 Peloponnisos	ukm Scotland	nl22 Gelderland
gr3 Attiki	ukm1 North Eastern Scotland	nl23 Flevoland
gr4 Nisia Aigaiou, Kriti	ukm2 Eastern Scotland	nl3 West-Nederland
gr41 Voreio Aigaio	ukm3 South Western Scotland	nl31 Utrecht
gr42 Notio Aigaio	ukm4 Highlands and Islands	nl32 Noord-Holland
gr43 Kriti	ukn Northern Ireland	nl33 Zuid-Holland
se Sweden		nl34 Zeeland
se01 Stockholm		nl4 Zuid-Nederland
se02 ostra Mellans-verige		nl41 Noord-Brabant
se04 Sydsverige		nl42 Limburg (NL)
se06 Norra Mellans-verige		
se07 Mellersta Norrland		
se08 ovre Norrland		
se09 SmAland med oarna		
se0a Vastsverige		

Table 2. Groups of regions by average growth rates between 1996 and 2000 of GDP and ICTE [total employment in high tech] in deviation from mean values

High GDP growth rates, High ICTE growth	High GDP growth rates, Low ICTE growth	Low GDP growth rates, High ICTE growth	Low GDP growth rates, Low ICTE growth	
be31 Prov. Brabant Wallon	gr14 Thessalia	be1 Region de BxlCapitale	be22 Prov. Limburg (B)	itc1 Piemonte
es13 Cantabria	gr25 Peloponnisos	be21 Prov. Antwerpen	be23 Prov. OostVlaanderen	itc3 Liguria
es21 Pais Vasco	gr23 Attiki	be25 Prov. West Vlaanderen	be24 Prov. Vlaams Brabant	itd3 Veneto
es22 Communidad de Navarra	es43 Extremadura	be34 Prov. Liege	be32 Prov. Hainaut	itd4 Friuli Venezia Giulia
es3 Communidad de Madrid	es62 Region de Murcia	be34 Prov. Luxembourg (B)	be35 Prov. Namur	itd5 Emilia Romagna
es53 Illes Balears	ukc1 Tees Valley and Dirham	de11 Stuttgart	dk Denmark	ite1 Toscana
es61 Andalucia	ukc2 Northumberland, Tyne and Wear	de12 Karlsruhe	de13 Freiburg	itf1 Abruzzo
es7 Canarias (ES)	ukd North West (including Merseyside)	de14 Tubingen	de21 Oberdayern	itf2 Molise
lu Luxembourg (GrandDuche)	ukd1 Cumbria	de23 Oberpfalz	de22 Niederbayern	itg1 Sicilia
nl23 Flevoland	ukd2 Cheshire	de24 Oberfranken	de25 Mittelfranken	itg2 Sardegna
nl31 Utrecht	ukd3 Greater Manchester	de27 Schwaben	de26 Unterfranken	nl11 Groningen
nl32 North Holland	ukd5 Merseyside	de73 Kassel	de3 Berlin	nl21 Overijssel
nl41 NoordBrabant	uke1 East Riding and North Lincolnshire	dea3 Munster	de4 Brandenburg	nl22 Gelderland

Table 2. (continued)

High GDP growth rates, High ICTE growth	High GDP growth rates, Low ICTE growth	Low GDP growth rates, High ICTE growth	Low GDP growth rates, Low ICTE growth	
se01 Stockholm	uke4 West Yorkshire	dea4 Detmold	de5 Bremen	nl34 Zeeland
ukd4 Lancashire	ukf1 Debyshire and Nottinghamshire	dee3 Magdeburg	de6 Hamburg	at11 Burgenland
uke2 North Yorkshire	ukf2 Leicestershire, Rutland and Northands	gr11 Anatoliki Makedonia, Thraki	de71 Darmstadt	at12 Niederosterreich
uke3 South Yorkshire	ukg1 Herefordshire, Worcestershire and Works	gr12 Kentriki Makedonia	de72 Giessen	at22 Steiermark
ukf3 Lincolnshire	ukg2 Shropshire and Staffordshire	gr23 Dytiki Ellada	de8 Mecklenburg Vorpommeern	at31 Oberosterreich
ukh1 East Anglia	ukg3 West Midlands	es11 Galicia	de91 Braunschweig	at32 Salzburg
ukh2 Bedfordshire, Hertfordshire	uki2 Outer London	es12 Pricipado de Asturias	de92 Hannover	at34 Vorarlberg
ukh3 Essex	ukj2 Surrey, East and West Sussex	es23 La Rioja	de93 Luneburg	fi13 Ita Suomi
uki1 Inner London	ukj3 Hampshire and Isle of Wight	es24 Aragon	de94 WeserEms	se02 Ostra Mellansverige
ukj1 Berkshire, Bucks and Oxfordshire	ukk3 Cornwall and Isle of Scilly	es41 Castilla y Leon	dea1 Dusseldorf	se07 Mellersta Norrland
ukj4 Kent	ukl1 West Walles and The Valleys	es42 Castillala Macha	dea2 Koln	se08 Ovre Norrland
ukk1 Gloucestershire, Wiltshire and North Somerset	ukm2 Eastern Scotland	es51 Cataluna	dea5 Arnsberg	
ukk2 Dorset and Somerset	ukm3 South Western Scotland	fr22 Picardie	dec Saarland	
ukk4 Devon		fr24 Centre	dee1 Dessau	

Table 2. (continued)

High GDP growth rates, High ICTE growth	High GDP growth rates, Low ICTE growth	Low GDP growth rates, High ICTE growth	Low GDP growth rates, Low ICTE growth
ukl2 East Wales		fr26 Bour-gonge	dee2 Halle
ukm1 North Eas-tern Scotland		fr3 Nord Pasde Calais	def Schleswig Holstein
ukm4 Highlands and Islands		fr41 Lorraine	deg Thu-ringen
ukn Northern Ire-land		fr51Pays de la Loire	gr24 Ste-rea Ellada
		fr52 Bretagne	gr43 Kriti
		fr62 MidiPy-renees	fr1 lle de France
		itc4 Lombar-dia	fr21 Champag-ne Arden-ne
		ite2 Umbria	fr23 Haute Norman-die
		ite3 Marche	fr25 Basse Norman-die
		ite4 Lazio	fr42 Alsace

Table 3. Variables concerned in the estimation procedure

	Labels in the estimation table
Variable	Explanation
Dep. var.	Per capita GDP growth rate between 1996 and 2000
lnGDPt	log of per-capita GDP in t
lnEHT	log of population share employed in high-tech in t
DlnEHT	r. of change of pop. share empl. in high-tech btwn t and t+4
lnHK	log of population share with tertiary education or more in t
n+d	Annual population growth rate and depreciation (0.05)
λ	Speed of convergence
*	statistical signif. at 10% (robust t-stats in brackets)
**	statistical signif. at 5% (robust t-stats in brackets)
***	statistical signif. at 1% (robust t-stats in brackets)

Table 4. Absolute and conditional β convergence

Dep. var.: gdp growth rates	Testing for convergence		
	Abs. Conv	Abs. Conv. (country)	Cond. Conv.
lnGDPt	−0.142	−0.017	−0.036
	(5.58)[c]	(−0.91)	(1.91)[a]
lnEHT			0.038
			(4.47)[c]
DlnEHT			0.038
			(1.88)[a]
lnHK			−0.069
			(3.44)[c]
n+d			0.085
			−1.05
Denmark		0.036	0.074
		(2.98)[c]	(4.93)[c]
Germany		−0.074	−0.031
		(6.27)[c]	(1.79)[a]
Greece		0.071	0.078
		(2.30)[b]	(2.25)[b]
Spain		0.066	0.012
		(4.33)[c]	(−0.6)
France		−0.014	0.003
		(−1.23)	(−0.27)
Ireland		0.365	0
		(11.97)[c]	(.)
Italy		0.025	0.026
		(1.95)[a]	(2.37)[b]
Luxembourg		0.19	0.213
		(12.85)[c]	(12.35)[c]
Netherland		0.043	0.066
		(2.28)[b]	(3.65)[c]
Austria		−0.023	0.037
		(1.97)[a]	(1.86)[a]
Portugal		0.112	0
		(2.55)[b]	(.)
Finland		0.105	0.102
		(3.94)[c]	(5.48)[c]
Sweden		0.016	0.048
		(−0.59)	(−1.3)
United Kingdom		0.348	0.337
		(26.46)[c]	(25.51)[c]
Constant	0.619	0.195	0.581
	(8.45)[c]	(3.37)[c]	(2.61)[c]
Observations	200	200	175
R-squared	0.11	0.92	0.94
λ	0.038	0.004	0.009

8 References

Acemoglu, D. (1998) Why Do New Technologies Complement Skills? Directed Technical Change and Wage Inequality. The Quarterly Journal of Economics, pp. 1055–1089.

Barro, R. J., X. Sala-i-Martin (1992a) Convergence. The Journal of Political Economy, 100(2): 223–251.

Barro R. J., X. Sala-i-Martin (1992b) Regional Growth and Migration: A Japan-United States Comparison. Journal of the Japanese and International Economies, 6:312–346.

Bramanti A., Maggioni M. A. (1997) La dinamica dei sistemi produttivi territoriali: teorie, tecniche, politiche. Franco Angeli.

Campanelli L. (1998) Competenze, apprendimento e teoria d'impresa. Economia e Politica Industriale, 98(1): 22–64.

Caselli, F., Esquivel, G., Lefort F. (1996) Reopening the convergence debate: A new look at cross-country growth empirics. Journal of Economic Growth, (1):363–389.

Castells, M. (2000) The rise of the network society. In The Information Age: Economy, Society and Culture. Oxford: Blackwell.

David, P., Foray D., (2002) An Introduction to the Economy of the Knowledge Society. Blackwell.

European Commission (2004) A new partnership for cohesion: convergence competitiveness cooperation. Third report on economic and social cohesion.

Fagerberg, J., Verspagen B. (1996) Heading for divergence? regional growth in Europe reconsidered. Journal of Common Market Studies, 34(3): 431–448.

Islam, N. (1995) Growth empirics: A panel data approach. Quarterly Journal of Economics, (110): 1127–1170.

Magrini. S. , (2003) Regional (Di)Convergence. Ca' Foscari N.D.L., 03(04).

Mankiw G., D. Weil, Romer P. (1992a) A contribution to the empirics of growth. Quarterly Journal of Economics, 107(2): 407–37, 1992a.

Mankiw N., Romer, D., Weil, D. (1992b) A contribution to the empirics of economic growth. Quarterly Journal of Economics, (107): 407–437.

Porter. M. E. (2003) The economic performance of regions. Regional Studies, 37(6-7):549–578.

Quah., D. (1993) Galton's fallacy and tests of the convergence hypothesis. The Scandanavian Journal of Economics, 95 (4):427–443.

Quah. D. T. (1996a) Empirics for Economic Growth and Convergence. European Economic Review, 40:1353–1375.

Quah. D. T. (1996b) Regional Convergence Clusters Across Europe. European Economic Review, 40:951–958.

Riggi, M. R., Bramanti, A. , Maggioni M. A., (2002) A Review of Existing Indicators Related to ICT and RegionalDisparities. a Stocktaking Exercise. New Economy Statistical Indicators System, Milano: CERTeT, Università Bocconi.

Rodriguez-Pose A., Fratesi. U., (2004) Between Development and Social Policies: The Impact of European Structural Funds in Objective 1 Regions. Regional Studies, 38(1):97–113.

Romer., P., (1986) Increasing Returns and Long-Run Growth. Journal of Political Economy, (94): 1002–1037.

Sala-i-Martin., X., (1996) Regional cohesion: Evidence and theories of regional growth and convergence. European Economic Review, 40(6):1325–1352.

Solow., R.M. (1956) A Contribution to the Theory of Economic Growth. Quarterly Journal of Economics, 70(1): 65–94.

Regional Disparities and the Effects of Innovation Activities on Regional Integration

George M. Korres[1,*], Constantine Tsamadias[2]
and Panagiotis Liargkovas[3]

[1] Assistant Professor, Department of Geography, University of the Aegean,
University Hill, Mytilene: 81100, Greece.
Also Visiting Fellow (Oct. 2006/ Feb. 2007) at the University of Leeds, Institute of
Communication Studies, Leeds LS2-9J, United Kingdom
[2] Assistant Professor with Harokopio University of Athens, Department of Home
Economics and Ecology. 70, El. Venizelou str., Athens 17671, Greece
[3] Associate Professor, University of Peloponesse, Department of Economics,
Tripolis, Greece

1 Introduction

The EU has played a major role in disseminating good practice in Research and Development (R&D) policy by helping to create a "European Research, Technology, Development and Innovation Community", where decision-makers, researchers, and other interested parties can communicate and work together, in both formal and informal ways, in official advisory committees, specific R&D programmes and policy exchange initiatives. By assisting in this, and through its influence on policy formation and implementation, EU policy has indirectly contributed to closing the R&TD and innovation gap between member states and regions, and, by changing the culture, it has, in some respects, improved the policy planning process.

To improve the quality of regional development strategies the Commission intends to support the latest ideas, which have not yet been adequately exploited. They are expected to provide the regions with the scope for experimentation, which they sometimes lack but need to meet the challenges of the information society and to make their economies more competitive.

* Email: gkorres@hol.gr

The Commission has laid down three working topics for ERDF innovative actions in 2000–2006: (1) Regional economies based on knowledge and technological innovation; (2) Information society at the service of regional development; and (3) Regional identity and sustainable development. The European Union is increasingly becoming a knowledge-based economy and society. The development of knowledge has a direct effect on competitiveness and employment as well as on the way society functions in general.

The only possible way for technologically weak countries to converge and *catch up* on the advanced countries is to imitate the more productive technologies. The outcome of the international innovation and diffusion process is uncertain; this process may generate a pattern in which some countries follow diverging trends or a pattern where countries converge towards a common trend. This article attempts to investigate and measure the role and effects of European innovation policy on the convergence process and elimination of regional disparities in member states.

2 Regional Disparities: Regional Domestic Product (RDP), Population and Employment

The economic development of a region is, as a rule, expressed in terms of its Gross Domestic Product (GDP). It is also an indicator frequently used as a basis for comparisons between regions. But what exactly does it mean? And how can comparability be established for regions of different size and different currencies?

Regions of different size achieve different GDP levels. However, a real comparison can only be made by indicating the regional GDP per inhabitant for the region in question. This is where the distinction drawn between place of work and place of residence becomes significant: Gross Domestic Product (GDP) measures the economic performance achieved within national or regional boundaries, regardless of whether this was attributable to resident or non-resident employed persons. Reference to GDP per inhabitant is therefore only straightforward if all employed persons engaged in generating this value are also residents of the region in question.

In areas with a high proportion of commuters, regional GDP per inhabitant can be extremely high, particularly in such economic centres, as for instance, London or Vienna, Hamburg, Prague or Luxembourg, and relatively low in the surrounding regions, even if these are characterised by high household purchasing power or disposable income.

Regional GDP is calculated in the currency of the country in question. In order to make GDP comparable between countries, it is converted into euros using the official average exchange rate for the given calendar year. However, not all differences in price levels between countries are reflected in exchange rates. In order to compensate for this effect, GDP is converted, which currency conversion rates being used, known as Purchasing Power Parities (PPPs), to an artificial common currency, called Purchasing Power Standards (PPS).

Prague (Czech Republic), the region with the highest GDP per inhabitant in the new Member States, has already risen to 16th place with PPS 31 639 (149% of the EU-25 average) among the 268 NUTS 2 regions of the countries examined here (EU-25 plus Bulgaria and Romania). It should be noted, however, that Prague is an exception. The next regions of those joining the EU in May 2004 follow a long way behind: Bratislavský kraj (Slovakia) is in 65th place with PPS 23 782 (112%), Közép-Magyarország (Hungary) is 147th with PPS 18 993 (89%), Cyprus is 157th with PPS 18 281 (86%), Malta is 179th with PPS 16 221 (76%) and Mazowieckie (Poland) 196th.

In 2001, the highest per capita GDP was more than twice the lowest in 12 of the 19 countries examined here incorporating NUTS 2 regions. The largest regional differences are in the United Kingdom, where there is a factor of 4.4 between the two extreme values (Inner London: 288% of the EU-25 average; Cornwall and the Isles of Scilly: 65%), and in Belgium, with a factor of 3.1. In ten countries, the highest regional per capita GDP is between twice and three times that of the lowest. Half of this group of countries is made up of the older Member States, plus four of the new Member States and Romania.

Therefore, comparatively marked regional disparities in per capita GDP therefore emerge in both the old and the new Member States. Moderate regional disparities in per capita GDP (i.e. factors between the highest and the lowest value of less than two) are, however, almost exclusively found in the older Member States. This is particularly true of Sweden (Stockholm: 159%; Norra Mellansverige: 98%) and Ireland (Southern and Eastern: 141%; Border, Midland and Western: 97%). Bulgaria (Yugozapaden: 40%; Yuzhen tsentralen: 24%) is the only country in this group that is not one of the older Member States.

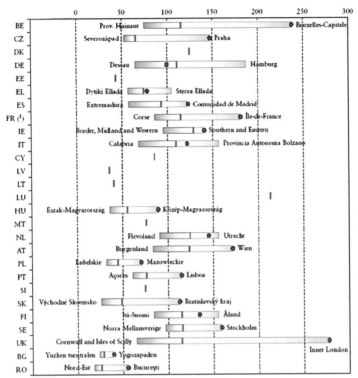

Fig. 1. GDP per capita (in PPS) 2001, NUTS 2 level, in percentage rate of EU-25 average (EU-25 = 100)

Economically dynamic regions, whose per capita GDP increased by more than one percentage point when compared with the average, are shown in orange and red. Less dynamic regions (those with a fall of more than one percentage point in per capita GDP as against the EU-25 average) are shown in yellow. Figures range from + 21.2 percentage points for Inner London in the United Kingdom to – 7.1 percentage points for Schwaben in Germany. Of the ten most dynamic NUTS 2 regions, three are in Greece and one each in the Czech Republic, Ireland, the Netherlands, Hungary, Slovakia, the United Kingdom and Romania. The fastest growing regions are therefore scattered relatively broadly across the 27 countries examined here.

Conversely, six of the ten least dynamic regions are in Germany, with two in the United Kingdom and each in Austria and Romania. Upon closer examination, we can see that between 1999 and 2001, numerous somewhat peripheral regions of the enlarged European Union managed to catch up by comparison with central regions with higher per capita GDP. This is particularly true of Ipeiros (+ 9.6 percentage points) and Peloponnissos (+ 9.3) in Greece, Região Autónoma da Madeira (+ 6.7) in Portugal and Pohjois-Suomi in Finland (+ 5.1), but also of Alentejo (+ 1.4) in Portugal, Andalucía (+ 1.4) in Spain and South Western Scotland in the United Kingdom (+ 1.3).

2.1 The Regional Employment

The employment rate of the 15–64 age group represents employed persons aged 15–64 as a percentage of the population of the same age group. In 2002, this employment rate was generally lower in Southern Europe. Poland's low employment rate was an exception in the northern part of Europe. There were 24 NUTS 2 regions with an employment rate below 50% — two in Spain, five in France (including all four overseas regions), six in Italy, one in Hungary and five each in Poland and Bulgaria. Of the six Italian regions below 50%, three (Campania, Calabria and Sardegna) had the lowest rates (41.9%) of all European NUTS 2 regions studied. In all Polish regions except two (Lubelskie, Mazowieckie), the employment rate of the 15–64 age group was less than 55%.

NUTS 2 regions in which the employment rate exceeded 75% in 2002 (altogether there were 21 of them) can be found in the Netherlands (4), Finland (2), Sweden (3) and the UK (11). Denmark (comprising one NUTS 2 region) also had an employment rate above this level. Among the new Member States, only six NUTS 2 regions exceeded 65%: four in the Czech Republic (the capital region Praha, Střední Čechy, Jihozápad, Severovýchod), one in Slovakia (the capital region Bratislavský kraj) and Cyprus (which, like Denmark, comprises a single NUTS 2 region).

In most countries, there was a positive trend in employment between 2001 and 2002. Only two of the former EU-15 Member States recorded a decrease in total employment (Germany 0.7% and Denmark 0.5%); the highest increase was observed in Spain (2%, representing an increase of 312,000 employed persons), Italy (1.9% or 315,000 employed persons) and Ireland (1.9% or 33,000 employed persons). The intensity of the decline in the new Member States, and especially Romania, was substantially greater: 9.5% in Romania (decrease of 1.01 million employed persons), 3% in Poland (decrease of 424,000 employed persons) and 5.5% in Lithuania (decrease of 81,000 employed persons). The biggest upturn was recorded in Latvia (2.5%, representing an increase of 24,000 employed persons) and Bulgaria (1.5%, or 41,000 employed persons).

In 17 countries, most NUTS 2 regions recorded a rise in 2001–2002 in total employment – this was the case for Ireland, the U.K., Spain, France, the Netherlands, Austria, Sweden, Finland, Italy, Greece, the Czech Republic, Hungary and Bulgaria and also the Member State Luxembourg, Cyprus, Latvia and Estonia, each comprising one NUTS 2 region.

The greatest decrease in total employment (more than 5%) was recorded in no fewer than seven Romanian regions, in Poland (Mazowieckie, Opolskie, Podlaskie, Warmińsko-Mazurskie), the Ionian Islands in Greece and Lithuania. In Poland, the greater absolute decrease (108,000 employed persons) was observed in the region of Mazowieckie; in Romania it was the region of Nord-Est (214,000 employed persons). At the other extreme, the most positive development in total employment in 2002 (increase of more than 5% in comparison with the previous year) was in Spain (Ciudad Autónoma de Melilla), France (Champagne-Ardenne, Poitou-Charentes, Languedoc-Roussillon and also two overseas regions, Guyane and Réunion, despite their high unemployment rates), Greece (Ipeiros, Sterea Ellada, Peloponnissos, Voreio Aigaio, Notio Aigaio) and Portugal (Região Autónoma da Madeira).

The unemployment rate, representing unemployed persons as a percentage of the economically active population (i.e. employed persons and the unemployed), stood at 7.7% in the former EU-15 Member States, at 14.9% in the new Member States, at 18.2% in Bulgaria and at 8.4% in Romania. Seventy-four NUTS 2 regions had unemployment rates below 5%: eight in Austria (only one Austrian region exceeded 5%), 19 in the UK, nine in Italy, three in the Czech Republic, eight in Germany, all 12 regions in the Netherlands, two in Hungary, three each in Portugal and Sweden, one each in Spain, Finland and Ireland, and the three single-region States of Denmark, Luxembourg and Cyprus.

In 22 regions unemployment was particularly high (i.e. those with an unemployment rate over 20%): three in Italy (Campania, Calabria, Sicily), all four French overseas regions, two regions in Germany (Dessau, Halle) and no fewer than half the regions in Bulgaria, Slovakia and Poland. In the case of Italy, there were big differences between the northern (low unemployment rate) and southern regions (high unemployment rate).

The situation in the labour market was more stable in the former EU-15 Member States, among which only Greece and Italy improved between 2001 and 2002 (decrease of 0.5 percentage points). Even though the unemployment rate rose the most in Portugal (by 1 percentage point), the overall level still remained very low (5.1%). The changes in the new Member States and in Bulgaria and Romania were more dynamic – with the biggest decrease of the unemployment rate being in Estonia (2.3 percentage points), Latvia (2.8 percentage points) and Bulgaria (2.1 percentage points), as well as notable increases in Poland (1.7 percentage points) and Romania (1.8 percentage points). In the case of Romania, the unemployment rate in 2002 was relatively low: 8.4%.

In 2002, an improvement of more than 0.5 percentage points in comparison with 2001 was observed in 57 NUTS 2 regions, whereas an equivalent worsening was noted in 107 regions. The greatest decline in the unemployment rate (over 2 percentage points) was recorded in Bulgaria (Severen tsentralen, Severoiztochen, Yugoiztochen, where the latter two had an unemployment rate above 20%), France (two overseas regions, Guyane and Réunion, both with high unemployment rates), Greece (Sterea Ellada) and the new Member States Estonia and Lithuania.

Regions with the largest increase in the unemployment rate (more than two percentage points) in 2002 were as follows: six Polish regions, two Spanish regions (La Rioja and Extremadura), two in Greece (Voreio Aigaio and Notio Aigaio), two in Romania (Sud-Est and Sud) and one French region (Franche-Comté).

In 2002 female unemployment in the former EU-15 Member States was 8.7% (countries with a rate higher than 10% were Spain (16.4%), Greece (15.0%) and Italy (12.2%)); in the new Member States, it stood at 15.6% (more than 10% in Lithuania (12.9%), Latvia (11.0%), Slovakia (18.7%) and Poland (20.9%)); in Bulgaria and Romania it was 17.3% and 7.7% respectively. At regional (NUTS 2) level, a female unemployment rate below 5% was recorded in eight regions in Austria, two each in Belgium, Portugal and Italy, 30 in the UK, six in Sweden, 10 in the Netherlands, nine in Germany, three in Hungary, one in Finland, Ireland and the Czech Republic. In Denmark, Luxembourg and Cyprus the female unemployment rate was also below 5%.

In 2002, regions with a female unemployment rate over 20% could be found in Poland (ten of the 16 regions), France (all four overseas regions, with Réunion exceeding 30%), three regions in Bulgaria and two each in Germany, Slovakia, Spain and Greece. The situation in Italy was marked by a big difference across the country – of the six regions in this category, Campania and Calabria were over 30%. In Germany the female unemployment rate was noticeably higher in the regions of the former GDR.

The youth unemployment rate represents unemployed persons aged 15–24 as a percentage of the economically active population of the same age group. However, there is a greater divergence between the former EU-15 Member States (14.9%), and the new Member States (32.4%), Bulgaria (37.2%) and Romania (23.2%). In the former EU-15 Member States, a youth unemployment rate of over 25% was observed in Italy (27.2%) and Greece (26.5%), whereas it was below 10% in Denmark (7.4%), Germany (9.7%), Ireland (7.8%), Luxembourg (7.0%), Austria (6.2%) and the Netherlands (5.0%).

In the new Member States, the only countries that to have less than 20% youth unemployment were Slovenia (16.5%), the Czech Republic (16.9%), Hungary (12.4%), Cyprus (7.7%), Malta (15.3%) and Estonia (17.6%). The highest level of this indicator was recorded in Poland (42.5%). Across the enlarged EU, Bulgaria and Romania youth unemployment was below 10% in 76 regions. At the other extreme, regional youth unemployment rates above 50% were observed in Bulgaria (Severozapaden), France (Guadeloupe, Martinique), Italy (Campania, Calabria, Sicily) and Poland (Dolnośląskie, Lubuskie, Warmińsko-Mazurskie, Zachodniopomorskie).

The long-term unemployment rate represents persons unemployed for one year or longer, as a percentage of the sum of those unemployed for less than one year and those unemployed for one year or longer. In 2002, relatively low long-term unemployment rates (below 20%) were recorded in five Swedish regions, 17 British regions, three Austrian regions (Salzburg, Tirol, Vorarlberg), one Spanish region (Illes Balears), one Italian region (Valle d'Aosta) and in Denmark. In spite of the high youth and female unemployment in the Spanish region of Andalucía, the long-term unemployment rate was relatively low here. The opposite situation was observed in Slovenia. A long-term unemployment rate of more than 65% was observed in four Bulgarian regions (Severozapaden, Yugozapaden, Yuzhen tsentralen, Yugoiztochen), all four French overseas regions, in four Italian regions (Lazio, Campania, Puglia, Sicily), two Greek regions (Western Greece/Dytiki Ellada and Inland Greece/Sterea Ellada), two Slovak regions (Západné Slovensko and Východné Slovensko) and in the Polish region of Podkarpackie.

2.2 The Regional Population

In general one could say that the ageing of the population is caused by a population dynamic which is too low: the relative influx of youngsters and outflow of older people is too low to compensate each other. Population dynamics are the result of demographic behaviour and are mainly influenced by mortality (the mean life expectancy), fertility (the average number of children born and the mean age at which women have children) and migration (the relative number of immigrants and emigrants and their age distribution). Figure 2 shows these working age people and their children.

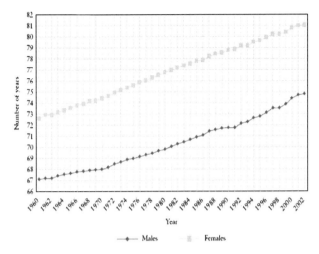

Fig. 2. Life expectancy at birth 1960–2002, EU-25

In the course of the 20th century, life expectancy increased considerably. In 1960 the average life expectancy at birth was 67.1 years for men and 72.6 for women. During the following years this expectancy increased for men by nearly eight years and for women by nearly nine years to respectively 74.8 and 81.1 years in 2002. However such an increase in the number of expected years to live at birth does not necessarily mean an increase in years of good health. Researchers have different opinions on this point: some say that the increase in life expectancy has been accompanied by an increasing frailty of people at higher ages, others hold the opposite view.

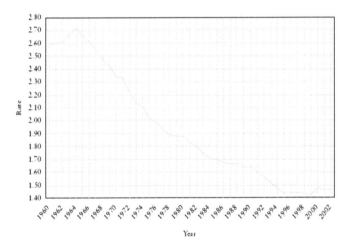

Fig. 3. Total fertility rate 1960–2002, EU-25

In most of the countries of the European Union, there were high numbers of births during the first 25 years after the Second World War. However, after 1970 birth rates dropped dramatically as women had fewer children and at a later age.

3 The Regional Policy in European Union

The European Union is one of the most prosperous economic areas in the world but the disparities between its member states are striking, even more so if we look at the EU's various 250 regions. To assess these disparities, we must first of all measure and compare the levels of wealth generated by each country, as determined by their Gross Domestic Product (GDP) mentioned earlier. For instance, in Greece, Portugal and Spain, average per capita GDP is only 80% of the Community average. Luxembourg exceeds this average by over 60 percentage points. The ten most dynamic regions in the Union have a GDP almost three times higher than the ten least developed regions.

3.1 Priority Objectives

The regulations adopted in 1993 for the period 1994–1999 established six priority Objectives for the Structural Funds:

- Objective 1: promoting the development and structural adjustment of regions whose development is lagging behind;
- Objective 2: converting regions seriously affected by industrial decline;
- Objective 3: combatting long-term unemployment and facilitating the integration into working life of young people and of those excluded from the labour market;
- Objective 4: facilitating the adaptation of workers to industrial changes and changes in production systems;
- Objective 5a: speeding up the adjustment of agricultural structures in the framework of the reform of the Common Agricultural Policy and facilitating the structural adjustment of the fisheries sector in the framework of the reform of the Common Fisheries Policy;
- Objective 5b: facilitating the development and structural adjustment of rural areas A further Objective for the Structural Funds was created by the Act of Accession for Austria, Finland and Sweden;
- Objective 6: promoting the development of regions with an extremely low population density.

3.2 The New Priority Objectives

Three priority Objectives have been established for the period 2000–2006:

- Objective 1: promoting the development and structural adjustment of regions whose development is lagging behind

The title of this Objective remains unchanged; the regulation stipulates that regions currently eligible under Objective 6 and the outermost regions as defined in the Amsterdam Treaty shall be integrated into Objective 1 for the 2000–2006 period.

- Objective 2: supporting the economic and social conversion of areas facing structural difficulties

This new Objective, which focuses on economic and social conversion, brings together Objectives 2 and 5b of the current programming period and extends them to cover other areas (urban areas in difficulty, areas in crisis dependent on the fishing industry, and areas undergoing conversion which are highly dependent on the services sector) facing the same problems due to a lack of economic diversity.

- Objective 3: supporting the adaptation and modernisation of education, training and employment policies and systems

This new Objective brings together the previous Objectives 3 and 4 and will take as its starting point the new title on employment introduced by the Amsterdam Treaty. It will assist regions throughout the EU except those covered by the new Objective 1, taking into account the general needs of areas facing structural difficulties with regard to economic and social conversion. It constitutes a reference framework for the development of human resources throughout the Member State, notwithstanding regional specificities. Measures previously funded under the former Objective 5a will henceforth be supported by the Guidance section of the EAGGF within the framework of the new Objective 1 programmes (as is currently the case, except as regards compensatory allowances for disadvantaged areas, which are financed by the EAGGF Guarantee section), and elsewhere in the European Union by the EAGGF-Guarantee section and the FIFG within the framework of accompanying measures to the Common Agricultural Policy and the Common Fisheries Policy.

Objective 2: converting regions seriously affected by industrial decline during the 1994–1999 period eligibilty under Objective 2 was linked to three conditions:

- an unemployment rate above the Community average;
- a percentage share of industrial employment exceeding the Community average;
- a decline in this employment category.

A series of secondary criteria meant that eligibility under Objective 2 could be extended to include adjacent areas, urban areas, and areas facing or threatened by a severe increase in unemployment, problems related to the regeneration of derelict industrial sites or the impact of the restructuring of the fisheries sector.

Objective 5b: facilitating the development of vulnerable rural areas during the 1994–1999 period, the general criterion for eligibility under Objective 5b was a low level of socio-economic development (assessed on the basis of per capita GDP).

There were three additional main criteria, two of which had to be met for an area to be eligible:

- a high level of agricultural employment;
- a low level of agricultural incomes;
- low population density and/or significant migration trends.

Eligibility could be extended to other areas not covered by Objective 1 but with a low level of development, if one or more of the following secondary criteria were met: the remote location of the area, sensitivity to trends in the agricultural sector or the restructuring of the fisheries sector, the structure of agricultural holdings and of the agricultural working population, the environment, etc.

Objectives 3 and 4: Objective 3: combating long-term unemployment and facilitating integration into the labour market. The current Objective 3 aims at combating long-term unemployment and facilitating the integration into working life of young people and those threatened by exclusion from the labour market. Objective 3 also promotes equal opportunities for men and women on the labour market. Interventions under Objective 3 are not limited to specific regions.

Objective 4: adaptation to industrial change. This objective facilitates the adaptation of the workforce to industrial changes and to changes in production systems. As for Objective 3, interventions under Objective 4 are not subject to regional limitation.

New Objective 3: development of human resources for the 2000–2006 period, the new Objective 3 will focus primarily on the adaptation and the modernisation of national and European policies for employment, education and training. Objective 3 funding will be available in all areas except those covered by the new Objective 1. The new Objective 3 will also serve as a reference framework for all human resource actions in the Member States. It will take into account the Employment Title in the Amsterdam Treaty and the new European employment strategy. The regulation takes into account the wide variety of policies, practices and needs in the different Member States based on their national action plans for employment and the ex-ante evaluation. In view of the length of the period covered (2000–2006), the areas in which the European Social Fund (ESF) will apply have been broadly defined. They include active labour market policies to combat unemployment, promote social inclusion and equal opportunities for men and women, strengthen employability through lifelong education and training systems, and measures to anticipate and facilitate adaptation to economic and social change.

3.3 The Structural Funds

The 1993 regulations list three Structural Funds:

* the European Regional Development Fund (ERDF);
* the European Social Fund (ESF);
* the Guidance section of the European Agricultural Guidance and Guarantee Fund (EAGGF). The Financial Instrument for Fisheries Guidance (FIFG) is not a Structural Fund as such, but finances structural actions in the fisheries sector within the framework of Structural Fund programmes.

The European Union's regional policy is based on financial solidarity inasmuch as part of Member States' – contributions – to the Community budget goes to the less prosperous regions and social groups. For the 2000–2006 period these transfers will account for one third of the Community budget, or 213 € billion:

* (a) 195 € billion will be spent by the four Structural Funds (the European Regional Development Fund, the European Social Fund, the Financial Instrument for Fisheries Guidance and the Guidance Section of the European Agricultural Guidance and Guarantee Fund);
* (b) 18 € billion will be spent by the Cohesion Fund;
* (c) 70% of the funding goes to regions whose development is lagging behind. They are home to 22% of the population of the Union (Objective 1);
* (d) 11.5% of the funding assists economic and social conversion in areas experiencing structural difficulties. 18% of the population of the Union lives in such areas (Objective 2);

- (e) 12.3% of the funding promotes the modernisation of training systems and the creation of employment (Objective 3) outside the Objective 1 regions where such measures form part of the strategies for catching up;
- (f) There are also four Community Initiatives seeking common solutions to specific problems, namely Interreg III for cross-border, transnational and interregional cooperation, Urban II for sustainable development of cities and declining urban areas, Leader for rural development through local initiatives, and Equal for combating inequalities and discrimination in access to the labour market.

According to the estimations of Hermin model, the estimated effect is to increase real GDP in 2006 by around 6% in Greece and Portugal and by 2.4% in Spain as compared with the situation without intervention. The effect is relatively modest in Ireland (1.8%), where the Community Structural Funds (CSF) only account for under 10% of total public expenditure. The CSF will increase investment by much more, especially in Portugal (by 23%) and Greece (14%), which will add to effective demand via multiplier effects and, over time, also tend to increase productivity, through improved infrastructure and human capital as well as the use of more modern, and therefore efficient, plant and equipment. Table 1 illustrates the annual breakdown of commitment appropriations for 2000 to 2006 (referred to in Article 7(1)) (€ million – 1999 prices).

The Structural Funds have three main priority objectives: Objective 1: facilitate the catch-up for regions lagging behind in development. Objective 2: promote the socio-economic conversion of industrial, urban or rural zones or zones which are dependent on fisheries. Objective 3: provide improved training and job opportunities. In addition, aid is also granted by Community initiatives which encourage cross-border, transnational and interregional cooperation throughout the EU (Interreg III) and equality in the labour market (Equal).

The Cohesion Fund supports environmental and transport projects in the least prosperous Member States. The followings Tables 2–7 illustrate the structural fund and FIFG interventions are divided as follows between the priority Objectives, the coherence between areas eligible for structural funds and eligible for regional state aid as a percentage of EU population, the cohesion Funds: resources committed by area of intervention,

Table 1. Annual breakdown of commitment appropriations for 2000–2006 [referred to in Article 7(1)] [€ million – 1999 prices]

2000	2001	2002	2003	2004	2005	2006
29,430	28,840	28,250	27,670	27,080	27,080	26,660

1993–1999, the effect of community structural intervention on GDP and Employment, 1989–1999, the population in regions eligible for Structural funds but not for regional state aid as a percentage (%) of total population in each country and the structural funds by broad area of intervention under Objective 1 as a % of total.

Table 2. Structural Fund and FIFG interventions are divided as follows between the priority Objectives

Objective 1	ERDF	ESF	EAGGF Guidance
Objective 2	ERDF	ESF	EAGGF Guidance
Objective 3		ESF	EAGGF Guidance
Objective 4		ESF	EAGGF Guidance
Objective 5a		ESF	EAGGF Guidance
Objective 5b	ERDF	ESF	EAGGF Guidance
Objective 6	ERDF	ESF	EAGGF Guidance

Table 3. Coherence between areas eligible for Structural Funds and eligible for Regional State Aid as a percentage of the EU population

	Regions eligible for Structural Funds		Regions not eligible for Structural Funds		Total	
	1994–1998	2000–2008	1994–1998	2000–2008	1994–1998	2000–2008
Areas eligible for regional state aid	44.0	35.6	2.7	6.7	46.7	42.3
Areas not eligible for regional state aid	6.6	5.8	46.7	51.9	63.3	57.7
Total	50.6	41.4	48.4	59.6	100	100

Source: European Union, Eurostat, DG-Regio.

Table 4. Cohesion Funds: resources committed by area of intervention, 1993–1999

	Transport: % total	Environment: % total	Total mill.€
Greece	51.2	42.3	2992
Spain	49.7	50.2	9251
Ireland	50.0	50.0	1496
Portugal	48.1	51.9	3006
Total	49.7	50.2	16761

Source: European Union.

Table 5. Effect of Community Structural Intervention on GDP and Employment, 1989–1999

	Greece		Ireland		Portugal		Spain	
	GDP	Unemploy-ment rate	GDP	Unemploy-ment rate	GDP	Unemploy-ment rate	GDP	Unemploy-ment rate
1989	4.1	–3.2	2.2	–1.4	5.8	–3.6	0.8	–0.4
1993	4.1	–2.9	3.2	–1.0	7.4	–4.1	1.5	–0.8
1999	9.9	–6.2	3.7	–0.4	8.5	–4.0	2.1	–1.6
2006	7.3	–3.2	2.8	0.4	7.8	–2.8	2.4	–1.7
2010	2.4	0.4	2.0	0.5	3.1	–0.1	1.3	–0.4

Source: European Union, estimates on the HERMIN model, 2000.

Table 6. Population in regions eligible for Structural funds but not for regional state aid as percentage (%) of total population in each country

	B	DK	D	EL	E	F	RL	I	L	NL	A	P	FIN	S	UK	EU-15
1994–1999	0	0	5.3	0	8.9	9.6	0	7.5	6.4	10.4	5.9	0	12.6	9.7	9.0	8.6
2000–2008	3.4	0.1	2.3	0	4.3	8.8	0	7.0	0.3	8.2	3.9	0	12.0	7.4	9.8	5.8

Source: European Union, Eurostat, DG-Regio.

Table 7. Structural Funds by broad area of intervention under Objective 1 as % of total

	1989–1993	1994–1999	2000–2006
Infrastructure	25.2	29.8	24.3
Human Resources	29.6	24.5	23.9
Productive Environment	23.6	41.0	24.9
Other	1.6	4.7	7.0

Source: European Union.

4 The European Innovation Policy

The European Union's 2010 goals in R&D, as set by the Lisbon summit strategy and endorsed by European Heads of State and Government in Barcelona in 2002, are to achieve a R&D intensity (R&D expenditure as percentage of GDP) of 3% for the Union as a whole as well as to have two thirds of R&D expenditure financed by the Business Enterprise Sector (BES). Sweden and Finland are ahead of most Member States for the EU 2010 R&D goals with R&D intensities well above the 3% mark and over two thirds of their R&D expenditure being financed by the BES.

In 2001, 55% of the EU-25's R&D expenditure was financed by the BES, still lower than the 66%-goal. With R&D expenditure representing

1.93% of its GDP, the EU-25 still had a lower R&D intensity than its Triad partners Japan (3.12%) and the United States (2.64%) in 2002. China's R&D intensity leapt from 0.70% in 1998 to more than 1.20% in 2002. In the ten years to 2002, the US's R&D expenditure grew more than twofold to over 225 billion constant 1995 PPS. The EU and Japan's amount of R&D likewise more than doubled in one decade. Table 8 illustrates the top 15 Eurpean Union regions in R&D expenditure and employment in high-tech and medium high-tech manufacturing, whereas, Table 9 indicates the top 15 regions in employment in the knowledge-intensive services and patenting.

Bearing in mind that the EU's enlargement to 25 Member States only took place in 2004, the inclusion of the ten new Member States would have already added about 4% of additional R&D expenditure to the then 15 Member States' Union's total R&D expenditure (in million constant 1995 PPS) between 1999 and 2002.

Denmark, Sweden, Finland are leading EU Member States in Research and Development, boasting among the highest R&D intensities (R&D expenditure as a percentage of GDP). Likewise, these three Nordic EU countries have the highest number of R&D personnel as a percentage of total employment in the European Union. More than three out of 100 employed people were active in R&D in Finland in 2002 and so was more than 2.5% of Sweden's workforce in 2001 and more than 2.25% of Denmark's in 2002. The European Union's percentage of R&D personnel among employed people is 1.44. Estonia, Latvia, Lithuania, Portugal and the Slovak Republic had among the highest shares of female researchers in the European Union.

In most countries, female researchers are especially concentrated in the GOVernment (GOV) and Higher Education (HES) Sectors. In most countries, a significant proportion of Business Enterprise Sector researchers (more than 40%) gets employed in large enterprises of more than 250 employees. Only in smaller countries such as Estonia, Cyprus or Malta is this less the case. In Estonia and Cyprus for instance, enterprises of one to nine employees attracted about respectively 20% and 30% of Business Enterprise Sector researchers. Tables 10 and 11 illustrate the leading region by Member States in R&D expenditure and employment in high-tech and medium high-tech manufacturing, respectively. Finally, Table 12 indicates the top 25 European Union regions and leading region by Member State in terms of GDP.

Table 8. Top 15 EU regions in R&D expenditure and employment in high-tech and medium high-tech manufacturing

Total R&D expenditure in 2001			Business R&D expenditure in 2001			Employment in high and medium high-tech manufacturing 2002		
Region	Mio current €	% of GDP	Region	Mio current €	% of GDP	Region	Thousands HC	% of total employment
Braunschweig (DE)	2896	6.99	Vastsverige (SE)	2445	5.19	Stuttgart (DE)	401	21.2
Stuttgart (DE)	6146	4.94	Braunschweig (DE)	2140	5.17	Tubingen (DE)	158	18.7
Oberbayern (DE)	6959	4.58	Stuttgart (DE)	5566	4.49	Braunschweig (DE)	121	17.5
Berlin (DE)	3222	4.22	Stockholm (SE)	3005	4.37	Franche – Comte (FR)	88	17.4
Pohjois – Suomi (FI)	5766	4.10	Oberbayern (DE)	5575	3.66	Kozep – Dunantul (HU)	76	16.6
Tubingen (DE)	1757	3.85	Eastern – NUTS 1 (UK)	4684	3.32	Karlsruhe (DE)	204	16.4
Karlsruhe (DE)	2949	3.77	Sydsverige (SE)	1017	3.11	Niederbayern (DE)	90	15.6
Dresden (DE)	1050	3.63	Tubingen (DE)	1423	3.10	Unterfranken (DE)	96	15.6
Etela – Suomi (FI)	2794	3.61	Pohjois – Suomi (FI)	435	3.09	Rheinhessen – Pfalz (DE)	138	15.4
Lansi – Suomi (FI)	1056	3.50	Noord – Brabant (NL)	1796	2.82	Freiburg (DE)	151	14.9
Ile de France (FR)	14132	3.36	Ostra Mellansverige (SE)	984	2.79	Schwaben (DE)	122	14.5
Midi – Pyrenees (FR)	1841	3.35	Lansi – Suomi (FI)	818	2.71	Mittelfranken (DE)	111	14.1
Noord – Brabant (NL)	2011	3.21	Mittelfranken (DE)	1273	2.56	Oberbayern (DE)	285	13.9
Koln (DE)	3675	3.18	Darmstadt (DE)	3394	2.54	Darmstadt (DE)	237	13.5
Mittelfranken (DE)	1551	3.10	Etela – Suomi (FI)	1948	2.52	Peimonte (IT)	235	13.2

Source: European Union.

Table 9. Top 15 regions in employment in knowledge-intensive services and patenting

	Employment in knowledge-intensive services in 2002			Patent application to the EPO in 2002			High technology patent application to the EPO in 2002		
	Region	Thousands HC	% of total manufacturing	Region	Number	Per million inhabitants	Region	Number	Per million inhabitants
1.	Inner London (UK)	788	59.14	Noord–Brabant (NL)	2593	1084	Noord–Brabant (NL)	1201	502
2.	Stockholm (SE)	532	54.84	Stuttgart (DE)	2952	749	Oberbayern (DE)	973	238
3.	Outer London (UK)	1118	50.35	Oberbayern (DE)	3034	741	Stockholm (SE)	305	168
4.	Ile de France (FR)	2353	46.80	Karlsruhe (DE)	1430	535	East Anglia (UK)	358	161
5.	Surrey, East and West Sussex (UK)	532	46.02	Mittelfranken (DE)	845	500	Sydsverige (SE)	181	141
6.	Vastsverige (SE)	395	45.45	Tubingen (DE)	871	492	Mittelfranken (DE)	211	125
7.	Berlin (DE)	552	45.07	Freiburg (DE)	1031	481	Gloucestershire, Wiltshire and North-Sommerset (UK)	228	103
8.	Ostra Mellansverige (SE)	318	44.49	Vorarlberg (AT)	100	456	Berkshire, Bucks and Oxfordshire (UK)	199	93
9.	Wien (AT)	332	44.46	Rheinhessen–Pfalz (DE)	912	454	Oberpfalz (DE)	95	88
10.	Noord–Holland (NL)	593	44.12	Sydsverige (SE)	582	454	Karlsruhe (DE)	221	82
11.	Denmark (DK)	1205	43.98	Darmstadt (DE)	1550	414	Stuttgart (DE)	315	80
12.	Berkshire, Bucks and Oxfordshire (UK)	510	43.78	Oberphalz (DE)	420	397	Ile de France (FR)	873	79
13.	Hamburg (DE)	344	43.44	Prov. Brabant Wallon (BE)	135	382	Bretagne (FR)	215	73
14.	Eastern Scotland (UK)	388	42.46	Koln (DE)	1598	372	Hampshire and Isle of Wight (UK)	125	70
15.	Etela–Suomi (FI)	530	41.79	Unterfranken (DE)	480	365	Prov. Antwerpen (BE)	97	59

Source: European Union.

Table 10. Leading region by member states in R&D expenditure and employment in high-tech and medium high-tech manufacturing

	Total R&D expenditure in 2001			Business R&D expenditure in 2001			Employment in high & medium high-tech manufacturing 2002		
	Region	Mio current €	% of GDP	Region	Mio current €	% of GDP	Region	Thousands HC	% of total employment
Poland	Mazawieskie	543	1.28	–	–	–	–	–	–
Portugal	Centro	338	1.44	Centro	233	0.90	Lisboa	65	4.90
Slovenia	Slovenia	341	1.50	Slovenia	197	0.80	Slovenia	85	2.22
Slovakia	Bratilavsky	59	1.00	–	–	–	Zapadne Slovenska	83	11.10
Finland	Pohjois – Suomi	570	4.10	Pohjois – Suomi	435	3.00	Lanse – Suomi	52	8.75
Sweden	–	–	–	Vastsverige	2445	5.19	Ostra Melansverige	71	2.87
United Kingdom	Eastern NUTS1	4505	3.80	Eastern NUTS1	4564	3.32	Hertfordshire, Worcestershire and Warks	75	12.04

Source: European Union.

Turnover from products which are either new to the market or just new to the enterprise accounted for about 30% of total turnover in Spain, Italy, Germany and Finland, for those enterprises with some form of product innovation. Over 80% of all large enterprises (250 or more employees) in Luxembourg and Austria had innovation activity. Too high innovation costs were generally cited by enterprises as the most important factor hampering innovation. In nearly all countries, the main highly important effect of innovation was cited as improved quality in goods or services.

The proportion of enterprises with co-operation arrangements for innovation activities (such as cooperation with other enterprises within the enterprise group or cooperation with suppliers) ranged from half of all enterprises with innovation activity (Finland, Latvia and Lithuania) to less than 10% (Italy). In general, enterprises with innovation activity had a higher propensity to undertake strategic or organisational change, compared to enterprises without innovation activity.

In summary, we can state that there is a widening tendency for differences between European regions in the fields of innovations and new technologies and in particular in the subjects of Research and Development Expenditures per inhabitant. According to econometric evidence, we can also state that the European Union should improve the distribution of regional funds for research and development, in order to diminish these differences and to support researchers in less favoured regions, and consequently to affect the socio-economic and regional growth and convergence of member states (Guisan, Cancelo and Diaz-Vazquez, 1998).

Table 11. Leading region by member states in R&D expenditure and employment in high-tech and medium high-tech manufacturing

	Employment in knowledge-intensive services in 2002			Patent application to the EPO in 2002			High technology patent application to the EPO in 2002		
	Region	Thousands HC	% of total manufacturing	Region	No:	Per million inhabitants	Region	No	Per million inhabitants
Belg.	Region de Bruxelles-Capita Brussels	168	49.71	Prov. Brabant Walon	135	382	Prov. Antwerp	97	59
Czech	Praha	245	40.27	–	–	–	–	–	–
Denm.	Denmark	1205	43.98	Denmark	1149	214	Denmark	240	45
Germ.	Berlin	852	45.07	Stuttgart	2952	749	Oberbayern	973	238
Eston.	Estonia	179	30.85	Estonia	12	9	Estonia	3	3
Greece	Atiki	467	29.80	Kriti	8	14	Kriti	2	3
Spain	Communidad deMadrid	874	37.08	Catalonia	384	62	Communidad deMadrid	51	10
France	Ile de France	2353	48.80	Ile de France	3407	313	Ile de France	873	79
Ireland	Southern and Esatern	405	35.40	Southern and Esatern	287	101	Southern and Esatern	104	30
Italy	Latzio	584	33.54	Emilia Romana	710	177	Valle d; Aossa	3	25

Table 11. (continued)

	Employment in knowledge-intensive services in 2002			Patent application to the EPO in 2002			High technology patent application to the EPO in 2002		
	Region	Thousands HC	% of total manufacturing	Region	No:	Per million inhabitants	Region	No	Per million inhabitants
Cyprus	Cyprus	83	28.17	Cyprus	7	10	Cyprus	1	1
Latvia	Latvia	245	24.83	Latvia	14	8	–	–	–
Lith.	Lithuania	351	24.73	Lithuania	9	3	Lithuania	4	1
Lux.	Luxembourg	72	38.05	Luxembourg	89	201	Luxembourg	3	8
Hung.	Kozep-Mayaskip	405	34.08	–	–	–	–	–	–
Malta	Malta	42	28.45	Malta	7	18	Malta	0	1
Neth.	Utrecht	209	45.20	North Holland	2503	1084	North Holland	1201	502
Austria	Wien	332	44.40	Vorsteng	103	450	Wien	77	48
Poland	–	–	–	–	–	–	–	–	–
Port.	Lisboa	399	30.88	–	–	–	–	–	–
Sloven.	Slovenia	211	22.82	Slovenia	85	18	Slovenia	7	3
Slovek.	Bratislavsky	117	38.93	–	–	–	–	–	–
Finl.	Aand	7	55.99	Ita-Suomi	57	84	Ita-Suomi	14	20
Swed.	Stockholm	532	54.84	Sydsverige	582	454	Sydsverige	350	168
U.K.	Inner London	788	59.14	East Anglia	771	340	East Anglia	358	181

Source: European Union.

Table 12. Top 25 EU regions and leading region by Member State in terms of GDP

Region	Top 25 EU regions in GDP per head in PPS in 2001		Leading region by Member States in GDP per head in 2001			
	Mio current €	PPS per head	Country	Region	Mio current €	PPS per head
1. Inner London (UK)	183.230	58.881	Belgium	Region de Bruxelles-Capitale Brussels	48.716	48.721
Region de Bruxelles (BE)	48.710	48.721	Czech	Praha	17.308	30.252
Luxembourg (LU)	22.020	43.601	Denmark	Denmark	177.871	26.851
Hamburg (DE)	73.650	38.275	Germany	Hamburg	73.669	88.276
Ile de France (FR)	420.878	36.915	Estonia	Estonia	6.668	8.791
Wien (AT)	57.970	35.459	Greece	Sterea Ellada	9.471	21.331
Berkshire, Bucks and Oxford-shire (UK)	80.380	33.297	Spain	Communida de Madrid	114.157	25.455
Oberbayern (DE)	152.530	33.163	France	Ille de France	420.878	26.915
Stockholm (SE)	88.807	32.488	Ireland	Southern and Eastern	92.092	28.698
Provincia Autonoma Bolzano – Bozen (IT)	14.059	32.124	Italy	Provincia Autonoma Botzano-Bozen	14.059	32.124
Utrecht (NL)	37.970	32.037	Cyprus	Cyprus	10.205	17.588
Darmstadt (DE)	133.544	31.906	Latvia	Latvia	9.227	7.659
Aland (FI)	921	31.796	Lithuania	Lithuania	18.505	8.341
North Easstern Scotland (UK)	17.719	30.530	Luxembourg	Luxembourg	22.020	48.601
Bremen (DE)	22.479	30.439	Hungary	Kopez-Magyaroszag	25.494	18.315
Praha (CZ)	17.308	30.252	Malta	Malta	4.294	15.379
Groningen (NL)	17.833	29.876	Netherl.	Utrecht	37.906	32.037
Noord – Holland (NL)	79.605	29.734	Austria	Wien	57.970	85.459
Lombardia (IT)	262.331	29.403	Poland	Mazowieskie	42.404	14.629
Southern and Eastern (IE)	92.092	28.693	Portugal	Lisboa	46.086	23.476
Emila-Romagna (IT)	100.082	28.227	Slovenia Rep.	Slovenia	21.845	15.296
Stuttgart (DE)	124.424	28.103	Slovekia Rep.	Bratislavsky	5.919	22.930
Salsburg (AT)	15.202	27.975	Finland	Aland	921	81.796
Prov. Antwerpen (BE)	47.123	27.701	Sweden	Stockholm	68.807	32.488

Source: European Union.

Therefore, by pursuing their own interests, regional authorities can increase the momentum towards the establishment of a European Research Area as well as ensuring its effectiveness and consistency. The establishment of a European Research Area, however, is not confined to the most central and competitive regions. The instruments available – the Framework Programme, the Structural Funds and action at national and regional level – should be used together in a more coherent way, each according to its objectives, in order to enable all regions to participate fully in the area

5 Conclusions

Technological progress has become virtually synonymous with long run economic growth. It raises a basic question about the capacity of both industrial and newly industrialized countries to translate their seemingly greater technological capacity into productivity and economic growth. In the literature there are various explanations for the slow-down in productivity growth for OECD countries. One source of the slow-down may be substantial changes in FDI, and in the industrial composition of output, employment, capital accumulation and resource utilization. The second source of the slow down in productivity growth may be that technological opportunities have declined; otherwise, new technologies have been developed but the application of new technologies to production has been less successful. Technological factors act in a long run way and should not be expected to explain medium run variations in the growth of GDP and productivity. The Regional Policy, supported through Structural Funds and a Cohesion Fund has created objectives that have thus far been moderately successful in reducing disparities between the regions of the EU15. Greece, Portugal, Ireland and Spain, the four countries, which qualified for the Cohesion Fund, witnessed almost an 11% average increase in per capita GDP from 1988–1998. On average, the poorest EU regions saw the per capita GDP rise by almost 7% over the same ten years. The funding provided through Regional Policy contributed significantly to these GDP increases.   Moreover, the European research and innovation policy has adopted an approach oriented more towards innovation than technological excellence as such, better addressing the deficiencies of less favoured regions as a result. An improvement in the interaction between the deployment of the Structural Funds and research policy is important to accelerating the "catching up" of lagging regions. The Structural Funds can provide the necessary support for firms and research institutes in the latter to participate on equal terms in future research programmes.

6 References

Acs Z.J., FitzRoy F., Smith I. (1999) High technology employment, wages and university R&D spillovers: Evidence from US cities. Economics of innovation and new technology vol 8, no1-2, 57-78

Armstrong, H. (1995) An Appraisal of the Evidence from Cross-sectional Analysis of the Regional Growth Process within the European Union, in H.W. Armstrong and R.W. Vicherman, ed: Convergence and Divergence Among European Regions, European Research in Regional Science, 5, pp. 40-65., Pion Limited, London.

Bernard A.B., Jones C.I. (1996) Technology and convergence, Economic Journal, 106, 1037-44.

Biehl, D., et al. (1986) The contribution of infrastructure to regional development. Comisión de las Comunidades Europeas, Luxemburg.

Breschi, S., Livoni, F. (2001) Localised knowledge spillovers vs. innovative milieux: knowledge 'tacitness' reconsidered, Papers in Regional Science, 80, pp. 255-273.

Castro, E.A., Jensen-Butler, C.N. (1991) Flexibility and the neo classical model in the analysis of regional growth, Institute of Political Scence, University of Aarhus, Denmark.

Clarysse, B., Muldur, U (2001) Regional cohesion in Europe? An analysis of how EU public RTD support influences the techno-economic regional landscape, in Research Policy, Vol. 30, No. 2, pp. 275-296.

Cooke, P., Clifton, N., Huggins., R (2001) Competitiveness and the knowledge economy, ESRC Social Capital and Economic Performance Project Research Paper 1, Centre for Advanced Studies, Cardiff University, UK (January 2001).

Cooke, P., Morgan, K. (1998): The Associational Economy: firms, regions and innovation. London, Oxford University Press.

Cuadrado, J.R. (1994) Regional disparities and territorial competition in the EC, en Moving Frontiers: Economic Restructuring, Regional Development and Emerging Networks, Eds. J.R. Cuadrado, P. Nijkamp, P. Salva, Hants (UK) 1994, pp. 3-23.

De la Fuente (1997) The empirics of growth and convergence, Journal of Economic Dynamics and Control, 21, 23-77

Durlauf S.N., Quah D.T. (1999), The new empirics of economic growth, Centre for economic Performance Discussion Paper no. 384 (Final version February 1999).

European Commission (1999) Structural and Cohesion Funds, Guidelines for programmes in the period 2000-2006,COM(1999) 344 final

European Commission (1999) Report on the Cohesion Fund (1999).

European Commission (2000a) The Regions in the New Economy – Guidelines for Innovative Measures under the ERDF in the Period 2000-06, Draft Communication from the Commission to the Member States, Brussels 11/07/00.

European Commission (2000b) The Regions in the New Economy, Fact Sheet, Brussels 14/07/00.

European Commission (2000c) The new programming period 2000-2006. Methodological working papers no. 3, Indicators for monitoring and evaluation: an indicative methodology, DG Regional Policy, European Commission, Brussels.

European Commission (2000d) 11th annual report on the Structural Funds, 1999, Brussels, 13.11.2000, COM(2000)698 final.

European Commission (2001) Second Report on Economic and Social Cohesion.

Gillespie, A., Richardson, R., Cornford, J. (2001) Regional development and the new economy, paper presented to the European Investment Bank Conference, Luxembourg, January 2001.

Carmen Guisan M., M. Teresa Cancelo, M. Rosario Diaz-Vazquez, (1998) Evaluation of the effects of European regional policy in the diminution of regional disparities, ERSA conference papers ersa98, p312, European Regional Science Association

Herzenberg, S. A., Alic, J. A., Wial, H. (1999) Toward a Learning Economy, in Issues in Science and Technology, Winter 1998-99, pp. 55-62.

Korres G (1998) Productivity and technical change on EEC countries, The Cyprus Journal of Science and Technology, Vol. 1, Number 4.

Korres G (2002) Technical Change, Diffusion and Innovation in a Context of a Growth Model, in Globalisation and Economic Growth: A Critical Evaluation, John Smithin, C. Paraskevopoulos, T. Georgakopoulos (eds.), APF (Athenian Policy Forum), Toronto/Canada, pp. 111-122.

López-Bazo, E, Vayá, E. Mora, A., Suriñach, J. (1999) Regional Economic Dynamics and Convergence in the European Union, The Annals of Regional Science, 22(3), pp. 1-28.

Lundvall BÅ (ed) (1992) National systems of innovation: Towards a theory of innovation and interactive learning (Pinter, London)

Maskell P., Malmberg A. (1999) Localised learning and industrial competitiveness Cambridge Journal of Economics 23, 167-185

Millard, J. (1999) New Methods of Work: Experience from the Fourth Framework Programme, Socio-Economic Preparatory Conference for the Fifth Framework Programme, Paris, 23 February.

OECD (1997) Regional Competitiveness and Skills, Paris,

OECD (1999) The Response of Higher Education Institutions to Regional Needs, Paris.

OECD (2001a) Innovative Networks. Co-operation in National Innovation Systems, Paris.

OECD (2001b) Science, Technology and Industry Scoreboard. Towards a knowledge-based Economy, Paris.

OECD (2001c) Special Issue on Fostering High-tech Spin-offs: A Public Strategy for Innovation. STI Science Technology Industry, Review No. 26, Paris.

OECD (2001d) Towards a knowledge-based economy – OECD science, technology and industry scoreboard, 2001 edition, Paris.

OECD (2002 a) Special Issue on New Science and Technology Indicators. STI Science Technology Industry. No. 27, Paris.

OECD (2002 b) Patent database, OECD, April 2002;

OECD (2002 c) STAN database, OECD, April 2002.
OECD (2004) Main Science & Technology Indicators, Paris.
Paci R. and Pigliaru F. (1999), Technological catch-up and regional convergence in Europe, Contributi di Ricerca Crenos, 99/9
Romer, P.M., (1990) Endogenous Technological Change, Journal of Political Economy, vol. 98, pp. S71-S102.
Sakurai, N., Papaconstantinou, G., Ioannidis, E., (1997) Impact of R&D and Technology Diffusion on Productivity Growth: Empirical Evidence of 10 OECD Countries, Economic Systems Research, vol. 9, pp. 81-109.
Europa Websites-Regional Policy and Parliament Fact Sheets
http://europa.eu.int/scadplus/leg/en/lvb/g24000.htm
http://europa.eu.int/scadplus/printvision/en/lvb/160020.htm
http://europa.eu.int/comm/regional_policy/sources/docoffic/ofical/reports/conclu34_en.htm
http://europa.eu.int/comm/regional_policy/sources/docoffic/ofical/reports/conclu34_en.htm
http://europa.eu.int/comm/regional_policy/intro/regions5_en.htm
http://europa.eu.int/comm/regional_policy/intro/regions7_en.htm
http://europa.eu.int/comm/regional_policy/intro/regions9_en.htm
http://europa.eu.int/comm/regional_policy/into/regions10_en.htm
http//www. europal. eu. int/factsheets/4_8_2_en.htm
http://www.europarl.eu.int/factsheets/4_1_5_en.htm

Part IV

Challenges and Prospects
for an Integrated Europe

Research and Technological Development Policy and Innovative Performance: The Greek Case Within the EU

John Hatzikian

Technological Institute of Athens, Department of Business Administration, Athens, Greece

1 Introduction

Today, it is becoming more acceptable that knowledge-intensive industries to found at the centre of a trend which moves towards a new type of economy: "the knowledge economy". That in general means an economy which is based on the production, the distribution and the utilisation of knowledge and information (OECD, 1996, p. 9). In a knowledge-driven economy, innovation has become central to achievement in the business world. In addition to traditional technological innovation, there is innovation through new business models, new ways of organising work and innovation in design or marketing. Managing and exploiting, to their best effect, all these different kinds of innovation represent a major challenge to businesses today.

The knowledge-driven economy affects the innovation process and the approach to innovation. The traditional idea that innovation is based upon research (technology-push theory) and inter-action between firms and other actors is replaced by the current social network theory of innovation, where knowledge plays a crucial role in fostering innovation (Foray, D., 2000, pp. 239-255). If the organisation is to stay responsive to external change, a flexible and adaptable organisational structure is a necessity. Organizations, large and small, have begun to re-evaluate their products, their services, even their corporate culture in the attempt to maintain their competitiveness in the global markets of today. The more forward-thinking companies have recognised that only through such reform can they hope to survive in the face of increasing competition.

Many organisations in both the public and private sector have launched initiatives to develop methodologies and tools to support entrepreneurship and management of innovation in business. Higher education establishments, business schools and consulting companies are developing appropriate methodologies and tools, while public authorities are designing and setting up education and training schemes aiming to disseminate best practices among businesses of all kinds. Strategic and organisational changes applied in business should take into account the challenge of the new knowledge economy.

Within the firms that actually implement strategic and organizational changes, the perspective involved is that strategic and organizational changes can help their firms to foster competitive advantages by increasing flexibility and efficiency, managing knowledge effectively, improving productivity and time-to-market, improving relationships with suppliers, gathering on-line marketing information, facilitating teamwork, integrating different sources of customer information, reducing costs by using IT-based solutions and eliminating redundant processes (European Commission-DG Enterprise, 2004, pp. 27-29).

Companies should tend to focus especially on techniques in the areas of project management, business plan development, outsourcing and benchmarking. This paper will examine the national policy for the research and the technological development in Greece from 1950 until today and the effect of the European Union on the national policy. The main questions, which will be attempted to be answered are: What was the development of national policy for research and technological development in the post-war period in Greece? What is the current policy for research and technology? What are the consequences of the European policy for research and technology? Furthermore, innovative activities of Greek and EU enterprises, operating in industry and service sectors, will be examined in order to understand and present processes of knowledge-generation and coordination.

2 Theoretical Framework

Initially, technological progress was assumed to be achieved through a linear process starting with basic scientific research and progressing through more applied levels of research into areas such as marketing and the final launch of a new product or process. Science was seen as the driver of innovation and, as a result, governments concentrated science policy.

New ways of considering innovation have brought about a change in thinking as regards innovation-related policies (European Commission, 2004, p. 12). The first explicit theory of innovation management is the "technology push theory or engineering theory of innovation". In this theory, innovation opportunities, i.e. the opportunities to improve products or the manufacturing processes, are found in the uptake of research results. According to this theory, basic research and industrial R&TD are the sources of new or improved products and processes.

The production and uptake of research follows a linear sequence from research to the definition of a product and specifications of production, and the application of technology to make a product that conforms to the specifications defined by research that has also produced patents and scientific publications. The limitations of engineering solutions were recognised in the 1960s, resulting in an alternative view that sources of ideas for solutions should originate from the market. This alternative view gave birth to the "market pull theory of innovation". This theory has still been playing gives a central role in the research as a source of knowledge to develop or improve products and processes.

This theory sees the first recognition of organisational factors as contributors in innovation theory; the technical feasibility was still considered as a necessary condition of innovation, but no longer sufficient in itself for successful innovation. Organisational competency had to be taken into account to ensure successful innovation (Schmookler, J., 1996; Myers, S. and Marquis, D.G., 1969). A new generation called the "chain-link theories" of innovation then emerged to explain the fact that linkages between knowledge and market are not as automatic as assumed in engineering and market pull theories of innovation. There were two phases: (a) At the beginning of the 1980s, more attention was given to linkages between research and the market via engineering, production, technology development, marketing and sales (Mowery, D.C. and Rosenberg, N., 1978) and (b) Later in the 1980s, the focus laid the stress on the information generated through the linkages existing between the firm and its customers and suppliers. In these theories, innovation management is explained by combinations of tangible forms of capital in conjunction with one intangible form of capital: data about customers and suppliers (Von Hippel, E., 1994). At the end of the 1980s and during the 1990s, a technological networks theory of innovation management was developed by a new group of experts under the label of "systems of innovation". Those theorists assumed that innovative firms are linked to a highly diversified set of agents through collaborative networks and the exchange of information.

This view stressed the importance of sources of information that are external to the firm: clients, suppliers, consultants, government laboratories, government agencies, universities, etc (Nelson, R.R., 1993; Niosi, J., 1993, pp. 77-95; OECD, 1999). Finally, "the social network theory" of innovation management is based on two earlier ideas and a new insight. The earlier ideas hold that innovation is determined by research (technology push theory) and by unordered interaction between firms and other actors (technological networks theory). The new insight is that knowledge plays a more crucial role in fostering innovation.

The growing importance of knowledge as a production factor and a determinant of innovation can be explained by the continuous accumulation of technical knowledge over time, and by the use of communications technologies that make that knowledge available very rapidly worldwide (Foray, D., 2000, pp. 239-255). The evolution from a technological network perspective of innovation management to a social network perspective has been led by the challenge to transform information into knowledge (e.g. information contextually connected to the development or improvement of products or processes). Knowledge-based innovation requires not one but many kinds of knowledge. Furthermore, it requires the convergence of many different kinds of knowledge retained by a variety of actors.

3 Methodological Background

In the context of this paper, the term "innovation" is defined as a new or significantly improved product (good or service) introduced to the market or the introduction within an enterprise of a new or significantly improved process (Oslo Manual; European Commission, 2004, p. 11 and 17). Innovations are based on the results of new technological developments, new combinations of existing technology or the utilisation of other knowledge acquired by the enterprise.

Innovations may be developed by the innovating enterprise or by another enterprise. However, purely selling innovations wholly produced and developed by other enterprises is not included as an innovation activity. Innovations should be new to the enterprise concerned; for product innovations do not necessarily have to be new to the market and for process innovations the enterprise does not necessarily have to be the first to have introduced the process.

Product innovators are defined as enterprises that introduced new and improved goods and/or services significantly with respect to their fundamental characteristics, technical specifications, incorporated software or other immaterial components, intended uses, or user friendliness. Changes of a solely aesthetic nature and the pure sale of product innovations wholly produced and developed by other enterprises are not included. Process innovators are defined as those who implemented new and significantly improved production technologies or new and significantly improved methods of supplying services and delivering products. The outcome of such innovations should be significant for the level of output, quality of products (goods or services) or costs of production and distribution. Purely organisational or managerial changes are not included.

Successful innovators are defined as enterprises that introduced or implemented product innovations process innovations, or both product and process innovations during the period 1998–2000. An innovation is successful if it has been introduced to the market (product innovation), or if it has been implemented (process innovation). Enterprises with only on-going and/or abandoned innovation activity are defined as enterprises that had on-going or abandoned innovation activities to develop or introduce new or significantly improved products (goods or services) or implement new processes, including RTD activity.

Enterprises with innovation activity are defined as enterprises that introduce new or significantly improved products (goods or services) to the market or enterprises that implement new or significantly improved processes. Innovations are based on the results of new technological developments, new combinations of existing technology or the utilisation of other knowledge acquired by the enterprise. The term covers all types of innovator, namely product innovators, process innovators, as well as enterprises with only on-going and/or abandoned innovation activities.

Enterprises without innovation activity are defined as enterprises that had no innovation activity whatsoever during the survey period. The statistical data are based mainly on Greek national data (Ministry of Development – GSRT), OECD and Eurostat: Community Innovation Survey (CIS 2 & 3). The Community Innovation Survey (CIS) had been jointly initiated and implemented by Eurostat and DG Enterprise under the aegis of the European Innovation Monitoring System (EIMS), part of the Innovation Programme. The methodology was developed in co-operation with Statistical Offices in the Member States, independent experts and the OECD.

The Community Innovation Survey (CIS) provided a major new source of information on innovation at enterprise level in all EU Member States, Norway and Iceland. The CIS has been carried out for the first time in

1992. CIS2 took place in 1996 and CIS3 in 2001. Data gathering and analysis has been supported under the various Community RTD Framework Programmes. Since 2000, the CIS has become a major data source of the "European Innovation Scoreboard". The methodological basis of the CIS is provided by the "Oslo manual", a joint publication of Eurostat and the OECD. Data collection made by the statistical offices or competent research institutes in the member states.

The results of the surveys are treated at national level, using a common methodology and further processed by Eurostat to increase cross- country comparability. The Oslo manual is currently under revision in order to account for new orientations of European innovation policy. Among other aspects, the next CIS should contribute to a better understanding of the "non-technical" aspects of innovation, such as management techniques, organisational change, design and marketing issues.

4 An Overall Review of RTD Policy in Greece: 1950–2005

The Greek sector of research and technology was developed substantially afterwards the creation of institutional framework for the scientific research in the country in the beginning of the 1980s, the domestic activity in Research and Technological Development (R&TD). Between 1950 and 1981 is almost non-existent both in the level of government policy and in the level of private enterprises.

At this period, the main perception underlying the Greek economy, was that the investment in activities of research and technological development was not for the interest of a small country as Greece and was considered, as wastefulness in the particular developmental course of the country (Vaitsos K. and Giannitsis T., 1987, p. 71 and 72).

This time period is characterized by the intense government interventionism, accompanied from a extremely protective frame, that created conditions of greenhouse for the existing enterprises and simultaneously undermined the developmental possibilities of country, and did not encourage the technological renewal (Sakellaropoulos T., 1993, p. 235).

The renewal and the technological modernisation were also impeded by an other factor that is a few big, monopolistic character industrial enterprises from the government owned banking system (Sakellaropoulos T., 1993, p. 236). This important restrictions undermined the competitiveness of economy and rejected the engagement of expenses in research and technology, lagging behind the economy of entire country technologically. The first institutional bases for a policy of research and technological growth are placed with law 706/77. A national program of financing of research is promoted. In 1982, the Ministry of Research and Technology is created, which three years later is changed in General Secretariat of Research and Technology (GSRT) that today depends in the Ministry of Development (Vaitsos K. and Giannitsis T., 1987, p. 73).

Basic institution of establishing and implementation of RTD policy in Greece is the General Secretariat of Research and Technology (GSRT), which depends on the Ministry of Development (YPAN). The GSRT coordinates the inquiring work that is financed by the structural programs of European Union. The entry of Greek economy in the European Union, influenced considerably also the research and technological policy of country.

The government strategy for the RTD from 1980 to 1999 included interventions for the enrichment of Greek research network and, circumstantially, for the aid of industrial research. That particular effort had as results the increase of expenses for the research from 0.33% of GDP (1986) in 0.67% of GDP (1999) and the doubling of enterprises with activities RTD (NTUA-ICAP, 2002, p. 65). RTD policy, that since then was practised, was applied via structural programs EPET I, STRIDE and EPET II at periods 1990–1995 and 1995–2000 respectively.

This programs, under the 1st and 2nd Community Support Framework (CSF) of corresponding periods, aimed, mainly, the improvement of infrastructure of the research and technological web of country via creation of RTD institutions of (research institutes and centres, liaison offices, etc.) and the aid of enterprises and their networking and partnerships with the research institutions aiming at the improvement of their competitiveness.

With the above programs, it has been achieved important improvement in the research infrastructure of Greece and partly familiarization of the enterprises with the RTD and the transfer of technology. "Operational Program E&T 1989–93 (EPET I)" had budget about 100 million ECU. Its main objective was the aid of RTD infrastructure and particularly that of government owned sector. The program "Community Initiative STRIDE" had similar budget with EPET I, about 80 million €, and was applied the same period.

A strand of action was the extension and the modernisation of RTD infrastructure. "Operational Program R&T 1994–99 (EPET II)" is the bigger action both in terms of duration (six years) and in terms of budget (public expense was about 400 million €). EPET II aimed mainly in the mobilisation of created infrastructure and at second in its enlargement. The objective for certain relative decentralisation of activities RTD was not achieved and the bigger part of resources (more than 50%) remained in Attica.

The Operational Programs for the RTD (EPET I and EPET II), applied from 1989 until 1999, contributed decisively in the enlargement, the differentiation but also the rise of quality of RTD system. Today, in the frame of 3rd CSF (2000–2006), it is aimed the enlargement but simultaneously and the balance of system of research and technological growth, giving priority in the action that concerns the enterprises. The main tool for the implementation of national RTD strategy is the Operational Program "Competitiveness, 2000–2006".

The total budget for the technological innovation and research, in the frame of Operational Program of Ministry of Development, is 497.1 (43.28%) million of Euros from which the 215.17 millions of € constitute the Community contribution, the 86.29 (17.35%) million of € the national public contribution and the 195.64 (39.35%) million of € the private contribution. Certain basic records of Greece in RTD at the decade of '90 are presented in Table 1.

In Table 1 is presented the percentage contribution of total of domestic expense in the research and the technological development as percentage of (%) GDP of member states of European Union, of EU, USA and Japan at time interval 1991 up to 1999. Sweden presents the higher and annually increasing rate of domestic expense in research and technological development (3.78% for 1999) in the decade 1990 and Finland follows (3.22%).

Afterwards these two countries, Japan follows (2.94%) and USA (2.64%). High percentage also Germany presents (2.44%). France (2.18%), Denmark (2.09%), the Netherlands (2.02%) and Belgium (1.96%) present higher percentage of mean of EU (1.93% for 1999). The United Kingdom (1.85%) and Austria (1.83%) present lower percentage but close to the mean of EU. Greece is precisely opposite Sweden and it is found in lower outmost of the scale, because it presents the lower rate of total domestic expense in the research not only in 1999 (0.67%) but all the duration of decade. Greece is found between the countries (Denmark, Austria, Portugal, Finland) that presents net increase of expense for research in entire the duration of decade 1990.

The United Kingdom, Italy and France present net reduction of expense in the research. Greece follows Portugal (0.76% for 1999). Greece at the last decade has made important progress and presents important improvements in the research and the technological development. The average annual rate of percentage of RTD of GDP showed constant increase at the time period 1991–1999. The percentage of domestic RTD expense of GDP was increased from 0.20% in the beginning of decade of '80 in 0.67% in 1999 (GSRT, 2003, p. 2). Greece between 1995 and 1999 presented higher average annual rate: 8.71% against 1.53% of EU (GSRT, 2003, p. 5).

Table 1. Total RTD expenditure in % of GDP

Country	1991	1993	1995	1997	1999
EU	1.94	1.92	1.84	1.82	1.93
Belgium	1.62	1.58	1.58	1.58	1.96
Denmark	1.64	1.74	1.83	1.89	2.09
Germany	2.54	2.42	2.31	2.31	2.44
Greece	0.36	0.49	0.49	0.51	0.67
Spain	0.84	0.91	0.85	0.86	0.88
France	2.37	2.45	2.34	2.24	2.18
Ireland	0.93	1.2	1.36	1.43	1.21
Italy	1.23	1.14	1.01	1.0	1.04
Netherlands	1.97	2.0	2.07	2.12	2.02
Austria	1.47	1.49	1.59	1.82	1.83
Portugal	0.51	0.62	0.58	0.65	0.76
Finland	2.04	2.21	2.35	2.78	3.22
Sweden	2.79	3.39	3.59	3.85	3.78
United Kingdom	2.07	2.15	2.02	1.87	1.85
USA	–	–	2.53[a]	2.56	2.64
Japan	–	–	2.77[b]	2.83	2.94

Note: [a] Concerns year 1996.
Sources: a) GSRT, Department of Scientific and
Technological Indicators Documentation,
b) Science and Technology Indicators for the European
Research Area (STI-ERA).

5 An Overall Review of Innovative Performance: The Case of Greece Within the EU

5.1 Development of Innovativeness of Enterprises

Table 2 shows that the innovative manufacturing enterprises represented the 26.5% in the first period (1994–1996), the 30.3% in the second period (1996–1998) and the 27.3% in the third period (1998–2000). This is evident that the Greek industry improves its competitiveness and reduces the gap with the European industry. Product innovators represented the 22.5% in the first period, the 25.2% in the second period and the 18.4% in the third period while process innovators represented the 18.5% in the first period, the 23.7% in the second period and the 17.5% in the third period. Although the number of enterprises introduced new or improved products to the market is relatively low, there is a positive trend of increase: 10.4% in the first period, the 14.0% in the second period and the 10.3% in the third period (Table 2).

The Greek industry performance in terms of the number of innovative manufacturing enterprises is almost at the same level with the Belgian (27.0%)

Table 2. Innovation Indices: Manufacturing enterprises: Greece

Indices	1994–1996[a]		1996–1998[a]		1998–2000[b]	
	% Share in population	% Innovative enterprises	% Share in population	% Innovative enterprises	% Share in population	% Innovative enterprises
Enterprises with innov. Activity	26.50	100	30.30	100	27.3	100
Product innovators	22.5	85.1	25.2	83.3	18.4	67.3
Process innovators	18.5	70.2	23.7	78.1	17.5	64.1
Intramural RTD	20.6	77.9	21.2	69.8	21.8	79.8
Research and experimental development	15.8	59.7	18.9	62.3	17.3	64.7
Continuous RTD	5.1	19.3	7.1	23.3	7.1	26.1
Occasional RTD	10.7	40.3	11.8	39.1	na	na
Enterprises with Cooperation arrangements on innov. Activities	4.7	17.7	6.5	21.4	5.1	19.9
Product innovators introduced new products to the market	10.4	39.2	14.0	46.0	10.3	37.8
Enterprises receiving public funding	11.4	43.1	10.9	35.8	17.0[c]	16.4

[a]>20 employees. [b]> 10 employees. [c]Central Government only.
Sources: Eurostat; GSRT, 2001 (CIS II); GSRT, 2004 (CIS III); European Commission, 2004 (CIS III).

and Spanish (29.0%) performance concerning the period 1996–1998 (GSRT, 2001, p. 17). In contrary, for the period 1998–2000, Greece is lagging behind comparing to the Belgian (59.0%) and Spanish (37.0%) performance (European Commission, 2004, p. 78 and p. 126). Nevertheless, the gap with the other European countries remains significant.

The average of European Union is at 53% for the period 1996–1998 and 47.0% for 1998–2000 (European Commission, 2004, p. 19). Ireland holds the maximum percentage: 73% for 1996–98 (GSRT, 2001, p. 17) and 75% for 1998–2000 (European Commission, 2004, p. 150) and Portugal the minimum one (26.0%) for the period 1996–1998 (GSRT, 2001, p. 17) and Greece the minimum one (27.0%) for 1998–2000 (European Commission, 2004, p. 114). The share of innovative enterprises in the service industry increased significantly from 11.1% in the first period to the 15.5% in the second period and the 31.9% in the third period of the enterprises with ten or more employees (Table 3).

Table 3. Innovation Indices: Service enterprises with ten or more employees: Greece

Indices	1994–1996		1997–1998		1998–2000	
	% Share in population	% Innovative enterprises	% Share in population	% Innovative enterprises	% Share in population	% Innovative enterprises
Enterprises with innovation activity	11.1	100	15.50	100%	31.9	100
Intramural RTD	4.2	37.5	6.2	40.0	6.6	20.3
Research and experimental development	8.3	75.0	13.0	84.0	16.1	72.0
Continuous RTD	5.6	50.0	5.6	36.0	10.5	32.0
Occasional RTD	2.8	25.0	7.5	48.0	na	na
Enterprises with Cooperation arrangements on innov. activities	6.3	56.3	5.6	36.0	12.8	39.1
Enterprises receiving public funding	2.1	18.8	3.1	20.0	15.5[a]	15.1

[a]Central Government only.
Sources: Eurostat; GSRT, 2001 (CIS II); GSRT, 2004 (CIS III); European Commission, 2004 (CIS III).

5.2 RTD and Innovation

The analysis of data from Greece and other European countries reveals that the development of innovations does not require the development of RTD activities within the enterprise. In Greece, the 59.7% in the first period, the 62.3% in the second period and the 64.7% in the third period of the innovative manufacturing enterprises carry out RTD. However only 19.3% in the first period, the 23.3% in the second period and the 17.3% in the third period of innovating firms perform RTD in a systematic manner.

In service sector, the percentage is much lower: the 8.3% in the first period, the 13.0% in the second period and the 16.1% in the third period of the innovative enterprises with ten or more employees carry out RTD. The 5.6% in the first and second periods and the 10.5% in the third period of innovating firms perform RTD in a systematic manner.

5.3 Information Sources and Networking

The majority of the Greek enterprises, 77.2% in the first period and 64.8% in the second period, (GSRT, 2001, p. 57) and 80.8% in the third period, (GSRT, 2004, p. 25) have limited or no interaction with other organizations during the innovation process. During the period 1994–1996 only 17.7% of the innovative enterprises have co-operated with other organizations, while during the period 1997–1998 this rate increased to 21.4% in manufacturing enterprises with 20 or more employees. In the period 1998–2000, this rate is 19.9%, but in manufacturing enterprises with ten or more employees. In service enterprises with ten or more employees, 56.3% of the innovative enterprises have co-operated with other organizations in 1994–1996, while during the period 1997–1998 this rate decreased to 36.0% and 39.1 in 1998–2000.

5.4 Government Assistance for Innovation Development

Government assistance for the development of innovation seems to have bore fruits, since it has led to the increase of innovative activities in enterprises during the examined periods. Furthermore, the government assistance is correlated with the increase of turnover share due to innovations during the period 1997–1998. The high percentage of the funded innovative enterprises (43.1% in 1994–1996, 35.8% in 1996–1998), in relation to the respective figures in the European Union that does not overcome the 21% (GSRT, 2001, p. 48), indicates dependence of the innovativeness of Greek enterprises upon the government assistance. In the service sector, the percentage of the funded enterprises is much lower, around 20% (18.8% in 1994–1996 and 20.0% in 1997–1998).

5.5 Barriers to Innovation by Economic Activities

The effects of obstacles to innovation were measured in terms of the following classification: projects which were seriously delayed, projects prevented from being started and projects that were burdened/encumbered with other serious problems. Table 4 shows that a large number of enterprises with innovation activity in Greece confronted a lot of obstacles in their effort to develop innovation activities.

Almost half of the enterprises with innovation activity both in industry (45%) and in services (45%) were burdened/encumbered with other serious problems. Table 5 shows, on the other hand enterprises with innovation activity in the EU and the first of these three categories was the most frequently cited as being experienced (37% in total, 31% for industry and 46% for services).

Table 4. Proportion of enterprises with innovation activity where innovation activity was hampered, by sector, Greece, 1998–2000 [%]

	Total	Industry[a]	Services
Seriously delayed	38	22	35
Prevented to be started	27	33	23
Burdened/encumbered with other serious problems	45	45	45

[a]Industry: Mining and quarrying, Manufacturing and Electricity, gas and water supply.
Source: Eurostat.

Table 5. Proportion of enterprises with innovation activity where innovation activity was hampered, by sector, EU, 1998–2000 [%]

	Total	Industry[a]	Services
Seriously delayed	37	31	46
Prevented to be started	22	21	24
Burdened/encumbered with other serious problems	22	22	22

[a]Industry: Mining and quarrying, Manufacturing and Electricity, gas & water supply.
Source: Eurostat.

Some 38% of enterprises with innovation activity in Greece (22% for industry and 35% for services) reported that innovation projects had been seriously delayed, while in the EU 22% of enterprises reported projects where obstacles had prevented them from starting to innovate. Delays in projects were more often felt in the services sector, by 35% of enterprises with innovation activity in Greece and 46% in the EU, compared to 22% for industry in Greece and 31% for industry in the EU. Some 23% of service enterprises with innovation activity had innovation projects that were prevented from being started in Greece and 24% in the EU, compared to 33% of industrial enterprises in Greece and 21% of industrial enterprises in the EU. A similar proportion of industrial and services enterprises reported that innovation projects had been burdened or encumbered with other serious problems (45% for Greece and 22% for the EU).

5.6 Hampering Factors by Economic Activities

The definitions of "Enterprises with innovation activity" and of "Enterprises without innovation activity" are provided in Sect. 3, "Methodological background". Hampering factors are divided into three main groups. The first covers economic factors and is sub-divided into excessive economic risk, high innovation costs and a lack of financial resources. The second covers internal factors, such as organisational rigidity, a lack of qualified personnel, a lack of information on technology or markets. The final category covers other factors such as insufficient flexibility of regulations or standards or a lack of customer responsiveness to new goods or services.

Among the economic factors that are listed (Table 6), as far as Greece is concerned, lack of appropriate sources of finance (34%) appear to be the most often cited reason why innovation activity is hampered in industry and innovation costs (31%) appear to be the most often cited reason why innovation activity is hampered in services. These factors are followed by innovation costs (30%) in industry and a lack of appropriate sources (29%) in services.

Within the EU, innovation costs appear to be the most often cited reason why innovation activity is hampered, followed by a lack of appropriate sources of finance and excessive perceived economic risks. Within the EU, almost one quarter of the enterprises with innovation activity cited the cost of innovation as a hampering factor (23% in industry and 26% in services), while 17% cited a lack of appropriate sources of finance in industry and 22% in services. As to the excessive perceived economic risks, they are 16% in industry and 19% in services.

Table 6. Proportion of enterprises with innovation activity where innovation activity was highly hampered, Greece and EU, 1998–2000 [%][a]

| | Industry[b] | | Services | |
	Greece	EU	Greece	EU
Economic factors				
Excessive perceived economic risks	26	16	26	19
Innovation costs too high	30	23	31	26
Lack of appropriate sources of finance	34	17	29	22
Internal factors				
Organisational rigidities within the enterprise	9	5	8	7
Lack of qualified personnel	19	15	14	19
Lack of information on technology	8	5	3	4
Lack of information on markets	7	5	4	5
Other factors				
Insufficient flexibility of regulations or standards	17	9	11	15
Lack of customer responsiveness to new goods or services	8	5	14	8

[a] Multiple answers allowed.
[b] Industry: Mining and quarrying, Manufacturing and Electricity, gas and water supply.
Source: Eurostat.

Comparing the different factors for enterprises with innovation activity to those without innovation activity, they also tend to cite innovation costs as the principal economic factor hampering innovation (Table 7).

Table 7. Proportion of enterprises without innovation activity where innovation activity was highly hampered, Greece and EU, 1998–2000 [%][a]

| | Industry | | Services | |
	Greece	EU	Greece	EU
Economic factors				
Excessive perceived economic risks	29	15	19	12
Innovation costs too high	30	20	22	16
Lack of appropriate sources of finance	27	13	20	12
Internal factors				
Organisational rigidities within the enterprise	7	5	4	5
Lack of qualified personnel	10	12	6	9
Lack of information on technology	7	5	4	4
Lack of information on markets	5	5	2	4
Other factors				
Insufficient flexibility of regulations or standards	11	7	7	9
Lack of customer responsiveness to new goods or services	11	8	9	6

[a] Multiple answers allowed.

However, among enterprises without innovation activity, the importance of excessive perceived economic risks (15% of industry and 12% of services) and a lack of appropriate sources of finance (13% of industry and 12% of services) are reversed when compared to the results for enterprises with innovation activity (Table 7). It should be noted that for all three economic factors, a higher proportion of enterprises with innovation activity cited these factors, as compared to enterprises without innovation activity.

As with economic factors, the proportion of enterprises without innovation activity that cited internal factors is generally lower than the corresponding share of enterprises with innovation activity (Table 7). This pattern did not hold for one of the internal factors, namely the lack of information on technology, nor for one of the other factors, where a lack of customer responsiveness to new goods or services is cited by a higher proportion of enterprises without innovation activity.

A comparison of the proportion of enterprises citing each of the factors shows that more enterprises generally felt constrained by economic circumstances than by internal factors, although a lack of qualified personnel is often viewed as one of the most important factors constraining innovation both in Greece and in the EU, but are reversed when compared to Greece and the EU (19% of industry and 14% of services in Greece and 15% of industry and 19% of services in the EU). In the EU, table 6 shows that the proportion of enterprises that cited the various hampering factors is generally higher among enterprises in the services sector.

In Greece, the largest difference in the proportion of enterprises with innovation activity citing each of these factors is six (6) percentage points (between industry and services), as regards insufficient flexibility of regulations or standards (in favour of industry) and lack of customer responsiveness to new goods or services (in favour of services). While the differences between industry and services are generally small, two of the nine factors (concerning a lack of information on technology and a lack of qualified personnel) hampered a greater proportion of enterprises in industry.

Within the EU, the largest difference in the proportion of enterprises with innovation activity citing each of these factors is six (6) percentage points (between services and industry), as regards insufficient flexibility of regulations or standards (in favor of services). While the differences between services and industry are generally small, only one of the nine factors (concerning a lack of information on technology) hampered a greater proportion of enterprises in industry. No matter which breakdown is studied, the most common hampering factors tended to be economic: high innovation costs, a shortage of financial resources and excessive economic risks. Within the EU, among enterprises without innovation activity, the proportion of enterprises where innovation activity was hampered was generally higher for industrial enterprises than for those from the services sector.

This was particularly true for economic factors, with the largest difference registered for high innovation costs, which were cited as a hampering factor of 20% for all industrial enterprises without innovation activity compared to 16% in the services sector. In Greece, enterprises without innovation activity showed similar behaviour.

6 The European Research Area and the National Policy

In January 2000 the European Committee in its statement proposed the creation of a European Research Area (EC, 2000, p.p. 26-27). The proposal in question offered a new horizon for scientific and technological activity and research policy in Europe. Its objective was the increase of financing of research as 3% of the total GNP of the European Union and the increase of the rate of financing of enterprises (European Committee, 2002, p.p. 2-8).The promotion of knowledge and innovation, that is based on research and technological development constitutes the corner stone of the strategy of Lisbon and Europe, falls short of its competitors as far as the investment of new knowledge is concerned, at the European meeting in Barcelona, in March 2002.

In this framework, Greece is called to follow. At the European meeting in Barcelona, in March 2002, its objective was the increase of financing of research as 3% of the total GNP of the European Union with the condition that two third of expenses will be financed by the enterprises, a thing which could lead to an increase of GDP of 0.5% and to 400,000 more places of work each year in the whole of the EU, up to 2010. Greece adopted the objective of increasing the GDP to 1.5% with enterprises contributing up to 40% of the financing (from 0.67% of GDP and from 24% in 1999, respectively) (GSRT, 2003, p. 14).

7 Conclusions

It is seen that for Greece government financing and Community financing mainly constitute the basic sources of financing of RTD and make the course, the direction, the objectives and the strategy for research and technology in our country completely dependent on this. The basic characteristic of RTD in Greece is, mainly, the transfer and diffusion of know-how via technological investments and education and not the growth of new products and new knowledge. Research activity supports more the assimilation and the adaptation of existing technology and not the creation of new knowledge. The technological modernisation of enterprises occurs mainly in the market of incorporated technology and innovation has a more commercial than technological content (NTUA-ICAP, 2002, p.p. 65-66). The Greek system henceforth has acquired an important experience in the planning and implementation of the policy for research and technological development and, also, has achieved certain positive results that concern the competitive human potential (increase and improvement of dexterities of human research dynamic), networking with foreign countries mainly via the CSF, and certain satisfactory results in the basic research and important improvements of infrastructure. However, the efficiency of the productive base of RTD system remains low.

The main reasons for this are the lack of comprehension of industry and firms for the necessity of undertaking RTD work the transfer of technology and innovation, the lack of collaboration between research institutions and industry, the relatively limited research potential, the lack of co-ordination of research activities, the lack of innovative – technological culture in Greece, the insufficient system of implementation, control and diffusion of RTD results and the delay against the RTD of developed economies (NTUA-ICAP, 2002, p.p. 22-29 ; GSRT, 2004, p.p. 69-73).

The perception that henceforth dominates the European Union is that investment in research and technology is an absolute necessity in order for European economy to become, not simply competitive but very competitive up to 2010. For Greece, this development signals the beginning of a new period in the sector of the policy for research and technological development, of which the general directions and objectives will be determined at European level, based on the joint analysis and the open method of co-ordination and will be determined by the conditions of other competition between the European Union, the USA and Japan and not at a level of a member state. The new policy of the European Union is directed to the increase of economic contribution of the private sector and enterprises in financing the work for research and technological development. I would like to characterise these new conditions of growth as "incubated" type of growth and it appears that those organisations that have the required resources and faculties in order to follow in the new direction will profit and these organisations and institutions will appear to make up a very small sector of the Greek economy.

This development, in our opinion, will strengthen still more the phenomenon of dualism in Greece, that is to say on the one hand the existence of big enterprises and organisations (academic and research institutions mainly) that are capable to of advancing international collaborations for the planning, implementing and promoting of research and technological work, products and services and on the other hand, the existence of an overwhelming majority of family , small to medium-sized enterprises, which do not have the research and technological base for the undertaking of similar activities in the sector of research and technological growth, with important social repercussions, particularly in employment. The "beneficiaries" up to date, appear to be between the academic and research institutions of Greece and the past teaches us that also in the new phase (from 2000 and onwards) of the European Research Area, the same "beneficiaries" once more will be a minimal number of enterprises that have the faculties and the resources, the internal organisation and the economic possibility, required for the implementation of the work for research and technological growth at an international level and networking. Greece is not a producer of research and technology, but has been a user of technology for decades. The basic partner in a new type of growth, that is to say the family, small to medium-sized enterprises in Greece do not appear to have the resources and the faculties that are required for this direction, not only because they are small enterprises that are activating in small size market, but, in our opinion, because there exists a factor concerning the lack of relative mentality, attitude and perception not only from Greek industry but also from the government owned sector, in general. New strategies can strengthen the European Union, as a distinguishable entity, for the reduction in the gap between the USA and Japan in the sector of research and technological growth, but for Greece this means importing technological modernisation and aid for the model of capitalistic economic growth, in the framework which will be intensified and legalised still more by the substitution of human workforce by technology. The information necessary for the development of innovation is derived mainly from within the firms showing an isolation of the firms from their environment.

This is actually obvious in both SMEs and large Greek companies. Greek enterprises, with weak linkages, try to make up for the lack of information by participating in exhibitions and workshops. In accordance to the above trend, co-operation for the development of innovations is low in all three above-mentioned periods; see Hatzikian (2003); Hatzikian (2004) for an extending discussion. Concluding, it can be said that the strengthening of networking, including vertical or horizontal collaborations and partnerships (innovation zones) among firms and collaborations between firms and technological or research organizations, appear as a central policy issue. Suitable policies to address the problem may include development of human resources, related with various aspects and levels of innovative activities in the framework of a national innovation system.

8 References

Christensen, C. (1997) The Innovator's Dilemma, Harper Collins.

Deniozos, G. (1993) Technology Perspective, in Giannitsis, T. (ed.) Industrial and Technological Policy, Themelio, Athens.

Drucker, P. (1997) Looking ahead implications of the present, *HBR*, Sept/Oct.

Edquist, D. (1997) Systems of Innovation. Technologies, Institutions and Organisations, London, Pinter.

European Commission, (1995), Green Paper on Innovation *COM(1995) 688*.

European Commission, (2000). Towards a European Research Area, COM (2000)06 of 18 January 2000.

European Commission (2004) Innovation Results for the EU, Iceland and Norway, Data 1998-2001 (CIS III), Luxembourg: Office for Official Publications of the European Communities.

European Commission-DG Enterprise (2004) Innovation Management and the Knowledge - Driven Economy, ECSC-EC-EAEC Brussels-Luxembourg.

Hatzikian, J. Comparative evaluation of the development of enterprises and the position of Greece in the innovation sector. In: Dioikitiki Enimerosi, 25, Jan 2003, pp. 74-83. Athens : Eidiki Ekdotiki, 2003, ISSN 1106-4749. (in Greek journal).

Hatzikian, J. (2004) The Research and Technological Development Policy: the Case of Greece, in Sakellaropoulos, Th., (ed.) (2004) Economy and Politics in Modern Greece, Vol. B', Athens: Dionikos, (in Greek).

Foray, D. (2000) Characterising the Knowledge Base: Available and Missing Indicators, pp. 239-255, in OECD. ed. Knowledge Management in the Learning Society, Paris, OECD.

GSRT (2001) National Innovation Survey (CIS II) in Greek Enterprises 1994-1998, Athens: Ministry of Development – GSRT.

GSRT, (2003) Research & Development in Greece, Ministry of Development, Athens.

GSRT (2004) National Innovation Survey (CIS III) in Greek Enterprises 1998-2000 Athens: GSRT - General Secretariat for Research and Technology - Ministry of Development, 2004 (in Greek).

Kitsos C. P., Hatzikian J., (2005) Sequential Techniques for Innovation Indexes. Sixteenth (16th) International Society for Professional Innovation Management – ISPIM Annual Conference: The Role of Knowledge in Innovation Management, Porto, Portugal, 19-22 June 2005.

Lundvall, B.A. (1995) National Systems of Innovation, London.

Machlup, F. (1962) The Production and Distribution of Knowledge in the United States. Princeton University Press.

Maskell, P. (1999) Social Capital, Innovation and Competitiveness, Oxford, Oxford University Press.

Mowery, D.C., Rosenberg, N. (1978) The Influence of Market Demand upon Innovation: a Critical Review of some recent Empirical Studies, Research Policy, 8, April.

Myers, S., Marquis, D.G. (1969) Successful Industrial Innovation,Washington, D.C., National Science Foundation.

Myers, P. (1996) Knowledge Management Tools, USA, Butterworth-Heinemann.

Nelson, R.R. (1993) National Innovation Systems: a Comparative Analysis, Oxford, Oxford Univ Press.

Niosi, J. (1993) National Systems of Innovation in Search of a Workable Concept, Technology in Society, 3, pp. 77-95.

NTUA, ICAP (2002) Evaluation of Partnerships and networking between research and industrial organizations (1995– 2001), Ministry of Development-GRST, Athens (in Greek).

OECD (1993) Frascati Manual, Paris.

OECD (1996) The Knowledge-Based Economy, Paris. STI Outlook.

OECD (1997) Creativity, Innovation and Job Creation Paris.

OECD (1997) Industrial Competitiveness in the Knowledge-based Economy, The New Role of Governments, Paris.

OECD (1999) Boosting Innovation. The Cluster Approach, Paris.

OECD (1999) Managing National Innovation Systems, Paris.

OECD (2000) Knowledge Management in the Learning Society, Paris.

OECD (2000) Innovative Clusters: Drivers of National Innovation Systems, Paris.

OECD (1993), Frascati Manual, Paris.

OECD (1996) The Knowledge-Based Economy. Paris. STI Outlook.

OECD (1997) Creativity, Innovation and Job Creation, Paris.

OECD (1997) Industrial Competitiveness in the Knowledge-based Economy, The New Role of Governments, Paris.

OECD (1999) Boosting Innovation. The Cluster Approach, Paris.

OECD (1999) Managing National Innovation Systems, Paris.

OECD (2000) Knowledge Management in the Learning Society, Paris.

OECD (2001) Innovative Clusters: Drivers of National Innovation Systems, Paris.

Patel, P., Pavitt, K. (1994) National Innovation Systems: why they are important and how they might be measured and compared, Economics of Innovation and New Technology, 3, pp. 77-95.

Sakellaropoulos, T., (1993) State and Economy in Greece. An historical typology", in Sakellaropoulos, T., Modern Greek Society. Historical and Critical Approaches, Critiki, Athens.

Soete, L., A. Arundel, (eds.), (1993) An Integrated Approach to European Innovation and Technology Diffusion Policy: A Maastricht Memorandum, Publication nr. EUR 15090 EN of the Commission of the European Communities, Brussels-Luxembourg.

Schmookler, J. (1996) Invention and Economic Growth, Cambridge, Harvard University Press.

Teece, D.J. (1992) Competition, Cooperation and Innovation: Organizational Arrangements for Regimes of Rapid Technological Progress, Journal of Economic Behavior and Organization, 18, pp. 1-25.

Teece, D.J., Pisano, G., Shuen, A. (1997) Dynamic Capabilities and Strategic Management, Strategic Management Journal, vol 18-7, pp. 509-553.

Tsipouri L. et. al., (1994) Research and Technology management in Enterprises : Issues for Community Policy, Case Study in Greece, Luxembourg.

Vaitsos, K., Giannitsis, T. (1987) Technological Transformation and Economic Development. The Greek experience and international perspectives, Gutenberg, Athens (in Greek).

Von Hippel, E. (1994) The Sources of Innovation, Oxford, Oxford University Press.

Winter, S.G. (1987) Knowledge and Competence as Strategic Assets, in Teece D. J. ed. The Competitive Challenge. Strategies for Industrial Innovation and Renewal, USA, Harper & Row.

World Bank (1998) Knowledge for Development, World Development Report, New York, Oxford University Press.

Financial Autonomy of Local Governments: Case Studies of Finland and Poland

Lasse Oulasvirta[1,*] and Maciej Turala[2]

[1] Department of Adminstrative Science, University of Tampere, Finland
[2] University of Lodz, Poland

1 Introduction

Local governments are a part of the economic, social and political system in all democratic countries. However, the role that is played by local governments, their importance and the level of autonomy varies a great deal among countries. Different approaches to the issue of local governments in different countries come about as a result of varying historical, cultural and social backgrounds.

This article deals with two local government systems whose path of development was greatly different – namely Finland and Poland. Since the mid-1940s both these countries operated under extremely different conditions. Although not a part of Soviet Union as such Poland was nonetheless a part of the Soviet-run block of Central and Eastern European countries. During nearly five decades of communist regime local governments were abolished in Poland. On the other hand Finland was a democracy and a market economy, where local governments operated and developed.

Only after 1990 did Poland start to chase the developed European countries. The political system changed, the economy became market-oriented and local governments were resurrected. This article attempts to present the current status of local governments in Poland and Finland in order to ascertain where the Polish model of local governance is on the map of development. The article emphasises the issue of financial autonomy and further develops the OECD research project entitled "Fiscal Design Across Levels of Government" regarding the concept of financial autonomy in sub-national government levels.

* Email: lasse_oulasvirta@uta.fi

Financial autonomy may be approached from two sides, namely the income source side and the expenditure side. The authors try to assess the income source based autonomy by analysing the income structure of local governments, and the decision-making power that the local authorities may exert over various types of income sources. On the other hand the authors attempt to assess the extent to which the expenditure is pre-determined by national legislation. This is done through allocating particular expenditure items on an expenditure autonomy continuum, ranging from voluntary tasks (expenditures) to commissioned tasks (expenditure) which are steered in detail by the central government. The article is concluded by an analysis of relationships between the income autonomy on the one hand and tasks as well as expenditure that they incur on the other hand. A matrix combining both these facets is constructed and presented in order to assess whether the income autonomy and the expenditure autonomy are balanced.

1.1 Organisation of the Local Government System in Poland

The contemporary history of local governments in Poland started in 1990. The current form of locally managed communes (*"gmina"*) was created by a Local Government Act passed by the Parliament on March 8, 1990. The Act has replaced the old system of so-called national councils, which were a relict of the communist era.

The role that the communes were to play in shaping a democratic Poland was at that time considered to be great (Stoker 1991, p. 1–20). The recreation of local governments was one of the first fundamental reforms undertaken after Poland had changed its political and economic system. The fact that the Local Government Act has been passed by the Parliament on the same day as the new Constitution, which was a confirmation of and a stepping stone for further transformation, speaks volumes for how significant the local governments were thought to be. The creation of autonomous local governments was to help stabilise the new democracy through political, fiscal and administrative decentralisation. It was considered vital to have local governments as allies in the struggle for strengthening and stabilising the democratic system in Poland during the time of system transformation in the early 1990s.

The communes have been the only level of local government administration for nearly nine years. On January 1, 1999 a new territorial division was implemented, which created two additional levels of local government – voivodships (*"województwo"*), which are also referred to as regions and are the largest of local governments, as well as an intermediate level between regions and communes – counties (*"powiat"*). This reform was meant to increase the effectiveness of the way in which the country was managed, make the society more actively involved in the matters of running the state and finally to adjust the territorial division of Poland to the requirements posed by the anticipated enlargement of the EU (Kot 2003, p. 82–83).

The local governments of all levels are not hierarchically subordinate to local governments of higher levels nor to the central authorities. Currently there are 16 regions, 381 counties and 2478 communes. The expenditure that is carried out by local governments amounts to slightly less than a third of all public expenditure. Within that amount Polish local governments take care of a wide array of tasks from spatial planning and environmental protection, through maintaining public facilities and infrastructure, supllying heat, gas and electricity, treating sewage and waste, providing local public transport, health care, social welfare, education and culture to ensuring public order.

1.2 Finnish Local Government System

The foundation for Finnish local government system was layed in 1865–1873 with laws on rural municipalities and cities. The present Local Government Act of 1995 treats both rural municipalities and cities in the same way. The present act gives more flexibility than former laws to organise municipal functions and administration. Local self-government is safeguarded in the Finnish constitution.

Finland has a one-tier local government system with 444 municipalities. There is no intermediate local government level with its own taxing powers and elected councils as in other Nordic countries. Instead, Finland has so-called municipal joint authorities, which have council members appointed by member municipalities. These joint authorities take care of hospitals and vocational schools and some other activities requiring wider population bases than separate municipalities have.

At the regional level, there are six regional general-purpose state authorities, provinces (*"lääni"*). Provinces are mainly regulatory authorities. Besides these provinces there are some special purpose regional state authorities.

The 1990s saw two important law reforms. Besides the enactment of the Local Government Act in 1995, also the grant system for local governments was reformed. The new system that came into power in 1993 replaced cost-based, specific government grants by estimated general type of grants which are determined by municipal expenditure needs and tax base differences.

The expenditure of local authorities and joint municipal authorities makes up nearly two-thirds of all public expenditure on consumption and investments in Finland. Most of the expenditure of local authorities and joint municipal authorities arises from the provision of basic welfare services. Staff costs are over half of local government expenditure. Employees in total are little over 400,000.

Local authorities run the country's comprehensive school system, upper secondary schools, vocational institutes, libraries, cultural and recreational services. Child day-care, welfare for the aged and the disabled and a wide range of other social services are also responsibilities of local authorities. Local governments provide preventive and primary health care services, specialist medical care and dental care, and also promote a healthy living environment. They even take care of planning and supervision of land use and construction in their area, water and energy supply, waste management, street and road maintenance and environmental protection.

2 Local Government Finance

2.1 Local Government Finance: The Case of Finland

Finnish local self-government derives its strength from an independent taxation right that is protected in the constitution. Local authorities fund nearly half of their operations out of their own tax revenues. These consist of a local income tax, a share of a corporate income tax and a real estate tax. Contrary to typical public economics' arguments of tax assignment, income tax is the most important local tax in Finland whereas property tax is of minor importance. In addition, local governments receive an annual share of revenues from corporate taxes (a shared tax).[1]

Each municipality decides independently on its income tax rate; no upper limit is set. The real estate tax has an upper and a lower limit prescribed in the tax law. Municipal income tax is a flat rate tax on the earned income of individuals. The average tax rate has been slowly increasing during the last decades. In 2002, the average local income tax rate was 18.03% of taxable income.

Government grants are another major source of income for local authorities, and amount to, on average, 15% of their income. A major grant reform was implemented in 1993 most of the grants that the municipalities received were changed from specific grants at actual costs to general

---

[1] of Finnish and Nordic municipal finance see Oulasvirta 1993 (p. 106–135), 2003a (p. 89–98) and 2003b (p. 340–349).

purpose grants related to objective criteria (non-matching grants). As the grants are not anymore matching and earmarked like before, the municipalities are expected to be more efficient in providing services according to local needs and circumstances. Currently, the system is made up of general grants and two-sector grants to social welfare and health care as well as to education and culture. Both the general and sector grants are by nature general purpose grants. The general grants are formed by grants per capita and tax revenue equalising grants, which are typical general and non-matching grants.

In addition to grants mentioned above, also *discretionary general grants* may be awarded to a municipality which, primarily due to exceptional or temporary financial difficulties, is in need of additional financial support. The applications are directed to the Ministry of Interior and the Cabinet makes the ultimate decision.

Operating revenues (fees and charges) make up about 26% of municipal income. Two-thirds of municipality income from fees and charges comes from publicly-owned enterprises, mainly energy, water and sewerage works and harbours. Within the limits laid down in the law, the local authorities may also use charges for social services and health care and for educational and cultural services. However, these charges are of minor significance in funding these services.

Loans bring in about 2–4% of municipal income. Local authorities normally use loans only to fund investments; they do not normally take loans to finance their running costs. They have the right to borrow independently on both the domestic and the foreign money market.

2.2 Local Government Finance: The Case of Poland

The system of financing local governments in Poland is slightly more complex from the Finnish one due to the fact that there are three separate tiers of local government authorities. Thus, the following analysis provides only the simplified view of the Polish financial system, while attempting to reflect the characteristic features of each level of local government (Table 1).

Table 1. Municipal finances in Finland during 1950–2000, %

	1950	1960	1970	1980	1990	2000
Tax incomes	50.8	50.4	54.4	40.2	39.4	51.0
Loans	11.5	5.2	5.3	3.9	4.5	3.0
Grants-in-aid	17.5	15.0	15.3	18.2	23.0	14.0
Other incomes	20.2	29.4	25.0	37.7	33.1	32.0
Total	100.0	100.0	100.0	100.0	100.0	100.0

Source: Statistics Finland and The Association of Finnish Local Authorities.

Tax incomes play a lesser role in financing Polish local governments than they do in Finland, despite the fact that there are ten different tax income sources available to local governments. Local taxes include eight of them: real estate tax, agricultural tax, forest tax, tax on means of transportation, dog tax, inheritance and gift tax, personal income lump-sum tax, tax on civil law contracts. All income from these local taxes goes to communal budgets. The remaining two tax income sources, namely the personal income tax and the corporate income tax are state taxes which are shared between the state and all local governments. As of January 1, 2004, the shares that are transferred to local government budgets have been raised quite significantly. This change is bound to change the income structure of local governments considerably.

Apart from tax incomes Polish local governments also have a number of other income sources that are considered as their own sources of income. The most prominent in this group are charges which the communal local government may collect: a treasury fee, an administrative charge, market dues, charges for some services provided by local governments, mineral royalties and other charges and fines. The group of local governments' own sources of incomes is concluded by various other sources including: incomes from property, inheritance and donations, interests etc.

The share of local governments' own sources of incomes in total incomes has been gradually decreasing ever since the local governments have been re-established in 1990. This is particularly clear in the case of communes – as far as counties and regions are concerned, the shares have been more stable (in the case of counties the share has even increased), but their level is much lower than for communes (see Table 2).

As a result of a weakening role of local governments' own sources of incomes the role of grants transferred from the state budget has been gradually increasing. The role of general grants has been growing particularly significantly. Similarly to Finland, the general-purpose grants are based and calculated according to a set of objective criteria. These include: local governments' per capita tax incomes, low population density, high rate of unemployment, level of expenditure on social welfare, etc. General-purpose grants are a major source of funding for all local governments in Poland.

Finally, the specific grants that are awarded to Polish local governments are conditional grants. They are awarded mainly for executing tasks in the field of government administration and other tasks which are commissioned by law or which derive from agreements. They are not as significant as general grants in financing communes but play a major part in financing counties as well as regions.

Table 2. Local government income structure 1991–2002, %

	Communes			Counties		Voivodships	
	1991	1999	2002	1999	2002	1999	2002
Own sources	45.4	34.3	34.7	4.3	9.5	1.6	2.9
PIT and CIT shares	28.9	18.2	15.2	1.9	1.3	16.4	12.8
General grants	13.5	32.1	35.2	44.4	47.0	34.7	35.8
Specific grants	12.0	15.4	14.9	49.4	42.2	47.3	48.5

Source: Reports on implementation of state budget – information on local government budgets, published by the Cabinet and Statistical Yearbooks published by the Main Statistical Office.

Table 2 shows the development of major components of the local government income structure since 1991 (a recreation of communal local government) and 1999 (establishment of counties and regions).

3 Financial Autonomy of Local Governments

3.1 The Relationship Between Central and Local Government

Usually, three crude models of the relationship between central and local government are mentioned. The relative autonomy model gives local governments a freedom of action within a defined framework of powers and duties. Central control is limited and local authorities are steered by legislation. Local authorities raise most of their revenue through direct taxation. In the agency model local authorities serve mainly as agencies for carrying out central government's policies.

This is guaranteed by detailed legislation, regulation and controls. There is therefore little need or justification for significant local taxation. Grants and other central funding make up the most of the local government income. The interaction model is something between the two extreme models. According to Stoker the political processes of central and local government are closely inter-related – possibly through a dual mandate – with issues being resolved by mutual discussion. In this model it is difficult to define responsibilities, since emphasis is on working together. Local government finance will consist of both taxes and grants, but taxes may be shared and grant levels protected (Stoker 1991, p. 6–7).

Stoker emphasises that normally no country can be simply described in terms of only one of these models. One must also observe that the pattern may vary between different activities in the same country (Stoker 1991).

It is certainly not true that any of these models is a universal one, the best solution irrespective of the phase of development in the country in question. Local government systems and central-local relations develop in their country-specific circumstances, culture and history. In Europe we may discern a modern trend that emphasises local democracy and decentralization from central government to regional and local levels, which has even been expressed in the European Charter of Local Self Government.

3.2 The Income Autonomy Concept

A comparon of financial autonomy between Polish and Finnish local governments requires that the analysis is based on comparable units that carry out a similar scope of tasks. That is why only local governments on the communal level in Poland are analysed and compared to their Finnish counterparts.[2] Similarly, the Finnish joint authorities are not taken into consideration. This approach is to safeguard the quality of the comparison and prevent the distortion of results and conclusions.

The concept of income autonomy is approached according to the classification of income sources prepared by the OECD (OECD 2001). According to that classification the sub-national government income sources may be ranked respective to the level of autonomy that they provide local governments with. Tax incomes are divided into three main categories of decreasing tax autonomy which are then subdivided into groups and ranked by decreasing order of control that the local governments may exert over a given income source. The grants are also classified and divided into smaller groups. The breakdown of local government income sources is presented in Table 3, together with the income structure of local governments in both analysed countries.

Before presenting a more detailed analysis of the income structure, let us first discuss shortly the features of particular groups of income sources with regards to financial autonomy. Tax incomes and other own sources of income are by far the most favourable sources of income as far as financial autonomy of local governments is concerned. Not only do they offer a possibility of deciding (to a greater or lesser extent) the amounts that are collected, but normally also provide local authorities with a priviledge of deciding freely how these funds will be spent. That is to say that tax incomes are not earmarked to any specific activities.

---

[2] The analysis is carried out for communes as well as large cities which have a status of counties, while being communes at the same time.

Table 3. Income sources of Polish and Finnish local governments

Tax incomes and other own sources of income:	Weight index	Finland 2002 [EUR, % of total incomes]	Poland 2002 [PLN, % of total incomes]
(a) Local government sets tax rate and tax base	100%		Income from property 2.89 billion, 4.58%
(b) Local government sets tax rate only	80%	Income tax 11.95 billion, 66.7% Real estate tax 1.49 billion, 8.3%	Real estate tax 9.77 billion, 15.48% Agricultural tax 0.82 billion, 1.30% Tax on means of transportation 0.53 billion, 0.84% Marketplace fee 0.24 billion, 0.39% Forest tax 0.11 billion, 0.18%
(c) Local government sets tax base only	70%		
(d1) Local government determines revenue split	65%		
(d2) Revenue split can only be changed with consent of subnational government	60%		
(d3) Revenue split fixed in legislation, may unilaterally be changed by central government	50%	Share of corporate tax 0.64 billion, 3.6%	Share of Personal Income Tax 8.80 billion, 13.94% Share of Corporate Income Tax 0.79 billion, 1.25% Tax on civil law contracts 0.87 billion, 1.38% Treasury fee 0.48 billion, 0.77% Mineral royalties 0.23 billion, 0.36% Lump-sum income tax 0.19 billion, 0.30% Inheritance and gift tax 0.18 billion, 0.29%

Table 3. (continued)

Tax incomes and other own sources of income:	Weight index	Finland 2002 [EUR, % of total incomes]	Poland 2002 [PLN, % of total incomes]
(d4) Revenue split determined annually by central government as part of the budget.	40%		
(e) Central government sets rate and base of local government tax.	40%		
Other own incomes	40%		Other own incomes 5.61 billion, 8.87%
General-purpose grants	40%		General grants 22.23 billion, 35.21%
Grants related to objective criteria	35%	Current grants 3.67 billion, 20.5%	
Grants also related to own tax effort	45%		
Specific grants	10%	Investment grants 0.16 billion, 0.9%	Specific grants 9.38 billion, 14.86%
Discretionary grants	0%		
Total taxes and grants		Total taxes and grants 17.91 billion, 100%	Total incomes 63.12 billion, 100%

Source: Finnish Local Government Association, 23.3.2004, www.kunnat. net; Report on implementation of state budget – information on local government budgets for 2002, published by the Cabinet in 2003 in Warsaw.

On the other hand, specific grants offer very little as far as the income side of financial autonomy is concerned. Furthermore, they are often very restrictive with regards to the expenditure side as well. Since they are awarded for a specific purpose (mostly tasks that are commissioned to local governments by legislation), it is necessary to use them exactly as the donor has specified. Should these funds be used otherwise, it is required that they are returned to the donor.

This means that the local governments' hands are tied – there is no freedom of using or allocating specific grants as the local authorities consider it best. It is therefore clear that specific grants are the least favourable group of incomes as far as financial autonomy is concerned. Finally, the general purpose grants lie somewhere in between the tax incomes and specific grants.

They do not offer much with regards to the income autonomy but have a distinct advantage over specific grants in that they may be used freely, as the local government authorities see fit. Table 3 presents the shares of incomes allocated to particular income sources ranked in accordance with the OECD report on tax autonomy. The classification of grants used in the table is slightly less complex than what the OECD report proposes. The reason for that being that such a detailed breakdown of grants is not fully applicable for our country comparison purposes.

The income sources of Polish and Finnish local governments have been allocated to appropriate classes in the table above. In the case of Polish local governments the grants have only been allocated to main groups as either general-purpose grants or specific grants. Also there remains a significant group of own incomes of Polish local governments that could not be allocated to specific groups due to the fact that the available statistics do not provide a required level of detail. This group accounts for 5.6 billion PLN (8.87% of total incomes). They have been included in a separate group called 'other own incomes'.

In the case of Finnish local governments, the current grants have not yet been allocated to the main groups of general-purpose grants or specific grants. This shall be tried later. Anyway, about 90% can be estimated to be general type of grants of the current grants. Investment grants are all specific grants. In the Finnish case, the percentages have been calculated from the income other than tax and grant income excluded.

The table above includes also the proposed **weighing indices** for all classes of incomes. These indices are to reflect, subjectively, what level of autonomy and decisionmaking power a given class of incomes provides the local governments with. These indices were used to weigh particular classes of incomes so that an income autonomy index could be worked out.

A calculation of such an index for Poland (based on the proposed values for weighing) gives the following result (the calculation is carried out by multiplying the shares of particular income sources through the weighing indices assigned to them and adding them to receive a joint index): **47.4%**. This means that Polish communes are capable of controlling and deciding over 43.1% of the incomes that they receive. Carrying out a similar calculation for Finland, (also based on data that is currently in the table) shows that the value of this index is **69.1%**. The difference is thus substantial.

3.3 Financial Autonomy of Local Governments – the Expenditure Autonomy Concept

The aforementioned OECD survey did not eloborate the expenditure side of financial autonomy. Although it is harder to measure the level of financial autonomy analysed from the expenditure side quantitatively, it is still necessary to at least do that in a more qualitative way and to explain the near concept of expenditure autonomy. In order to do that we classify expenditure into three crude categories, based on the type of tasks that are performed:

- (a) Voluntary local tasks completely decided by the local government council;
- (b) Obligatory tasks defined in a more flexible way by framework laws. In this case the citizen may not demand the service in a specific mode irrespective of local government budget appropriations reserved to that service;
- (c) Obligatory tasks defined in detail by legislation. The strongest case of this category is a law that gives the client a subjective right to get a certain service from the local government. The local government must provide it irrespective of its budget appropriations.

These three groups of tasks create a continuum of decreasing expenditure autonomy, meaning the extent to which the expenditure is generated and controlled by locally made decisions. Depending on the local government model that is adopted tax incomes, other own sources of income and general-purpose grants may therefore be allocated to financing more or less restrictively defined tasks, thus providing local governments with varying scope of financial autonomy. Specific restricted grants may also give some latitude depending on the expenditure autonomy in the specific task in question. In the Polish case most of expenditures are related to tasks belonging to groups (b) and (c) thus the level of financial autonomy (its expenditure side) is not as great as it could be. In the Finnish case most of the tasks are in the category b).

3.4 Combining the Income and Expenditure Autonomy for Fiscal Autonomy

In this section we combine the assessment of financial autonomy from both the income and the expenditure side. Only after doing this one can make an evaluation of the consistency of the central government policy towards local governments.

So, let us briefly compare the expenditure side of financial autonomy of Polish and Finnish local governments with the income one. Firstly let us look at the income structure in 2002, which is presented in Table 4:

Table 4. The income structure of Polish and Finnish local governments in 2002

Income sources	Poland [%]	Finland [%]
Tax incomes and other own sources	49.93	78.6
General-purpose grants	35.21	20.5
Specific grants	14.86	0.9
Total	100.00	100.00

Source: prepared by the authors.

It is clearly visible that the income structure is more favourable in the case of Finnish local governments. Specific grants, which are the most restrictive group of incomes, do not play virtually any role in financing Finnish municipalities. However, also in Poland the role of specific grants in financing communes is relatively small (it is much greater in the case of counties and regions), although one issue needs to be raised here. It is the fact that the amounts of specific grants that are transfered to communes are insufficient for financing all the tasks that were commissioned to communes (and which were meant to be financed fully by specific grants). This has led to a situation where local authorities need to cover some of the costs of commissioned tasks out of their tax incomes or general-purpose grants, which ought to be devoted to other issues.

The last issue that needs to be considered here is the type of tasks that are carried out using tax incomes, other own sources of income and general-purpose grants. It has already been stated that in Poland most tasks are obligatory tasks which vary as far as the level of detail provided by legislation is concerned. They are classified to categories (b) and (c). In the Finnish case most are in class (b).

These three classes of tasks together with three main categories of incomes create a matrix of financial autonomy which measures the extent to which the expenditures and incomes are generated and controlled by locally made decisions. In order to assign Poland and Finland to certain positions on this continuum the authors have identified the countries in the matrix in the conclusion section. Figure 1 presents the matrix of financial autonomy which combines the income and the expenditure aspect of financial autonomy.

The strongest possible financial autonomy would mean that local governments have no centrally decided (by law) obligatory tasks and that they could themselves decide what kind of taxes, fees and charges and so on they use. If own incomes would be added with grants from central government that are general-purpose grants with no strings attached to them, the financial autonomy would still be very strong.

	Expenditure decision-making autonomy		
	(a) Free volun-tary tasks	(b) Obligatory tasks (frame laws)	(c) Obligatory tasks (detailed specific laws)
1. Tax own incomes and other own in-comes	Strongest autonomy		X
2. General-purpose grant income			
3. Specific grant in-come	X		No autonomy at all

(Income source autonomy)

Source: Prepared by the authors.

Fig. 1. The matrix of financial autonomy

The opposite situation would be if local governments had no own taxes but only specific grants awarded to perform only obligatory tasks defined by specific detailed laws. The specific grants would have tight rules how to use the money. If local governments have also some tax income but the central government decides both base and rate unilaterally without local government having any decision-making power on these matters (actually shared taxes), the autonomy would not be much stronger either.

We would emphasize that we do not take a normative stand that claims that box 1a (strong autonomy) is always better than box 3c (weak or no autonomy). There are situations when strong autonomy is not a good solution – for instance, if there are not enough preconditions for local authorities to practice good governance and democracy at the local level. Globally there are wide differencies in competency and integrity of local authorities and economic resources of local communities. This means that local power will not always mean responsible and efficient decision-making for the best of the majority of local citizens. One must also take into consideration that the optimal level of autonomy varies between different tasks. In elementary education, we need certainly some country wide standards and central supervision. In recreation and sports services there are normally not so strong central interests and intervention needs.

Still, our argument is that central government should aim to provide consistency. If the central government decentralization policy is consistent, then the cells marked with an "X" should be avoided. If no expenditure autonomy is given, then the money should be given centrally or in a centrally steered way to all local governments. The specific grants ought to be graded in a way that would take into consideration different expenditure needs of particular municipalities. Other boxes than the two with X lie within the consistency area, although three diagonal boxes – 1a, 2b and 3c represent the highest consistency.

Also should the services and expenditures that they cause be completely freely decided upon at the local government level, then the income responsibility should also lie with local tax payers. In this case there would still be a need for grants in order to equalise disparities in tax bases but this could be done with general-purpose grants.

4 Conclusions

In the Fig. 2 we have allocated Finland and Poland onto the matrix which we presented in the previous section.

In Finland the development has gone during the local government history from the top left-hand corner in the beginning to the bottom right-hand corner and finally has settled more or less in between those two extremes. During the second hald of the 19th century and at the beginning of the 20th century municipalities had very few obligatory tasks and financing responsibilities lay mainly on local tax-payers. After the independence and more notably from the 1960s to 1980s, during the welfare state building, local governments got many new obligatory tasks and specific grants directed to those obligatory tasks.

This combination was very effective to enlarge the welfare service provision at local level. This meant also a growth of local governmment expenditure and specific grants. In the late 1980s and especially during the recession in 1990s the welfare state model had to be revised. For the local governments this meant general grants spurring to economy and rationalizing in municipalities. This meant also grant cuts which further enhanced

	Expenditure decision-making autonomy		
	a) Free voluntary tasks	b) Obligatory tasks (frame laws)	c) Obligatory tasks (detailed specific laws)
1. Tax own incomes and other own incomes	Finland (1860s–1920s)		
2. General-purpose grant income			
3. Specific grant income			Finland (1960s–1970s)

Income source autonomy (left vertical label)

Source: Prepared by the authors.

Fig. 2. The matrix of financial autonomy – comparison of Poland and Finland

economizing in municipalities. At the same time – even if detailed laws had been changed more and more to frame laws – there were still many obligatory tasks with heavy expenditures. From the local government point of view the central government steering model in the 1990s became unbalanced. Consistency would have required that if central government cuts grants so strongly as Finnish cabinets did in 1990s, also task responsibilities should have been diminished accordingly. This did not happen and that is why many municipalities had to resort to deficit budgeting.

Going over to the Polish case, it needs to be said that the contemporary history of Polish local government is not nearly as long as the Finnish one. In Poland local governments were reestablished in 1990 after a 50-year long period when there had been no local governments. Initially, in the early 1990s, Polish communes enjoyed a significant amount of autonomy. They were financed mainly by the tax incomes, other own sources and general-purpose grants. As time went on the communes were obliged to carry out an increasing number of commissioned tasks. They were financed primarily by grants transfered from the state budget. Initialy those were mainly specific grants which were later replaced by general-purpose grants. That is why the current income autonomy is at a visibly lower level than ten years ago. As for the expenditure autonomy, it needs to be said that legislation provides for most tasks in detail.

4.1 Policy Recommendations

We urge for consistency in the central government policy. In order to have the information basis for this, there should be a negotiating system between central government and local governments and a common data basis agreed upon and relied upon. The data base is necessary to follow the expenditure and income development in the local government sector.

The system should also include reliable forecasting of the influences of the central government prepareded laws and budget decisions on local government economy. This should create the preconditions for a balanced steering policy and consistent level of financial autonomy consisting of both income and expenditure autonomy for the local government sector. When central government does not aim to ensure balanced steering and consistent financial autonomy for local government sector, this should be done in a transparent way with all the political consequences.

We need to remember that both Poland and Finland have ratified the European Charter of Local Self-Government. Article 9 of the charter says that "local authorities shall be entitled, within national economic policy, to adequate financial resources of their own, of which they may dispose freely within the framework of their powers". Further the same paragraph says that the financial resources shall be commensurate with the responsibilities provided for by the constitution and law. Article 9 is thus clearly speaks about a balanced steering of local government sector and for strong financial autonomy within the framework of the country specific circumstances.

From the point of view of local governments stability and predictability are also important in fiscal relations between local and central government. Sudden changes in grant and tax systems that affect local government finances – especially in a negative way – may decisively harm local government economic planning and may cause hasty decision making at the local level.

5 References

Batley, R. Stoker, G. (1991) (eds): Local Government in Europe. Trends and Developments MacMillan, London.

European Charter of Local Self-Government (1986) Euriopean treaty series No. 122, Council of Europe, Strasbourg.

Kot, J. (2003) Zarządzanie rozwojem gmin a praktyka planowania strategicznego (Managing the development of communes and the practice of strategic planning), Lodz University Press, Lodz.

OECD (2001) Fiscal Design Across Levels of Government, Year 2000 Surveys Summary Note, OECD, Directorate for Financial, Fiscal and Enterprise Affairs.

Oulasvirta, L. (1993) Municipal Public Finance in the Nordic Countries. In (ed. By Gibson & Batley) Financing European Local Governments, Frank Cass, London.

Oulasvirta, L. (2003a) Equalisation and the Finnish Local Government Grant System: Regional Outcome and Fiscal Justice. In Regional Public Finances (editor J Mönnesland), European research in regional science 13, Pion Limited, 2003, London.

Oulasvirta, L. (2003b) Local Government Finance and Grants in Finland. Finnish Local Government Studies 4/2003 (A special number of the Finnish journal Kunnallistieteellisen aikakauskirja).

Stoker, G. (1991) Trends in Western European Local Government, in: Batley, Richard & Gerry Stoker (eds): Local Government in Europe. Trends and Developments. MacMillan, London.

From Closed to Open Regionalism in Central America: a Preliminary Assessment of the Proposed Belize-Guatemala Free Trade Agreement

Michael J. Pisani

Professor, School of Business Administration, University of Michigan, Mount Pleasant, MI, USA

"Belize and Guatemala should use their best endeavors to commence negotiation of a Free Trade Agreement (FTA) and a Bilateral Investment Treaty (BIT), at the earliest practicable date, with a view to their entering into force as soon as possible after the commencement of the Treaties of Settlement" (Ramphal & Reichler 2004, p. 193).

1 Introduction

Belize and Guatemala lie at the northernmost reaches of Central America, buttressed by Mexico to the north, the Caribbean Sea to the east, the Pacific Ocean to the west and Honduras and El Salvador to the south (see map). They share a common border demarcated by dense jungle, scattered squatter settlements, a single paved road, and a history of irredentist territorial claims and counter-claims. Though both countries were settled in pre-Columbian times with Amer-Indian populations, most notably the Maya, European contact in the region gave rise to the Spanish and British colonial possessions of Guatemala and British Honduras (later Belize), respectively. The colonial competition fostered by Spain and Britain created a bi-national rivalry between the "offspring" of colonization whereby

Guatemala holds a tenuous claim to much of Belize.[1] As part of the modern talks to settle the boundary dispute, both countries are exploring the development of a bilateral free trade agreement, the subject of this essay. "Guatemala"… "free trade"… each term may invoke passionate debate amongst Belizeans. And these issues taken together – the Guatemala claim and free trade (globalization) – according to Barry (1995, p. 31), are the most "salient foreign policy concern[s]" facing Belize. As a settlement of the Guatemalan question seems likely sometime in the near future, an assessment of one key element of the post-settlement process – free trade – deserves further elucidation.

The commercial interchange between Belize and Guatemala is readily apparent at the Western Border crossing area just west of Benque Viejo del Carmen, Belize and east of Melchor de Mencos, Guatemala. Cross-border shopping, tourism, and money exchange are visible manifestations of the commercial relations between uneasy neighbors. Less visible, but equally notable at this border area are the illicit crossing of people, goods, and U.S. dollars.

Other areas scheduled for economic development along the western border include: the export of electricity from the Chalillo project (when completed, possibly in 2005) from Belize to Guatemala to help power the Petén in return for hard currency; a free trade zone at Benque Viejo del Carmen á la the Corozal Free Trade Zone; and the advancement of the Plan Puebla-Panama which will enhance the road infrastructure between Belize and Guatemala as well as Central America (Pisani, Yoskowitz, & Label, 2003). With an emphasis upon Belize, this chapter seeks to explore the prospects of enhanced economic interaction and integration between Belize and Guatemala as a possible result of political rapprochement involving the two neighbors.

The remainder of this essay is organized as follows: section two defines a free trade area; section three compares Belize and Guatemala utilizing macroeconomic variables; section four takes a deeper look at trade between Belize and Guatemala through the discussion of trade patterns and the notion of revealed comparative advantage; part five offers a discussion on the proposed free trade agreement; and the last section concludes the paper.

---

[1] See Murphy (2004) for a history of the territorial dispute.

Map of Central America

Source: www.eia.doe.gov/emeu/cabs/centam.html.

2 What Is a Free Trade Agreement (FTA)?

Free trade is simply the exchange of products without barriers; that is, economic agents (e.g. firms, consumers) engage in an unfettered exchange process: goods for money and vice-versa. A free trade agreement allows for this exchange process to occur between signatory countries. Typically, free (or open) trade is discussed as an exchange process between different national economic agents, such as a consumer in Belize and a firm in the United States, though the discussion is also germane at the national level. The international exchange process is primarily driven by price differentials in the marketplace rooted in the comparative advantages of firms operating around the globe (the topic of comparative advantage is addressed in detail in part four below).[2] Nobel Prize winning economist Joseph

---

[2] Other factors such as product quality and delivery options also influence purchase behavior in the marketplace. Though the early nineteenth century origin of the term "comparative advantage" focused on the competitive nature of the nation, the basic unit of analysis in the global economy today is the firm.

Stiglitz (2002, p. ix) believes this international exchange process is at the heart of "globalization – the removal of barriers to free trade and the closer integration of national economies." It is the integration of economies that is the root of free trade agreements.

The four major models of economic integration, in order of the depth of integration, are: (1) free trade areas; (2) customs unions; (3) common markets; (4) economic unions. Free Trade Areas (FTAs) abolish tariffs (taxes on imports) and quotas (numerical limitations of imports) among member nations. FTAs are the minimalist approach to economic integration allowing for the free movement of goods and services while retaining maximum political sovereignty between members. And permitted outside of the membership, FTA partners are able to exercise unique external relations with other nations. NAFTA (the North American Free Trade Agreement), with its members Canada, the United States and Mexico, is an example of a free trade area. The Ramphal and Reichler (2004) proposal seeks a minimum level of economic integration between Belize and Guatemala.[3]

Customs unions go a step further, as member nations agree to a common set of external tariffs and quotas. Belgium, The Netherlands, and Luxembourg formed a customs union between the World Wars. Common markets deepen integration to include the free movement of land, labor, capital and labor (factor resources). Both CARICOM (the Caribbean Community) and MERCOSUR (the South American Common Market) are near examples of common markets. And lastly, economic unions create a supra-national political and economic framework such as a common currency and legislative bodies (see Table 1). The European Union (EU) is the clearest example of an economic union with the adoption of a single currency (the Euro), a central bank, a parliament, a court of justice, European Commission (day-to-day administration), Council of Ministers (policy-setting institution), a single constitution, etc.

---

[3] The proposed FTA was again cited in a Government of Belize press release following the talks of May 3–6, 2004, which stated in part: "The delegations discussed the establishment of a Joint Commission that would examine a comprehensive list of new confidence building measures including a mutual legal assistance treaty, *a free trade agreement*, facilitation of the transit of goods of both countries and the joint promotion of tourism" (italics added) (Ministry of the Attorney General and Foreign Affairs, 2004a).

Table 1. Models of economic integration

Type of Economic Integration	Abolition of Tariffs and Quotas	Common External Tariff and Quota System	Free Movement of Factor Resources	Harmonization and Unification of Economic and Political Institutions
Free Trade Area	Yes	Yes	Yes	Yes
Customs Union	No	Yes	Yes	Yes
Common Market	No	No	Yes	Yes
Economic Union	No	No	No	Yes

The harbinger of the EU was a limited scope FTA initiated in part to quell political angst among rivals. Since the creation of the European Coal and Steel Community over four decades ago, the EU has evolved into a peaceful association of nation-states. The politics of an FTA suggest that closer economic cooperation and integration diminishes the possibilities of political violence (à la the European Union). The facilitators in the continued Guatemalan claim hope that a Belize-Guatemala FTA would bring about a similar political future; hence the FTA clause in the facilitators' proposals.

Furthermore, neither Belize nor Guatemala is a stranger to economic integration or integration initiatives. Belize is a full member of CARICOM; CARICOM also has temporary preferential trade agreements with Colombia and Venezuela. Guatemala is an integral member of the Central American Common Market and is signatory to two FTAs with the Dominican Republic and Panama. Guatemala has also signed a bilateral investment treaty with Chile (SICE Website, 2004). Additionally, Belize and Guatemala are party to the Plan Puebla-Panama, a pseudo-economic integration initiative in Mesoamerica; the Association of Caribbean States, primarily a forum for Caribbean states and issues; SICA (the Central American Integration System), the political umbrella organization for the Central American Common Market; and the Free Trade Area of the Americas (FTAA), the proposed FTA for the Western Hemisphere (Pisani & Label, 2003).

In the larger framework of globalization, Steger (2002) has suggested five general claims of globalism (the ideology of globalization) as central to the globalization argument:

1. *Globalization is about the liberalization and global integration of markets* [markets bring about rationality and efficiency leading toward greater social integration and material progress];

2. *Globalization is inevitable and irreversible* [the last finest triumph of mankind];
3. *Nobody is in charge of globalization* [globalization is in the hands of the marketplace];
4. *Globalization benefits everyone* [economic growth and progress is bound up with the process of globalization];
5. *Globalization furthers the spread of democracy around the world* [free markets and democracy are synonymous].

For the most part, Belize has attempted to navigate within these claims, accepting most and redefining others. As a member of CARICOM, SICA, the Plan-Puebla Panama, the FTAA, the IMF (International Monetary Fund), and the WTO (the World Trade Organization), Belize is moving towards economic integration first in the regional arena and eventually within the global marketplace. In essence, Belize has taken the position that it cannot stop the process of globalization so it ought to help mold its pace and outcome as a member of CARICOM. Barry (1995, p. 31) adroitly states: "The common opinion in the Caribbean was that the free trade train was coming, like it or not, and it behooved them to join the negotiations rather than get left behind."

Though the free market is a major player in globalization, it is buffeted by national and supranational organs that manipulate a nation's entry and participation within the global economy. Belize, largely, has been protected from the harsh competition of world markets through preferential access to U.S. and European markets. These protections are waning in an America and Europe less patient with structural trade preferences for small, dependent economies. As such, Belize has chosen the closed integration of CARICOM to the open integration of CACM, continues to press for long transition periods in trade negotiations,[4] and accepts the positive externality of democracy as a legacy of globalization.[5]

For Belize, globalization is omni-present in the form of international tourism; the selection of foreign, particularly consumer, products (Wilk, 1990); television programming; labor movements (through the temporary employment permits, Belize legally imports a few hundred to a few thousand workers annually while Belizeans have left by the tens of thousands

---

[4] Bhagwati (2004, p. 254–256) suggests the "how slow, how fast" of trade liberalization is dependent upon the local political environment and the robustness of the local economy.
[5] See Nicholls, Samuel, Colthrust & Boodoo (2001) for a fuller discussion of this topic.

to work in the U.S.); the establishment of free trade zones along the Mexican and Guatemalan borders; the illegal drug trade; and commodity prices for cane sugar and orange juice concentrate.

3 Country Comparisons

For better or worse, Guatemala and Belize lie at the northern part of the Central American Isthmus and share a 516 kilometer long border. Mexico is the primary neighbor and regional hegemon (Pisani, 2001) for both countries comprising 57.0% and 48.4% of the territorial land boundary with Guatemala and Belize, respectively. Though the border between Belize and Guatemala is sparsely populated, the border encompasses the primary land boundary for Belize (51.6%) and the second largest land boundary for Guatemala (15.8%). The primary link between the two nations occurs at the junction of Benque Viejo del Carmen, Belize and Melchor de Mencos, Guatemala. The term "distant neighbors" aptly describes the relationship between the two countries.

Guatemala is the most populous country in Central America and dwarfs Belize by comparison: Guatemala has more than 47 times the number of citizens than Belize. Measured by territory, Guatemala is more than three times the size of Belize. And the Guatemalan economy is more than 27 times larger than Belize's. Yet this aggregate data alone does not illustrate the level of the quality of life in each nation. Indicators such as literacy, life expectancy, per capita income and the Human Development Index (HDI) allow for deeper comparisons. Belizeans enjoy a substantially higher rate of adult literacy, live almost nine years longer and earn nearly 1.7 times more than their Guatemalan counterparts (see Table 2). Additionally, the distribution of national income, as measured by the GINI coefficient,[6] indicates a very unequal distribution in Guatemala, similar to that found in Brazil, and a somewhat uneven distribution in Belize, though in line with countries like the United States and China. Lastly, though unemployment rates are relatively high (albeit similar), the Guatemalan figure masks the widespread informal economy present in Guatemala.

---

[6] A GINI coefficient of zero indicates perfect income equality and a GINI coefficient score of one denotes perfect income inequality within a nation.

Table 2. Country Comparisons [2002][a]

Indicators	Belize	Guatemala
Population	253,000	12,000,000
Land Area (sq. Km.)	22,960	108,900
GDP ($US)	843,100,000	23,300,000,000
Per Capita Income ($US)	2,970	1,760
Adult Literacy (%)	77	70
Life Expectancy (years)	74.1	65.5
HDI (2002 World Ranking)	99 (of 177)	121 (of 177)
2002 Composite HDI Score	.737	.649
Exports (Value $US)	158,335,000	2,466,000,000
Export as % of GDP	19	11
Imports (Value $US)	524,515,000	6,044,000,000
Imports as % of GDP	62	26
GDP by Sector (%)		
Primary	15	22 (2001)
Secondary	19	19 (2001)
Tertiary	66	59 (2001)
Employment by Sector (%)		
Primary	27	50
Secondary	18	15
Tertiary	55	35
Unemployment Rate (%)	10	8 (2003)
Total Number in the Labor Force	94,172	4,500,000
GINI Coefficient	.400	.558 (1998)
Military Expenditures as % of GDP (2003)	2	1

[a]Statistics are for 2002 unless otherwise noted. Percentage statistics have been rounded.
Sources: http://www.worldbank.org/, http://hdr.undp.org/, http://www.intracen.org, http://www.gov.cso.bz/, http://www.odci.gov/ , http://www.cia.gov/.

A holistic measure of poverty is the Human Development Index (HDI) conducted annually by the United Nations Development Programme. The HDI is a composite index[7] which summarizes the general welfare of the population based upon health, knowledge, and standard of living, with age, adult literacy and school enrollment, and per capita GDP as the appropriate proxies, respectively (United Nations Development Programme, 2001). In

---

[7] To interpret these scores, the following scheme is used by the United Nations Development Programme: High Human Development, HDI scores range from .8–1; Medium Human Development, HDI scores range from .5–.79; and Low Human Development, HDI scores below .5.

2002, Belize ranked 99th in the world out of 177 countries surveyed. Guatemala placed far worse, 121st in the world. Yet the quality of life gap is closing between the two nations with Guatemala making steady progress and Belize backtracking over the last time period measured (see Fig. 1).

A closer look at the macroeconomy indicates a similar breakdown of the sectoral distribution of Gross Domestic Product (GDP) within each nation. For both Belize and Guatemala, the primary (e.g. agriculture, fishing, mining, logging) and secondary (e.g. manufacturing) sectors account for about one-fifth of total production. The tertiary sector (e.g. services) comprises the largest segment of production, around 60%. These trends are not carried forward as percent of the labor force employed in each sector, where primary, secondary and tertiary activities employ 27%, 18% and 55% of the Belizean labor force, respectively and 50%, 15% and 35% of the Guatemalan labor force, respectively.

In each nation, the high levels of primary sector (mostly agricultural) employment as compared to output indicate structural weaknesses (inefficiencies) and subsistence farming. This is even more evident in Guatemala where half of the economically active population is engaged in primary sector pursuits, a practice of its Maya past. And though the relative proportion of the workforce in relation to total population is similar, 37% in Belize and 35% in Guatemala, the size of the Guatemalan labor force dwarfs that of Belize by a factor of 45. The differential in economic power is complemented by military power where Guatemala annually outspends Belize by a ratio of 11 to 1.

Lastly, a brief discussion of the external trade sector serves as a segue to part four below. The Belizean economy is highly dependent upon international trade, which accounts for a whopping 81% of GDP (19% based on exports and 62% from imports). Guatemala, on the other hand, has a more

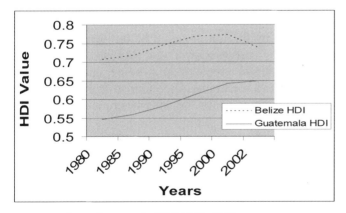

Fig. 1. Belize - Guatemala HDI 1980-2002

normalized pattern of international trade as a percentage of GDP: 37% (11% from exports and 26% based on imports). And as for scale, Guatemala trades over $8.5 billion, Belize less than $700 million.[8] Nonetheless, both nations support a structural trade deficit which can only be legally financed by domestic savings, international borrowing, remittances from nationals working abroad (mostly the United States), foreign aid, and/or Foreign Direct Investment (FDI). Both nations rely heavily upon borrowing, less so on FDI and remittances.

4 Trade Patterns and Revealed Comparative Advantage

In the classical sense, comparative advantage refers to a nation's ability to produce a good or service better than most other nations. With this productive ability comes the opportunity to exchange products with other countries that have alternative comparative advantage in different product(s). And the benefits of comparative advantage are maximized through specialization and trade in a just foreign exchange rate system. As noted international economist Mordechai Kreinin (1987, p. 224) has written:

Nations trade with each other for fundamentally the same reasons that individuals or regions engage in exchange of goods and services: to obtain the benefits of specialization. Since nations, like individuals, are not equally suited to produce all goods, either because they are differently endowed or for other reasons, all would benefit if each specialized in what they could do best and obtained its other needs through exchange.

In today's global economy, the ability to produce primarily resides at the individual firm level and as such comparative advantage more aptly refers to the ability of a firm located in a nation-state to produce goods and services better than most other firms situated in other nation-states.[9] The benefits (or gains from trade) of such productive abilities accrue to those who successfully navigate the international economic system. Kreinin (1987, p. 224) elaborates:

Asked why she engages in foreign trade, any businessperson can promptly offer a superficial, yet correct answer: she purchases a commodity abroad if and when it is cheaper abroad than at home, and she sells a commodity abroad when it fetches a higher price abroad than it does domestically. She buys where it is cheapest and sells where it is dearest in

---

[8] All monetary figures appearing in this paper have been converted to U.S. dollars.
[9] Taken one step further, a firm's comparative advantage within its domestic market has been dubbed competitive advantage in today's business lexicon. More recently, the term competitive advantage has expanded its meaning to include firm-level competencies in all markets.

order to maximize her profit. In other words, relative prices at home and abroad determine which goods are exported and which are imported by any given country.

Until recently, trade between Belize and Guatemala remained insignificant, but structurally weighted to the benefit of Guatemala (see Table 3). As late as 2000, bi-lateral trade between Belize and Guatemala made up less than .2% of total Guatemalan trade and 1.8% of Belizean total trade. Since 2003, however, bi-lateral trade between Belize and Guatemala has blossomed. A survey of the composition of the first trimester of 2004 trade reveals that the Guatemalan export basket to Belize is rather diverse, 20 product categories with an export value above $100,000 each and punctuated with agricultural inputs and household consumption (see Table 4). Belizean exports to Guatemala, on the other hand, are comprised of mainly third party petroleum products, electrical machines and tools, and vehicles and transport equipment – that is, these products are not made in Belize, but rather obtained and re-sold to Guatemala. This set of non-indigenous exports (i.e., arbitrage) to Guatemala does not bode well for long term Belizean comparative advantage.

Revealed Comparative Advantage (RCA) is a basic international trade measurement device which empirically presents those products that a nation (and by proxy, national firms) have a price or comparative advantage in the global marketplace. Specifically, RCA compares the ratio of national imports and exports as a share of total imports and exports in the world. Furthermore, a country is successfully specialized in today's world

Table 3. Belizean Trade with Guatemala 1994–2003 [in $US 1,000s]

Year	1994	1995	1996	1997	1998
Exports to Guatemala	143.6	1,013.9	471.8	1,989.3	967
Imports from Guatemala	5,140.9	3,926.2	6,307.9	6,934.4	7,206.9
Balance	–4,997.3	–2,912.3	–5836.1	–4,945.1	–6,239.9
Total Trade	5,284.5	4,940.1	6,779.7	8,923.7	8,173.9

Year	1999	2000	2001	2002	2003	2004[a]
Exports to Guatemala	604.5	1,227.6	2,394	1,951.1	30,104.3	6,101.5
Imports from Guatemala	10,890	12,977.3	13,763.5	21,387.1	31,670.5	9,263.2
Balance	–10,285.5	–11,749.7	–11,369.5	–19,436.0	–1,566.2	–3,161.7
Total Trade	11,494.5	14,204.9	16,157.5	23,338.2	61,774.8	15,364.7

[a]January thru April 2004.
Source: Central Bank of Guatemala (http://www.banguat.gob.gt/).

economy when its *share of world exports of a specific product is greater than its share of world trade as a whole.* That is, the country is producing something that the world wants in greater proportion than its overall participation in world trade. RCAs have been calculated for Belize and Guatemala over three time periods (1998–2002, 1997–2001, and 1996–2000) and appear in Table 5. These overlapping periods emphasize sustained comparative advantage.

Table 4. Primary composition and listing of Belizean-Guatemalan trade, First Trimester of 2004 [by value in US $1000s]

Product	Imports from Guatemala	Product	Exports to Guatemala
Animal Feed	1,901.4	Other Derived Petroleum Products	5,365.4
Plastics	1,147.7	Electrical Machines & Tools	429.2
Other Derived Petroleum Products	674.6	Vehicles & Transport Materials	177.8
Fertilizers	556.9	Scrap Metal	69.6
Vehicles & Transport Materials	544.0	Pipes	13.8
Cooking Oil/Lard	426.8	Skins & Hides (leather)	7.1
Insecticides	388.2		
Propane	326.2		
Pharmaceuticals	292.6		
Iron & Steel	276.2		
Paper & Cardboard	244.9		
Chemicals	227.8		
Glass	223.3		
Prepared Food: Cereals	217.5		
Detergents/Soaps	185.6		
Furniture	132.3		
Tires & Tubes	128.5		
Prepared Food: Meats	119.3		
Wood Manufacturers	115.7		
Other Metal Manufacturers	107.4		
Fireworks	86.6		
Vinegar	79.3		
Ceramics	70.6		
Cosmetics & Perfumes	69.9		
Ketchup & Condiments	65.3		
Candies	57.5		
Other	597.1		52.4
Total	9,263.2		6,101.5

Source: Central Bank of Guatemala (http://www.banguat.gob.gt/).

Table 5. Revealed Comparative Advantage for Belize and Guatemala

	Belize – RCA Score			Guatemala – RCA Score		
Product	98-02	97-01	96-00	98-02	97-01	96-00
Processed Food	12.97	24.10	12.39	5.41	4.74	4.00
Fresh Food	10.31	–	8.96	8.27	8.07	10.79
Clothing	–	–	3.96	–	–	–
Chemicals	–	–	–	1.33	1.39	1.16
Wood Products	–	–	–	.99	1.19	–
Basic Manufacturers	–	–	–	–	1.05	–

Note: Scores above 1 indicate that the country is specialized in that sector.
Source: Http://www.intracen.org (International Trade Center, UNCTAD/WTO).

Both nations are internationally competitive in processed and fresh foods. Additionally, Guatemala is an economic force in chemicals, wood products and basic manufactures. And Belize has lost its advantage in clothing, a result that would have come anyway with the expiration of global textile protection negotiated under the Uruguay Round (tariffs expire at the end of 2004). These results suggest that Belize is relatively uncompetitive in global markets; Guatemala is less so.

5 Discussion

Both Belize and Guatemala are relatively uncompetitive for most products in global markets. Guatemala has achieved some measure of export success regionally, particularly in the Central American community (snack/processed foods, cosmetics, textiles and handicrafts, toiletries, agricultural inputs, and construction materials) and the United States (fresh produce, coffee, textiles). Guatemala too has emerging ethno-tourism and archaeological-tourism industries. Ethno-tourism comprises Spanish-language learning schools and anthropology of contemporary Maya society. Impressive archaeological sites of Tikal and Queztaltenango showcase the Classic Maya while the city of Anitgua artfully displays the Spanish colonial past. Nonetheless, civil strife over the past 50 years has curtailed tourism in Guatemala from blossoming more.

Belize's chief exports not related to a preferential trade treatment (e.g. sugar, bananas, citrus) are tourism and marine products (e.g. shrimp). Tourism is not traditionally considered an export and thus does not show up in RCAs, but foreign tourists do spend money, and the tourism industry[10] contributes upwards of 20% of Belizean GDP and this sector (tourism)

---

[10] Tourism in Belize is a catch-all phrase for cruise-tourism, ethno-tourism, eco-tourism, historical/archaeological-tourism, and beach-tourism.

must be considered part of Belize's comparative advantage. Shrimping is a new industry to Belize and will continue to contribute in a growing and important way (shrimp exports were $50 million in 2003). These two Belizean exports may have the potential to become world class in orientation with the ability to compete unfettered on the global stage.[11] In summary, Guatemala is the better positioned to undertake regional trade while both Belize and Guatemala have the potential for site specific comparative advantages related to tourism.

Belizean officials (and policy) have maintained a "go slow" approach to economic integration, liberalization, and globalization as recently commented upon by Attorney General and Foreign Trade Minister Eamon Courtenay:

In the current global political environment, we believe greater integration into the international economy can assist us to reach our growth potential, broaden our economic base, while also ensuring that all segments of the population benefit from increased economic welfare. We therefore underscore the principle that any integration agreement (between asymmetric parties) must take due account of the special needs of developing countries and the vulnerabilities endemic to small developing states (Ministry of the Attorney General and Foreign Affairs, 2004b).

Though not explicitly stated in the quote above, "special needs" is a code word suggesting integration at a snail's pace, protecting national economies in a gradual movement toward globalization. This author agrees with this "go slow" approach for Belize.[12] Notwithstanding tourism and marine products, Belize is simply not ready to open up its markets to free trade overnight or in the near future. This is even more of a concern in areas where local manufacturers produce for the local marketplace and would be quickly displaced with trade liberalization.

And since Belize does not have internationally competitive products (RCAs) outside of those already produced at similar levels in Guatemala, there is little advantage for Belizean exporters to be found in the Guatemalan market with the exception of tourism integration. For most indicators, Guatemala dwarfs Belize. Belize is already a member of a trade diverting

---

[11] Another Belizean product just beginning its global competitive journey is Marie Sharp's. Beginning in the fall of 2004, Marie Sharp products are scheduled to appear in 345 Wal-Mart Stores, 600 Publix Stores and 53 Winn-Dixie Stores all located in the United States (Ramos, 2004a).

[12] In a related study of a liberalizing country in Central America, Pisani (2003) found that an abrupt opening to free trade had a deleterious effect on Nicaraguan income in the 1990s.

pact,[13] CARICOM (McBain, 2001), and adding Guatemala would simply continue trade diversion with another partner. At this time, the question of a Belize FTA with Guatemala boils down to the following: Does Belize wish to reward Guatemala through increased trade at the expense of CARICOM?

Interconnected to this discussion is the plight of the Belizean consumer who continues to be penalized through harsh national tariff and tax regulations and structural trade deficits (with Guatemala and the world). A more balanced approach would be to free up international trade in those areas not foreseen to be endemic to Belize, such as consumer electronics, automobiles, etc. The tax code should also consider lowering the basic costs of living (and production) for households (and producers) in Belize, such as lowering the onerous fuel tax, in order to sustain and build competitive advantages yet unforeseen.[14] Lastly, the voracious appetite for imported goods, accounting for about one-third of GDP (Pisani, Yoskowitz & Label, 2003), continues to be paid for in part by borrowed hard currency forcing up the price of money in Belize (i.e. higher domestic interest rates). The structural trade deficit should be offset by export promotion, FDI, and tourism receipts, and not sustained at its current level only to be paid for by future generations of Belizeans.[15]

6 Conclusion

This paper has sought to provide a preliminary assessment of the proposed free trade agreement between Belize and Guatemala. In doing so, the paper reviewed the definition of an FTA within the larger context of globalization, compared the two nations at a macro level, and evaluated the current trade linkages between Belize and Guatemala.

It must be reiterated that the proposed FTA is linked to the ongoing Guatemalan dispute and possible resolution. Nevertheless, no matter how politically expedient an FTA between Belize and Guatemala, Belize is simply not ready or well positioned for a free trade agreement with

---

[13] Trade diversion refers to higher cost import replacement from integration member(s) vis-à-vis the global marketplace. Trade creation, on the other hand, refers to trade which lowers the costs of products in intra-regional and intra-industry trade.

[14] The government has made steady progress in infrastructure development, notably the Southern Highway, but much remains to be accomplished in this area.

[15] See Pisani and Yoskowitz (2002) for a related discussion on dollarization and trade.

Guatemala. And even if Belize were ready for increased economic integration, there are more deserving and supportive nations in line ahead of Guatemala (e.g. Mexico and the United States) not to mention the move towards deepening Belize's participation in CARICOM (Ramos, 2004b). The time is not right for open trade with Guatemala. Perhaps a limited scope agreement[16] beginning with integrated tourism through already established institutions like the Ruta Maya and the Plan Puebla-Panama may placate the politicians and add value to the economies of both nations.

7 References

Barry, T. (1995) Inside Belize: The Essential Guide to Its Politics, Economy, Society, and Environment, with Dylan Vernon, Albuquerque, NM: The Interhemispheric Resource Center.

Bhagwati, J. (2004) In Defense of Globalization, New York, NY: Oxford University Press

Kreinin, M. E. (1987) International Economics: A Policy Approach, 5th Edition, New York, NY: Harcourt Brace Jovanovich, Publishers.

McBain, H. (2001) Open Regionalism: CARICOM Integration and Trade Links, in Victor Bulmer-Thomas (Ed.), Regional integration in Latin America and the Caribbean: The political economy of open regionalism, London, UK: University of London, Institute of Latin American Studies, 275-294.

Ministry of the Attorney General and Foreign Affairs (2004a), Belize/Guatemala Talks Continue, Press Office, Government of Belize, May 7. (Accessed at http://www.belize.gov.bz/pressoffice/press_releases/07-05-2004-3214.shtml)

Ministry of the Attorney General and Foreign (2004b), Belize's Trade Policy Reviewed by WTO, Press Office, Government of Belize, July 14. (Accessed at http://www.belize.gov.bz/pressoffice/press_releases/14-07-2004-3334.shtml)

Murphy, J. S. (2004) The Guatemalan Claim to Belize: A Handbook on the Negotiations, Belmopan, Belize: Print Belize, Ltd.

Nicholls, S., Samuel, G., Colthrust, P., Boodoo E., (2001) Open Regionalism and Institutional Developments among the Smaller Integration Schemes of CARICOM, the Andean Community, and the Central American Common Market, in Victor Bulmer-Thomas (Ed.), Regional integration in Latin America and

[16] Perhaps with the influence of this paper domestically which appeared in the fall 2004 issue of the Journal of Belizean Studies, but certainly after this paper was originally completed in August 2004, Belize and Guatemala signed a joint communiqué (dated November 22, 2004) moving forward with a framework for negotiating a FTA, beginning with a partial scope agreement. In December 2004, the government of Belize solicited the local business community as to specific local products of export promise to Guatemala for inclusion the partial scope trade talks.

the Caribbean: The political economy of open regionalism, London, UK: University of London, Institute of Latin American Studies, 141-164.

Pisani, M. J. (2003) The Negative Impact of Structural Adjustment on Sectoral Earnings in Nicaragua, Review of Radical Political Economics, 35(2), 107-125.

Pisani, M. J. (2001) Mexico: The Colossus of the North, Western Hemispheric Trade Digest, 1(5), 4-5.

Pisani, M. J. Label, W. A. (2003) Plan Puebla-Panama: Toward FTAA or Regionalism, Business Horizons, September-October, 46(5), 33-40.

Pisani, M. J., Yoskowitz, D. W. (2002) Dollarization! Journal of Belizean Studies, 24(2), 19-27.

Pisani, M. J., Yoskowitz, D. W., Label, W. A. (2003) Belize and the Plan Puebla-Panama: Prospects and Challenges, Journal of Belizean Studies, 25(2), 3-17.

Ramos, A. (2004a) Marie Sharp Hot in the US, Amandala, July 11, p. 39.

Ramos, A. (2004b) CARICOM Region Presses Ahead with CSME, CCJ, CARICOM Passport, Amandala, July 18, p. 39.

Ramphal, S., Reichler, P. S., (2004) Belize-Guatemala Territorial Differendum: Proposals from the Facilitators, in James S. Murphy, The Guatemalan Claim to Belize: A Handbook on the Negotiations, Belmopan, Belize: Print Belize, Ltd., Appendix 5, 182-196.

SICE (Organization of American States Foreign Trade Information System) Website (2004), http://www.sice.org, assessed July 26, 2004.

Steger, M. (2002) Globalism: The New Market Ideology, Lanham, MD: Rowman & Littlefield Publishers, Inc.

Stiglitz, J. E. (2002) Globalization and its Discontents, New York, NY: W.W. Norton & Company.

United Nations Development Programme (2001) Human Development Report, 2001, New York, NY: Oxford University Press.

Wilk, R. (1990) Consumer Goods, Cultural Imperialism and Underdevelopment in Belize, in SPEAR (Ed.) Third Annual Studies on Belize Conference, Belize City, Belize: Central America: SPEAR Reports No. 6, 135-146.

Aspects of Regional Social Governance. Welfare Reform in the US Implications for a Global Policy Against Exclusion

George Tsobanoglou

Assistant Professor, BA, BA (Honors), MA, PhD (Carleton), Department of Sociology, University of the Aegean, Mytilini, Lesvos, Greece and Chair, International Sociological Association, RC # 26, Sociology Department, University of the Aegean. Also Visiting Fellow (Oct. 2006/ Feb. 2007) at the University of Leeds, Institute of Communication Studies, Leeds LS2-9J, United-Kingdom

1 Introduction

Given the nature of recent economic trends, workforce development policies are necessary to combat unemployment among the poor and socially excluded. This is the general principle behind recent policy initiatives in the U.S. such as "workfare" and Individual Development Accounts (IDAs). These policies ideally deal with the negative effects of the new economy centered in service industries, and more particularly, the mismatch of skills that has served to create a class of outsiders (a rather "permanent underclass"). They do this by facilitating the development of socially needed skills and social capital in the form of higher education, property ownership, and personal savings, all of which are prerequisites for participation in the evolving institutions of civil society and the "new" economy.

Perhaps the most astonishing developments in the US context are the blurring of distinctions between social and economic skills, and between economic and social capital. For instance, the provision of competitive medical and care services which require research and other associates activities have become growth areas, as are quality of life investments in the working and general urban environments. Ironically, the main concern of the Europeans' that the welfare regimes are being disassembled in the US is in reality a turn to a healthy dosage of an expanded and expanding social reproduction sphere aiming at the direct provision of "services of recuperation" or restoration. The associated sports and kinetic culture enhance human activity and turn into important areas of commercial activity such aspects of human reproduction as dietary habits and healthy lifestyles. Similarly, the displacement of workers from the "industrial" sector or better the recomposition of business is met with high quality educational services made possible by the development of a well operating regional vocational educational system.

As the service industries become the leader in employment, welfare to work programs gain significance. Technological innovation in vocational education (community colleges with continuous training processes) are increasingly providing the skills necessary for such applications in industry, while research and development activities implemented at universities is leading to key innovations in the bio-medical, engineering and communication fields.

My main focus of this paper will be on the institutional context in which the Local Partnership Organizations (LPOs) operate and on the role of the Federal Government in the U.S. As we will see, related developments in the State of Michigan were key policy experiments that led to the overall establishment of the welfare to workfare program in 1996. Several developments in the US are linked with social and institutional innovations that started in that State. Available day of this program present an opportunity to evaluate the prospects of social reform tied to wealth creation and socio-economic development.

State policy makers, both Democratic and Republican, typically perceive that the most effective way to meet the new economic challenges is to improve the business environment. States in the US compete at all levels for business, especially for "clean" industries (or industries understood to contribute to overall quality of life). Generally, the term "business climate" refers to the perceived idea that the State attracts and retains corporate actors by measures of tax incentives, overlooking at times labor and environmental standards so as to allow greater profitability in order to be attractive to business. New trends are being directed into designing policies that improve the conditions for profitability and job creation involving also the not-for profit sector, the third sector.

The basic issue that seems to preoccupy the current level of US Federal policy makers is to have a holistic approach to community development that has one clear focus: *asset formation at local level*. Assets matter, provide an economic cushion and enable people to make investments in their future. Local assets also provide a psychological orientation towards the future, one's children and having a stake in one's community. Community stakeholders are the main issues that appear to govern recent economic governance directives in the US.

According to the Corporation Enterprise Development (CFED) in the US:

- One-half of American Households have less than $1,000 in net financial assets;
- One-third of American households (60% of African American households) has zeroed or negative net financial assets;
- Almost 40% of white children and 73% of African American children grow up in households with zero or negative net financial assets;
- Up to 20% of All-American households don't have a checking or savings account.

Generally, the seemingly boundless prosperity of the past decade has left some Americans behind. In 1998, one of eight Americans and almost one in five children were poor. This has been defined as living on an income of less than about $17,000 a year in a family of four. Recent demographic and social changes such, as the increase of women in laborforce, led households to an increase in child poverty.

There is a policy debate about the causes of poverty, unemployment and social inequality. Socio-economic changes such as globalization, new technologies and the growth of knowledge-based industries provide higher wages as well as the integration of populations with currently inadequate or inappropriate skills.

Formerly excluded areas both geographically and socio-economically, a matter that comes out of educational opportunities and social mobility bring about new conditions that define the issues of poverty and exclusion. While wages of unskilled workers have declined, the salary differential between men with and without a college degree has more than doubled since the early 1980s.

In terms of socio-cultural changes, single parent families seem to be increasing dramatically which double income families appearing also to be on the increase. Such changes can explain the rapid increase in child poverty and the income inequality among families due to the rise of female participation in professional jobs. Single parent families have the majority of poor children. Childcare and transportation are essential services for the eradication of some of the heaviest burdens for such families.

More than two-thirds of all mothers of pre-school children are now in the workforce. Most poor mothers, who might once have relied on welfare, must now work. Quality childcare is very important, but it is costly.

Democrats have promised to expand childcare assistance by $21 billion over the next five years.

The Republican policy is directed towards a stronger voluntary sector and tries to enforce a moral-ethical economy. In education, the Federal Government provides 7% of the nation's K-12 education bill. The so-called "categorical programs" take a slice of the federal budget. Such programs serve the poor (Title I) and handicapped (special education) students. Very few pennies do go on average students from the Federal Government.

For the purpose of this paper reference will be made only to category Title I (poor children), as it relates directly to a social category, i.e. welfare policy.

Title I remains the biggest federal education program for grades K-12, and costs about $8.4 billion a year. It is distributed to schools with high concentration of poor students. Title I is a funding stream, not a program with a specific educational strategy. Schools and counties use the funding in a variety of ways, and it is commingled with State and local programs and funds. A school needs to be 60% poor to qualify for a federal aid. At present, there are a number of problems associated with the burdensome rules and regulations set by the Federal Government that lead to the formations of state bureaucracies utilizing as much as 40% of the budget thus leaving local initiative on hold. Methodologies for evaluating the effect of the program need to be set in place. (Tom Loveless and Diane Ravitch "Broken Promises. What the federal Government Can Do To Improve American Education", The Brookings Review, Spring 2000, Vol. 18 No. 2.).

2 The State of Michigan Reforms

In Michigan, the institutional panoply in the social reform process includes the Program "To Strengthen Michigan Families" (TSMF). This is a comprehensive Welfare reform program operated statewide by the Michigan Family Independence Agency (MFIA) from October 1992 to September 1996. In October 1996 Michigan became one of the first States in the US to have certified as complete its New welfare program under the rubric for a law that radically changed welfare policies and programs in the US that is the Personal Responsibility and Work Opportunity Reconciliation Act (PRWORA) of 1996.

The Act gave States wide discretion to manage the TANFs (Temporary Assistance for Needy Families) in replacing the 65-year-old Aid to Families with Dependent Children (AFDC). Because Michigan's TANF program, the Family Independence Program (FOP) and TAM share most policies, their study offers important insights into the future of welfare reform.

After four years of operations, TAM has consistently increased the employment and earnings and reduced the welfare dependence, of families which were on welfare when the program started in October 1992. The program has mixed results for families entering welfare after that date. Although TAM reduced welfare dependents for all of those later welfare families, it increased employment only for those families that entered welfare from October 1994, when the program implemented a number of internal policy changes.

3 US Institutional Reforms

The American Community Renewal and New Markets Empowerment Act is a bi-partisan package that reflected the agreement between President Clinton and Speaker Hatter. The Senate expanded additional bi-partisan initiatives that will provide more opportunities for economic recovery, resources to local governments, improved access to new technology, more home ownership, and employability development. Such provisions are:

- (a). *Individual Development Accounts (IDAs):* In order to encourage wealth creation nationwide, IDAs are special matched savings accounts which provide tax credits that will enable more working low-income families to save, build wealth and enter the financial mainstream through the use of an innovative new financial instrument. Because of their importance IDAs are further presented later on
- (b). *Empowerment Zones/Enterprise Communities*: Fully funds Round II of the Urban/Rural Empowerment Zones and Enterprise Communities program. Urban Empowerment Zones include Boston, Mass, Cincinnati, Oh. Gary/East Chicago, East St. Louis, Illinois, Ironton, Oh. Columbus, Oh;
- (c). *Rural Empowerment Zones* include Southernmost Illinois Delta Empowerment Zone, Illinois (parts of Alexander, Johnson, and Pulaski Counties), while a great number of Indian reservations falls under this category;
- (d). *Low-Income Housing Tax credit*: As an incentive to create more and better affordable rental housing for low-income individuals, a tax credit is available to owners of rental properties that are rented to low-income individuals and meet certain other requirements. The amount of

low-income tax credits available in each State is currently limited by an annual volume limit of $1.25 per State resident. The bill would immediately increase the amount to $1.74 per state resident in 2001 and adjust subsequent increases to inflation;

- (e). *Renewal Communities:* Creates 50 Renewal Communities with targeted, pro-growth tax benefits, regulatory relief, brownfields clean up, and homeownership opportunities (the Clinton/Hastert package includes 40 Renewal Communities). At least 20 percent of the communities identified must be located in rural areas. Requirements for communities applying for Renewal Community status include high poverty rates and a local commitment to reducing local regulations, zoning restrictions and tax rates. Each State will have one Renewal Community;

- (f). *Charitable Choice Expansion*: Expansion of the current charitable choice provisions in welfare reform and Community Services Block grants. Allows charitable and faith-based organizations to compete for contracts or participate in voucher programs on an equal basis with other private providers whenever a state chooses to use non-governmental providers to deliver services to the poor. The provision preserves the religious character of faith-based institutions, without diminishing the religious freedom of the beneficiaries;

- (g). *The New Millenium Classrooms Act*: To increase the amount of computers donated to schools, libraries, seniors centers, and non profit vocational training centers in economically disadvantaged areas, the New Millenium Classrooms Act would expand the parameters of the current tax deduction and add a tax credit.

4 IDAs

Individual Development Accounts (IDAs) pose a unique alternative to traditional anti-poverty programs by bringing into the market and the community those left behind. IDAs are a federally exercised instrument of the social inclusion process. For this reason, it is worth to focus on the full mechanics of this instrument.

An IDA is a matched savings account set up in the name of an *individual* and restricted to high return investments such as *post-secondary education, starting a business or buying a home.* IDAs are designed to increase savings and investments for primarily low-income families (typically the working poor or welfare recipients). IDAs embody recognition of the fact that it is possible to escape poverty through asset building.

Community investors are secondary investors in that they match the savings of the individual only after the individual has met the investment and learning commitments agreed upon.

An IDA account is established in local financial institutions under a qualified individual's name. That individual must meet selection criteria, (the ethical qualities are important criteria), complete a financial literacy course and maintain consistent monthly (usually 12 months to 24 months) deposits (typically $20 to $50) into their account. Community investors then match the deposits of the individual (typically 1:1 up to 4:1), and these community investments are held in a separate account. When the participant meets the agreed upon goals, withdrawals are made from the individual and matching accounts to realize the savings, for example, for home ownership, education or small business start-up.

IDAs are emerging as a tool to integrate low-income families into the economy by helping them build assets. The process of family development, community building, and neighbourhood revitalization begins with low-income earners themselves. Without assets, poor families are likely to remain poor. Poor families can be empowered to own, not just owe. IDAs can begin to endow low-income families with productive assets as part of a strategy to move them into the economic mainstream.

At present, 32 States include IDAs in plans for using TANF (Temporary Assistance for Needy Families) funds. Twenty-nine States have passed IDAs legislation for TANF recipients and/or low-income citizens, including: Michigan, Illinois and Ohio. Twelve states and Washington, D.C. have ADD (American Dream Demonstration) sites (American Dream IDA Demonstration sites), including: Illinois (2 sites).

5 Community-based IDA Programs

It is estimated that over three hundred-community-based IDAs programs have been initiated or are in the planning stages in the US. There are non-profit organizations in at least 46 states running or planning IDAs programs – with and without State IDAs legislation.

All in all the IDAs Program is likely to be set within the Department of Economic Development to encourage individuals at poverty level to establish individual savings acounts. Funds in the account may be used to include costs of vocational training, post-secondary education, small business creation, first time home-ownership as well as home improvement to a primary residence. Individual account holders may deposit funds in the account, which will be matched at a specified ratio, which may vary in each State. The ministry then is to solicit proposals from community development organizations, defined as not-for-profit religious or charitable associations, to implement the program. Such proposals must include the requirement that individual account holders make financial contributions to their accounts. These community development organizations are also authorized to oversee the program's reserve fund, which is to be used for administrative costs and matching funds. Matching funds are to be held in the reserve fund until distributed to a specified vendor or service provider at the time of acquiring the account holder's chosen asset.

The former President Bill Clinton had this to say about IDAs: "As hard as they work, they still don't have the opportunity to save. Too few can make use of IRA.'s and 401 (k) plans. We should do more to help all working families save and accumulate wealth. That's the idea behind the Individual Development Accounts, the IDAs. I ask you to take that idea to a new level, with new retirements savings accounts that enable every low and moderate – income family in America to save for retirement, the first home, a medical emergency or a college education. I propose to match their contributions, however small, dollar for dollar, every year they save. And I propose to give a major new tax credit to any small business that will provide a meaningful pension to its workers. Those people ought to have retirement as well as the rest of us". Presidential State of the Union, 1999–2000.

Al Gore's social policy objective called "Retirement Savings Plus" was keen to the Universal Savings Account (USA) proposed by former President Clinton to address the issue of partially privatized social security. The USA account is following the method of IDAs. Families would deposit savings in voluntary individual retirement accounts, and the federal government would deposit tax credit funds in their accounts based on the levels of savings deposits and family income. The tax credit would be refundable so that even a family with no income taxability would receive the full matching amount.

The federal grant phases out so that a couple making $100,000 would receive only a $500 credit it made a $1,500 deposit a 1-for-3 match. The families could withdraw money earlier for catastrophic medical expenses, college tuition or to buy a first home. Financial institutions would be restricted to offer investment options based on broad-based mutual funds for equities, bonds and government securities.

The refundable tax credits and the matches of funds are in inverse relation to family income. The beneficiaries of the proposal would be low and moderate-income families. The plan requires families to save in order to get government benefits. Saving is hard for low-income families but this is the very essence of the new welfare to work process. (Gore's proposal leaves the Federal Insurance Contribution Act (FICA of 1977) payroll tax at its current high levels. About 80% of households pay more in FICA payments that in federal income taxes, and the FICA tax falls more heavily on low-and moderate-income families than on the wealthly ones. IDAs also provide training for financial literacy within a life-long education framework.

Other similar policy instruments include the American Community Renewal and New Markets Empowerment Act (ACRNMEA). This represents a comprehensive Legislation that would create economic incentives to invest in low-income communities, enhance educational and housing opportunities and help low-income families save and invest for the future.

Senator Lieberman has been very active on the issue of building assets via IDAs considering their nation-wide expansion of key importance for the empowerment of low income Americans. It is the policy of inclusion that constitutes the real re-engineering aspects of this situation. The existing legislation on IDAs for Michigan, Ohio and Illinois – as mentioned above – has been as follows:

- IDAs are included in the State welfare reform plan;
- Illinois passed IDA legislation at the end of the 1997–98 sessions. SB1350, "Individual Development Accounts", was introduced by Senator Judith Myers and representative William Black. (To read the text of the legislation pleases sees: http://www.legis.state.il.us/ publicacts/ pubact90/acts/90-0783.html).

The legislation was advocated by the Women's Self-Employment Project (WSEP), in Chicago, and created a statewide IDA as a pilot program. The pilot program has been being administered by WSEP and implemented by the Illinois Community Action Association. WSEP communicates program information to the agencies by scheduled conference calls, provides technical assistance, and produces reports to the State. Several bills were introduced in the 1998 legislative session.

HB 4786 sponsored by Rep. Hubert Price was passed and signed into law by the Governor. (Legislation is found in: http://198.109.122.10/ txt/publicAct/1997-1998/pa036198.htm).

The Governor of Michigan included a line item in his budget proposal for FY 2001. This provides $5 million dollars in surplus TANF funds for IDAs (June 21, 2000). The Family Independence Agency, in collaboration with the Council of Michigan Foundations, will administer the statewide program. The Charles Stewart Mott Foundation has proposed raising $5 million to match the State contribution. Community based non-profits, chosen by RFP, will administer the program, in cooperation with Michigan's

Community Action Agency Association, and establish a funding pool for the account matches.

Uses include post-secondary education, small business start-ups and building a principal residence. IDA legislation was passed in 1997. (Legislation is found in http://ohioacts.avv.com/122/hb408/home.htm).

The State Department of Human Services will oversee the county IDAs programs and will collaborate with Ohio Community Development Corporations (CDCs) to pilot the demonstration. IDAs may be established for home ownership, small business capitalization, or education. IDAs holders' income must be at or below 150 percent of the federal poverty level. Contributions for matching funds are tax deductible while interest earned is tax exempt for IDAs holders.

The IDAs Policy in the States of Illinois, Michigan and Ohio are as described below:

- IDAs Legislation has been passed and State Supported Program Operating. (All in all there are 12 States in this scheme with matching funds with three with no matching funds.) Michigan has a Coalition Building in States that have passed IDAs legislation. In Illinois, Michigan and Ohio Participant Eligibility requirements are TANF or TANF eligible;
- In Michigan, the program "To Strengthen Michigan Families" (TAM) is a welfare reform program operated statewide by the Michigan Family Independence Agency (MFIA) as referred to earlier. The evaluation the TSMF introduced an expectation that adult welfare recipients must enter into a "Social Contract" under which they agreed to engage in personally-and /or socially-useful activities for at least 20 hours/week;
- --TSMF allowed welfare clients to keep more of their grant while earning income on the job,
- --TSMF broadened AFDC (Families with Dependent Children) eligibility for two-parent families; and
- --TSMF allowed AFDC children to earn and save without affecting program benefits.

These provisions were operative on October 1, 1992. Welfare reform in Michigan continued to evolve building on the practices of the program, which led to additional TSMF provisions, being implemented on October 1, 1994, upon approval by the Department of Health and Human Services.

A new requirement for job search and job placement was implemented as a major employment strategy for AFDC applicants and recipients. MFIA and the Michigan Jobs Commission (MJC) – the agency responsible for oversight of Michigan's Job Training Partnership Act (MJTPA) programs – operated the new program, called Work First and jointly strengthened the connection between the Social Contract and the MOST Programs. The 1994 TSMF policies eliminated most current exemptions from participation in MOST, Michigan's employment and training program for AFDC recipients.

All adult AFDC recipients who were not required to participate in MOST under current exemption policy had to comply with the Social Contract: anyone not complying for 12 months was enrolled in MOST and became subject to financial penalties for non compliance applying heavier financial sanctions for noncompliance. Before October 1994, members of AFDC families who were mandated to participate in MOST and failed to comply could be disqualified from the assistance grant; that is, the monthly AFDC check could be reduced by an amount equal to that member's share.

After the interim TSMF policy changes of 1994, the sanction for an individual's failure to comply with Work First and MOST requirements was 25 percent of the family's grant until the individual complied. If the individual was non-compliant for a year, the entire family's AFDC case could be closed until the individual complied with Work First requirements.

Allowing deductions for investments supporting self-employment, TSMF allowed self-employed clients to include the purchase of capital assets and payments on business loans as deducible business expenses when considering AFDC eligibility and benefits extending some of the AFDC policy changes to the Food Stamp Program (FSP). After October 1994, TSMF applied roughly equivalent rules regarding sanctions, self-employment expenses, and vehicle exclusions to the FSP.

In brief, TSMF policies were instrumental in changing the culture of dependence on welfare and providing employment and long-term financial independence. TSMF increased adult's employment and earnings after four years, and increased the last group's employment by the end of the year. TSMF reduced welfare participation as well as benefits for ongoing families and the middle group of families.

Adults in TSMF were generally more likely to combine work and welfare, and less likely to remain on welfare without working. TSFM increased total family income for ongoing families (The Evaluation of "To Strengthen Michigan Families" Abt Associates Inc). *The future welfare reform in the TANF framework (TANF clients are required to find work within two years of receiving assistance and States may not use TANF funds for assistance to individuals for more than five years over their lifetime).*

TSMF allowed AFDC children to earn and save without affecting program benefits. The best welfare to workfare developments in the US have been those of the State of Michigan. Workforce and economic development therefore are undoubtedly linked to welfare, social cohesion, poverty alleviation and social inclusion policies in general. Michigan was the essential socio-political theater in the 1996 – welfare-to-workforce reform, which spread across the Mid-West, Northwest and the whole of the US.

Activities related to workforce development and those related to economic development seem to be complex but are not distinct. It so seems that both the TSMF and the TANF programs constitute social governance instruments.

The Federal to State and County partnerships are of paramount importance, new technologies added-new dimension to work organization and had an immense impact on the creation of new labor ecology. Labor is now more fluid in terms of its skill requirements. The new public administrative space allows for continuous valuation of work places and the New Skill Requirements that ought to be both cheaper and easier to apply. Training is the main antidote for exclusion, and it must be the main social policy focus. Developments in the work environment, the city and the region are becoming knowledge-based environments that provide workers with feed back on knowledge and vice versa. Thus, training should become specific but also general and should be provided on a mass scale.

Community Colleges develop simulations of work places and attempt to provide the link with production becoming part of a continuous work process in line with enterprises. This process continuously defines those turned redundant at a point in the work process and may need to get retrained. The high job rotation and increased redundancies are the name of the situation that couples with increased mobility produced by the TANF, IDA and TSMF programs.

Thus, welfare changes are becoming closer to social production needs, since the new programs provide greater labor mobility. At the same time, asset building provides for the social integration process. In a way, savings and asset building denote Education and Human Capital, both necessary requirements of knowledge economy. The emergence of communal approaches to job re-training and constant upgrading of standards denotes that the labor market is regulated by the State on a mass scale.

Special purpose accounts (IDAs) during the 1990s became an important element of welfare reform as expressed by the Personal Responsibility and Work Opportunity Reconciliation Act of 1996 (PRWORA). This Act gave impetus to the setting up of IDAs by permitting States to use their TANF grants to fund IDAs. Similarly, the Assets for Independence Act (Public Law 105-285, enacted in October 1998) provided Federal funds for the operation of IDAs.

In this context, the State valorizes the market and expands by the very undertaking of the socialization of the cost of reproduction of labor. The Aid for Families with Dependent Children (AFDC) program offerred cash assistance to needy children in lone parent families. In 1996, it was reformed as Temporary Aid for Needy Families (TANF). The aim was to get AFDC recipients off welfare. The work requirements in force under AFDC were tightened with a maximum period of support introduced (five years).

The block grant system of TANF has been of a rather competitive nature, a matter that translates into higher mobility for recipients. At the same time, the States seem to bear the full costs of any dollar spent on these programs. The IDAs are a novel component that aims to build local micro-savings drawing on female led households with poor children. The matching of savings by the federal budget stimulates female participation in the labor market and creates a new market for the non profits who must develop day care and transport facilities to allow women access into the job market.

6 Conclusions

In this paper, I tried to delineate those acts and regulatory frameworks that played a key role in the welfare reform in the US, which started out in Michigan among other places, a reform that is responsible for the current state of affairs that associates workforce development with (socio) economic development.

In this paper I focused on the significance of recent workforce development trends in the US and Michigan by looking on the importance of social initiatives that lead to greater workforce participation such as the family and children support schemes, for "social minorities" that are in the core of the poverty trap. Such target groups with the successful application of an asset-building program represents the real acid test for the success or failure of local employment development programs. The key is to be found in the population category targeted. In Michigan I have had a number of positive factors in the communities that led to their building social capital and social cohesion with socio-economic development. Employability has been associated with asset building for poor families and minorities. Unemployment remained the lowest in the US, and the State remained the highest foreign direct investment destination in the US. It is such reforms that a European Social Policy at regional level could develop.

7 References

DREES (1999) Collection MiRe Comparing social welfare systems in Nordic Europe and France.

DREES (1999) Collection MiRe (100), Maison des Sciences de L'Homme Ange-Guepin, Nantes, (1999) Vol. 4 Copenhague Conference France-Nordic Europe.

DREES (2000) Collection MiRe, Maison des Sciences de L'Homme Ange-Guepin, Nantes, Information on IDA's has been taken from the network of the Corporation for Enterprise Development, http://www.cfed.org/cfedpublications/

Eaton, G. E. (2000) Pension Capitalism and Issues of Governance, York University, Department of Economics, (mimeo) Toronto, Canada.

Haughton, G., Jones, M., Peck, J., Tickell, A., While, A. (2000) Labor Market Policy as Flexible Welfare: Prototype Employment Zones and the New Workfarism, Regional Studies, Vol. 34, 7, pp.669-680.

Tom, L., Ravitch, D. (2000) Broken Promises What the federal Government Can Do to Improve American Education, The Brookings Review, Spring 200, Vol. 18, No.2, Pages 18-21.

Minnow, N. (2000) Watching the Watchers: Corporate Governance in the 21st Century, Blackwell Publishers.

Navarro, V. (1999) The political Economy of the Welfare State in Developed Capitalist Countries, International Journal of health Services, Volume 29, Number 1, pages 1-50.

OECD (2000) The Jobs Study: Facts, Analysis, Strategies, Paris.

Pacolet, J. (1992) The state of the welfare state in the EU anno 1992 and five years later, Higher Institute for labor Studies, Catholic University f Leuven, Belgium.

Peck, J.A. (1999) New Laborers: making a New Deal for the workless class, Envirn. Plann. C. 17(3), pp. 345-72.

Peeters, D. (1999), Changing Work patterns and Social Security, 1999 Yearbook of the European Institute for Social Security, Kluwer Law International, The Hague.

Therborn, G. (1999) The Unemployment Iceberg: What is Beneath, Behind and Ahead?, International Journal of health Services, Volume 29, number 3, Pages 545-563.

Abbreviations

ACRNMEA	American Community Renewal and New Markets Empowerment Act
ADD	American Dream Demonstration
ADF	Dickey and Fuller Test
AFDC	Aid to Families with Dependent Children
AIC	Akaike Test
BEA	Bureau of Economic Analysis
BES	Business Enterprise Sector
CARICOM	the Caribbean Community
CEE	Central Eastern European
CFED	Corporation Enterprise Development
CIS	Community Innovation Survey
CRDW	Cointegrating Durbin Watson Test
CSF	Community Support Framework
EAGGF Guidance	European Agricultural Guidance and Guarantee Fund
EC	European Community
ECM	Error Correction Model
EHT	Employed in High-Tech
EIMS	European Innovation Monitoring System
EMU	European Monetary Union
ERA	European Research Area
ERDF	European Regional Development Fund
ERM	Exchange Rate Mechanism
ESF	European Social Fund
EU	European Union
FIFG	Financial Instrument for Fisheries Guidance
FDI	Foreign Direct Investment
FICA	Federal Insurance Contribution Act
FIP	Family Independence Program
FTA	Free Trade Agreement
FTAA	Free Trade Area of the Americas

GDP	Gross Domestic Product
GNP	Gross National Product
GMM	Generalized Method of Moments
GSRT	General Secretariat of Research and Technology
HICP	Harmonised Index of Consumer Prices
HDI	Human Development Index
HI	Herfindalh Index
IC	Industrial Concentration
ICT	Information Technology and Communications
IDAs	Individual Development Accounts
IMF	International Monetary Fund
ISCED	International Standard Classification of Education
ISPA	Instrument for Structural Policies for pre-Accession
IT	Information Technology
LPOs	Local Partnership Organizations
MERCOSUR	South American Common Market
MFIA	Michigan Family Independence Agency
MJC	Michigan Jobs Commission
MJTPA	Michigan's Job Training Partnership Act
NAFTA	North American Free Trade Agreement
NUTS	Nomenclature of Territorial Units for Statistics
OECD	Organisation for Economic Cooperation and Development
PLN	Poland
PP	Phillips and Perron Test
PPS	Purchase Power Parity
PRWORA	Personal Responsibility and Work Opportunity Reconciliation Act
RCA	Revealed Comparative Advantage
RD	Research-Development
R&D	Research and Development
RDH	Research and Development Activities per Inhabitant
RDP	Regional Domestic Product
RTD	Research, Technology and Development
RTD&I	Research and Technological Development and Innovation
SIC	Schwartz Test
SICA	Central American Integration System
SCE	Symmetric Cooperative Equilibrium
SNE	Symmetric and Nash Equilibrium

TANFs	Temporary Assistance for Needy Families
UK	United Kingdom
UN	United Nations
UNCTAD	United Nations Conferences on Trade and Development
US	United States
U.S.A.	United States of America
USA	Universal Savings Account
YPAN	Ministry of Development in Greece
WSEP	Women's Self-Employment Project
WTO	World Trade Organization

Index